ILLUSTRATED LETTERS OF THE PASTON FAMILY

PRIVATE LIFE IN THE FIFTEENTH CENTURY

# Illustrated Letters
## OF THE
# Paston Family

EDITED BY ROGER VIRGOE

MACMILLAN
LONDON

First published 1989 by
MACMILLAN LONDON LIMITED
4 Little Essex Street, London WC2R 3LF
and Basingstoke.

Associated companies in Auckland, Delhi, Dublin, Gaborone,
Hamburg, Harare, Hong Kong, Johannesburg, Kuala Lumpur,
Lagos, Manzini, Mexico City, Nairobi, New York,
Singapore and Tokyo.

A CIP catalogue record for this book is available from the
British Library.

ISBN 0–333–48099–6

Typeset by Florencetype Ltd, Kewstoke, Avon, England.

Printed by Cayfosa, Barcelona.

# Contents

*Endpapers: Letter in the hand of Sir John Paston to Margaret Paston, 17 January 1476.*
*The translation of this letter appears on page 244.*

# Chronology

| | |
|---|---|
| 1378 | Birth of William Paston I |
| 1419 | Death of Clement Paston |
| 1420 | Marriage of William and Agnes Paston |
| 1421 | Birth of John Paston I |
| 1 September 1422 | Accession of Henry VI |
| 1429 | William Paston appointed Judge of the Common Pleas |
| | Coronation of Henry VI |
| | Coronation of Charles VII in France |
| 1432 | Death of John Mowbray, 2nd Duke of Norfolk: succession of John, 3rd Duke |
| 1435 | Congress of Arras – Burgundy defects to France |
| | Death of the Duke of Bedford |
| 1436/40 | Marriage of John Paston with Margaret Mauteby |
| 1437 | Personal Rule of Henry VI |
| 1442 | Birth of John Paston II |
| 1444 | Birth of John Paston III |
| 13 August 1444 | Death of William Paston I |
| 22 April 1445 | Marriage of Henry VI to Margaret of Anjou |
| 1447 | Death of the Duke of Gloucester and Cardinal Beaufort |
| 1448–51 | The Gresham Dispute |
| July 1449 | French conquest of Normandy begins |
| 2 May 1450 | Murder of William, 1st Duke of Suffolk |
| June–July 1450 | Jack Cade's Rebellion |
| August 1450 | French conquest of Normandy completed |
| Aug–Sep 1450 | Dukes of York and Somerset return to England |
| From August 1450 | Action against Tuddenham and Heydon in Norfolk |
| July 1453 | Battle of Castillon and final loss of Aquitaine |
| August 1453 | The King's insanity begins |
| 13 October 1453 | Birth of Prince Edward |
| April 1454 | The Duke of York appointed Protector |
| 25 December 1454 | The King recovers and York's protectorate ends soon after |
| 22 May 1455 | First Battle of St Albans |
| Nov 1455 – Feb 56 | York's second protectorate |
| August 1456 | The Court moves from Westminster to Coventry |
| 1458 | Marriage of Elizabeth Paston with Robert Poynings |
| 1459 | Death of Sir John Fastolf and beginning of litigation over his inheritance |
| 23 September 1459 | Battle of Blore Heath |
| 12 October 1459 | The encounter at Ludford |
| November 1459 | Coventry parliament and the attainder of York |
| 10 July 1460 | Battle of Northampton |
| October 1460 | York claims the throne |
| 31 December 1460 | Battle of Wakefield – death of Duke of York |
| 1460, 1461 | John Paston I, knight of the shire for Norfolk |
| 3 February 1461 | Battle of Mortimer's Cross |
| 17 February 1461 | Second Battle of St Albans |
| 4 March 1461 | Edward IV proclaimed king |
| 29 March 1461 | Battle of Towton |
| 28 June 1461 | Coronation of Edward IV |
| 22 July 1461 | Death of Charles VII of France: accession of Louis XI |
| December 1461 | Death of 3rd Duke of Norfolk: succession of John, 4th Duke |
| 1461–64 | Campaigns against Lancastrians in North and Wales |
| February 1462 | Execution of John, 12th Earl of Oxford |
| 1463 | John Paston II knighted |
| 1 May 1464 | Marriage of Edward IV to Elizabeth Woodville |
| 1465 | Hellesdon and Drayton seized by John, 2nd Duke of Suffolk |
| 21/22 May 1466 | Death of John Paston I |
| 1467 | John Paston II, knight of the shire for Norfolk |
| 15 June 1467 | Death of Philip the Good of Burgundy: accession of Charles the Rash |
| 3 July 1468 | Marriage of Duke of Burgundy with Margaret of York |
| 1469 | John Paston's betrothal to Anne Haute |
| June 1469 | Warwick and Clarence ally against the King |
| 26 July 1469 | Battle of Edgecote followed by the killing of Earl Rivers and the capture of the King |
| August 1469 | Siege of Caister |
| October 1469 | The King regains power |
| 1469 | Marriage of Margery Paston with Richard Calle |
| 1470 | John Paston II, probably knight of the shire for Norfolk |
| 1470 | Caister recovered |
| April 1470 | Warwick and Clarence flee to France |

| | |
|---|---|
| **July 1470** | Agreement between Queen Margaret and Warwick |
| **2 October 1470** | Edward IV flees from England – the 'Re-adeption' begins |
| **14 March 1471** | Edward IV lands in England |
| **14 April 1471** | Paston brothers fight at the Battle of Barnet |
| **4 May 1471** | Battle of Tewkesbury |
| **May 1471** | Death of Henry VI |
| **1472** | Caister lost to the Duke of Norfolk |
| **1472** | Birth of Anne, daughter and heir of the Duke of Norfolk |
| **From 1472** | Pastons' connection with Lord Hastings and Calais |
| **July 1475** | Edward IV's invasion of France – Treaty of Picquigny |
| **17 January 1476** | Death of 4th Duke of Norfolk |
| **1476** | Marriage of John Paston III with Margery Brews |
| **1476** | Marriage of Anne Paston with William Yelverton |
| **5 January 1477** | Defeat and death of Charles of Burgundy at Nancy |
| **January 1478** | Marriage of Anne Mowbray with Richard, Duke of York |
| **18 February 1478** | Execution of Duke of Clarence |
| **1479** | Death of Agnes Paston<br>Death of Walter Paston<br>Death of Sir John Paston<br>Birth of William, son of John Paston III and eventually heir to all the Paston lands |
| **1480** | Death of Anne Mowbray |
| **1483** | John Howard created Duke of Norfolk and his son, Thomas, Earl of Surrey |
| **9 April 1483** | Death of Edward IV |
| **25 June 1483** | Deposition of Edward V and accession of Richard III |
| **31 August 1483** | Death of Louis XI of France: accession of Charles VIII |
| **November 1484** | Death of Margaret Paston |
| **August 1485** | Death of Duke of Norfolk and attainder of his heir |
| **22 August 1485** | Battle of Bosworth and accession of Henry VII |
| **From 1485** | John, 13th Earl of Oxford, dominant in East Anglia |
| **1485–86** | John Paston III is Sheriff of Norfolk and Suffolk and MP for Norwich |
| **June 1487** | John Paston III knighted |
| **16 June 1487** | Battle of Stoke |
| **1489** | Thomas, Earl of Surrey, released from Tower and sent to the North |
| **Oct – Nov 1492** | Invasion of France – Treaty of Etaples |
| **1495** | Death of Margery, wife of John Paston III |
| **1496** | Death of William Paston II |
| **1496/1504** | John Paston III marries Agnes Morley |
| **1497** | Suppression of Perkin Warbeck's and Cornish Rebellions |
| **1504** | Death of Edmund Paston |
| **28 August 1504** | Death of John Paston III |
| **21 April 1509** | Death of Henry VII: accession of Henry VIII |

# Calendar of Important Religious Feasts

**Christmas** 25 December
**Epiphany** 6 January
**Hilary** 13 January
**Candlemas** (The Purification of the Virgin) 2 February
**Annunciation of the Virgin** 25 March
**Midsummer** (Nativity of St John the Baptist) 24 June
**Lammas** (St Peter's Day) 1 August
**Michaelmas** (St Michael's Day) 29 September
**Hallowmas** (All Saints Day) 1 November
**Martinmas** (St Martin's Day) 11 November

MOVEABLE FEASTS DEPENDENT ON THE DATE OF EASTER
**Lent** 40 weekdays before Easter
**Ash Wednesday** First day of Lent
**Palm Sunday** 6th Sunday in Lent
**Good Friday** Friday before Easter Day
**Easter Day** A Sunday between 22 March and 25 April
**Rogation Sunday** 5th Sunday after Easter
**Ascension Day** Thursday following Rogation Sunday
**Pentecost, Whitsunday** 7th Sunday after Easter
**Trinity Sunday** 8th Sunday after Easter
**Corpus Christi Day** Thursday after Trinity Sunday

# Dramatis Personae

## THE FAMILY

**Clement Paston**    Son of William Paston of Paston. A yeoman who built up a substantial holding in and around Paston. Married Beatrice, sister and heiress of Geoffrey Somerton. He died on 17 June 1419 and was buried at Paston, apparently leaving only one child.

**William Paston I**    Born in 1378; inherited lands at Paston from his father and at Somerton from his maternal uncle. Very active as a lawyer in East Anglia; on many commissions and steward to the Duke of Norfolk and the Bishop of Norwich. Serjeant-at-law 1418 and Judge of the Common Pleas October 1429. He bought land and acquired more by his marriage, and died on 13 August 1444. He was buried in Norwich Cathedral.

**Agnes Paston (née Berry)**    Born about 1405 and married William Paston in 1420. She had four sons and one daughter who survived to maturity. She inherited lands in Norfolk and Hertfordshire from her father in 1433, and her husband settled Oxnead, Paston and other lands on her for life. During her widowhood she lived first at Norwich and Paston, but later with her second son, William, in London, where she died on 17–18 August 1479.

Children of William and Agnes.

**John Paston I**    Born on 10 October 1421. Educated at Cambridge and the Inner Temple. Perhaps a Yeoman of the Stables to the King in 1438–9 but had married Margaret Mauteby by 1440. A lawyer, he spent much time in London, but became a trusted councillor to Sir John Fastolf who made him the main heir to his extensive property. MP for Norfolk in 1460 and 1461 and JP in Norfolk from November 1460, he became a major figure in the county, but the property also brought him much trouble. He died on 21–22 May 1466 and was buried at Bromholm Monastery.

**Margaret Paston (née Mauteby)**    Born at Reedham, her mother's family home, in the early 1420s, she inherited her father's estates in 1433 and was soon snapped up for his son by his executor, William Paston. She raised four sons and two daughters to maturity while, in the frequent absence of husband and sons, acting as estate and household manager, as well as attempting to keep the peace within the family. A high proportion of the letters were written to or for her. She died early in November 1484 and was buried at Mautby.

**Edmund Paston**    Born in 1425 and possibly educated at Cambridge before training as a lawyer at Clifford's Inn and the Inner Temple. His father bequeathed him some land but he died unmarried in March 1449, when his property passed to his brother, John. He asked to be buried either in the Temple or in the Whitefriars Priory in London.

**William Paston II**    Born in 1436, he was at Cambridge and an Inn of Court and practised as a lawyer. His father had left him a little land but he was able to purchase a good deal more. Later he lived mainly at Warwick Inn in London. He was a councillor to the 12th Earl of Oxford and his widow until 1475, then to the Duke of Buckingham, who probably found him parliamentary seats at Newcastle-under-Lyme in 1472 and Bedwin, Wiltshire, in 1478 and 1491. He was a JP in Norfolk in 1465–71 and 1473–4. His grand marriage to Lady Anne Beaufort probably brought him more prestige than money and he engaged in a long dispute with his nephews over his parents' lands. He died in 1496, leaving two daughters, and was buried at the Blackfriars Priory in London.

**Clement Paston**    Born in 1442, he spent some time at Cambridge and then probably at an Inn in London. Not heard of after 1466, he probably died soon after his brother, John.

**Elizabeth Paston**    Born on 1 July 1429, she did not marry, in spite of many attempts, until November 1458. Her first husband, Robert Poynings, was killed at the Battle of St Albans in 1461, leaving her with an infant son, but she later remarried Sir George Browne of Betchworth, Surrey, by whom she also had children. He was executed in 1483 and she died on 11 February 1488. Her lengthy will makes no reference to her Norfolk kinsmen.

## Children of John and Margaret

**John Paston II**    Born in 1442, nothing is known of his education, but it clearly fitted him for life at the King's Court, to which he was sent by his father in 1461 and where he was knighted in 1463. He was on bad terms with his father, but was made executor of his will and inherited the bulk of his lands and his claims to the Fastolf estates. He was MP for Norfolk in 1467 and 1470 and JP from July 1466 but spent much more time in London than Norfolk, leaving his mother and brother to deal with the local problems of the estates while he lobbied at Court and Council. After 1471 he became closely associated with Lord Hastings and spent time in the Calais garrison, though sitting in the parliaments of 1472 and 1478. For long betrothed to Anne Haute, he never married, though he left an illegitimate daughter when he died in November 1479. He was buried at the Whitefriars Priory in London.

**John Paston III**    Born in 1444, nothing is known of his education, but he was living at home and acting as secretary for his mother by 1459. He joined the household of the young 4th Duke of Norfolk in 1462 and retained useful contacts there even after he ceased to be a full-time servant. He played an active role as local agent for his brother from 1466 to 1469 and, in spite of temperamental differences, relations between the two

were normally affectionate and trusting. Many letters refer to his attempts to find a bride, his brother often acting as surrogate wooer, but his long wait was well rewarded, for his eventual marriage was both eminently 'suitable' and a love-match. He succeeded to his brother's position in 1479, was a JP in 1480–3 and MP for Norwich in 1483. After 1485 he was one of the leading figures in the county, sheriff in 1485–6, JP and MP for Norwich in 1485. He was knighted at the Battle of Stoke in 1487. On his first wife's death he remarried but had no further children. He died on 28 August 1504. No will survives and his place of burial is unknown.

**Margery Paston (née Brews)**    Born about 1460, one of the many children of Sir Thomas Brews by his second wife. Hurdles had to be overcome before the marriage with John could take place, but the enthusiasm of Margery certainly helped. The couple set up house at Swainsthorpe but after Margaret's death had a variety of residences. She bore three children who survived to adulthood. She died in 1495 and was buried at the Whitefriars Priory at Norwich.

**Edmund Paston**    Born about 1450, he may have been educated at Cambridge and was certainly at Staple Inn in London during the 1460s. Later he spent time at home, when he wrote some of his mother's letters, and as a soldier at Calais. He was on good terms with both his elder brothers. He eventually secured some property by his marriage to a widow, in about 1480, and on her death married a twice-widowed heiress. Though he had at least one son, no child seems to have survived when he died in about 1502–3.

**Walter Paston**    Born about 1456, he was apparently his mother's favourite child and destined for a clerical career. He graduated from Oxford in 1479 but died two months later.

**William Paston III**    Born in 1459 and probably the last of Margaret's children. He was educated at Eton which he left about 1479. By 1487 he had entered the service of the Earl of Oxford and stayed in his household until 1503 when he was sent home to his brother as 'crazed in his mind'. He probably died soon after.

**Margery Paston**    Born before 1450, marriage was being considered for her by 1458, but none was finalised and in 1469 she revealed that she had been clandestinely married to the Pastons' servant, Richard Calle. The consequent furore even temporarily overshadowed the loss of Caister. She and Richard had three sons and a daughter but she was probably dead by the time her mother made her will in 1482.

**Anne Paston**   Born in the late 1450s, she spent some of her time in the Household of Sir William Calthorpe during the late 1460s. She was suspected of an attraction to another Paston servant, John Pamping, but in 1477 was respectably married to William Yelverton, grandson of the judge. They had two children who survived to maturity, and Anne may have died in childbed in 1494–5, as their son and heir was five years old on his father's death in 1500.

Children of John and Margery

**William Paston IV**   Born in 1479, he was educated at Cambridge and was later a member of Henry VII's Court. He married early and lived until 1554. He was one of the major gentlemen of Tudor Norfolk and the ancestor of all later Pastons.

SERVANTS OF THE FAMILY

**Richard Calle**   From Framlingham, he entered the Pastons' service on the recommendation of the Duke of Norfolk. By the late 1450s he was the chief manager of their estates and remained so until the falling-out over his marriage with Margery. He continued to act for the Pastons in the 1470s and wrote letters for Margery during that time. After the marriage he is invariably styled 'gentleman' and his children by Margery and by a second wife were accepted among the lesser gentry of Tudor Norfolk. Still living in 1503, he probably died soon after.

**John Daubeney**   Younger son of William Daubeney of Sharington, Norfolk, he was in the Pastons' service by 1461 and was used by them as a soldier and general administrator; he also wrote some letters for Margery. He made his will at the beginning of the siege of Caister and was killed there a few weeks later, much regretted by Margaret and John III.

**James Gloys**   Probably from the family of Wighton in North Norfolk, he served the Pastons from at least 1448 to his death. Although in holy orders and primarily employed as the family chaplain, he performed many other duties, and was not averse to donning helmet and armour. He frequently acted as Margaret's secretary and sometimes John's. Although, as an old family retainer, he was resented by the younger generation in the 1470s, he was much trusted by Margaret, who was no doubt responsible for his appointment to the rectory of Stokesby in 1472 and who accepted the administration of his will on his death the following year.

**James Gresham**   Of Holt, Norfolk, he was an attorney and active in the courts from 1435. He became clerk to Judge William Paston, whose death-bed he attended, and after his death continued to be an active agent for his son, receiving a retaining fee for his services. He continued to be attached to the Pastons after John's death but was impoverished by taking an office – perhaps as under-sheriff – and John II threatened to sue him for debt in 1470. Margaret had to remind her son 'how kind and true-hearted he has been to us, to his power'. He disappears from the letters after April 1471 and probably died that year.

OTHER CORRESPONDENTS AND CHARACTERS

**Friar John Brackley**   Probably of a Norwich family, John Brackley entered the Franciscan convent there in 1418. He studied at university and became a Doctor of Theology; in 1443 he was Warden of the Norwich Convent, when he became involved in the conflict between the City and the Priory, which was supported by the Duke of Suffolk and his followers. A partisan man, hostile to what he called the 'cursed covy' of John Heydon and his allies, and loyal to Sir John Fastolf, whose confessor he became, and to the interests of the Pastons after 1459, he protested to the end that Fastolf's last will had been valid. He died shortly before John Paston I in 1466.

**Sir John Fastolf**   The son of a Norfolk squire, Fastolf was a professional soldier for most of his life. Although still a simple esquire at the start of Henry V's campaigns, he rapidly earned promotion and, under the Duke of Bedford, he became one of the leading captains. He was personally engaged in the great Battle of Verneuil and at the battles around Orleans in 1429. He was made a Knight of the Garter and wrote papers on the strategy and tactics of the war. Fastolf made a fortune from successful warring: from wages, offices, plunder and ransoms. Most of his gains were sent to England to buy land – mostly in East Anglia. He settled at Caister, the house that he had built, in the 1450s and during this time John Paston became one of his closest friends and his legal adviser. He died on 5 November 1459, and since his wife had died in 1446, and he had no surviving child, John Paston was the main beneficiary of his will. The validity of the will was questioned by Fastolf's other legal advisers, and the disputes and litigation over his inheritance continued for twenty years.

**William, Lord Hastings**   Replaced Archbishop Neville as the Pastons' main patron after 1471. Hastings' influence stemmed mainly from his intimacy with the King: he had been a retainer of Richard, Duke of York, but after the accession of Edward in 1461 he was appointed Chamberlain of the Royal Household; he was also created a peer and given great estates in the Midlands. His outstanding attribute was his loyalty to the King, whom he accompanied into exile in 1470 and whom he helped to restore the following year. As part of his reward he was made Lieutenant of Calais, while retaining his Household post. His womanising in the King's company angered the Queen and her Woodville kinsmen. The rivalry with the Woodville faction led Hastings to support Richard of Gloucester's claim to the protectorship in 1483. When it became clear that he would not support the deposition of Edward's son, he was considered too powerful to be left alive, and his murder in June was an essential preliminary to Gloucester's seizure of the throne.

**Thomas Howes**    Servant and chaplain to Sir John Fastolf by 1445, when he was appointed Rector of Castlecombe by his master, he was one of Fastolf's closest and most trusted servants, though treated as harshly by him as any of the others. He was engaged in lengthy litigation through the 1450s because of actions taken on Fastolf's behalf without much help or sympathy from his master. Fastolf nevertheless made him one of his two active executors and for the first years after 1459 he supported John Paston in his efforts to retain the lands. He was appointed to the rectories of first Mautby, then Blofield in 1460 and four years later became rector of Pulham, also in Norfolk. He later broke with Paston and joined the ranks of his opponents, though personal relations seem to have recovered after John's death, judging by Margaret's reference to the loss the family had suffered by his death in February 1469.

**John Heydon**    Born about 1405 of obscure parentage – his original name was Baxter – he must, like William Paston, have had patronage to help him train in the law and, by the late 1420s, begin a very successful career which brought him great wealth. He used some of this to purchase an estate at Baconsthorpe, only a few miles away from the Pastons' main manors, and to begin the building of a great house there. He acted as counsel and steward for many individuals and institutions, including Norwich Cathedral, but from 1435 he was particularly associated with William, Earl, then Duke of Suffolk. With Sir Thomas Tuddenham of Oxborough, he was the dominant force in East Anglia during the 1440s, thriving on the patronage of the Duke, and was seen by the Pastons then and later as their main local enemy. He made other enemies, too, including Sir John Fastolf, and on Suffolk's fall in 1450 he suffered considerable reversals, but recovered quickly and continued to be extensively employed in the courts and as trustee and executor. He died in 1479 and like William Paston, was buried in the Cathedral. The family feud ended in the 1490s with the marriage of his grand-daughter, Henry's daughter, to the son and heir of John Paston III.

**William Lomnour**    A lawyer, he was a kinsman and neighbour of the Pastons and frequently acted as their adviser and agent. In the 1460s he was building 'a poor house' at Mannington, which still survives in part. He died there in 1481. He married an heiress who later became the second wife of Edmund Paston II.

**William Worcester**    Born in 1415, he was educated at Oxford, was in the service of Sir John Fastolf by 1438 and was one of his most trusted and active servants. He married the niece of his fellow-servant, Thomas Howes. Against the advice of his brother, John Paston seems to have treated him very ungenerously after Fastolf's death and Worcester proved a persistent and crucial opponent in the struggle over his old master's property. Relations with the family were restored after John's death and Worcester settled in reasonably comfortable circumstances, first at Cambridge, then at Norwich, where he died in 1482–3. His last years were partly spent travelling through England and writing up his antiquarian notes. Though much has been lost, what survives makes it clear that Worcester was England's first great antiquarian scholar and much of what we know about the families and buildings of fifteenth-century East Anglia derives from his observation and recording.

**William Yelverton**    Roughly contemporary with John Heydon, he was another very active and able lawyer who was retained by Fastolf, among others, during the 1430s, and who continued to be friend and adviser to him after his promotion to Judge in 1443. He made his main seat at Rougham in West Norfolk but retained property in the east of the county and often visited Caister. His friendship with the Pastons was broken by the disputes over Fastolf's will, but may have been mended by the marriage of Anne Paston to his grandson a year before his death in 1478.

# The World of the Pastons

THE EFFECTS of the Black Death of 1348-9 and the epidemics which succeeded it were still very visible in the Pastons' England. The countryside with its sprinkling of market towns had lost more than half its population and was not to begin to fill up again until the end of the century. There were probably fewer than two million people in England – scattered at a density of roughly 40 per square mile compared with more than 900 today, although this average conceals wide variations between the sparsely populated 'Highland Zone' north and west of a line from the Severn to the Humber, and the South-East and East Anglia, where most of the people lived.

## The Country and its Communities

Fewer people meant fewer houses and smaller settlements. In many parts of the country, including the western regions of Norfolk, arable fields had turned to pasture or had reverted to waste, and crumbling houses and decayed churches would have been common sights for the Pastons and their contemporaries. Some smaller settlements on poorer soils had already been abandoned and hundreds of others had diminished in size so as to be hardly viable as communities. The effects of depopulation may have been exacerbated by a deterioration in the climate, for fifteenth-century England seems to have been rather colder and wetter than before, making some land less productive. A rising sea-level was eating away at parts of the East Coast, gradually destroying, for example, the large port of Dunwich in Suffolk.

Since there was now quite enough land to support the smaller population, there was no need to plough the poorer soils, and there was a move from arable farming to pasture in many places. An Italian observer at the end of the century commented that: 'Agriculture is not practised in this island beyond what is required for the consumption of the people, because were they to plough and sow all the land that was capable of cultivation they might sell a quantity of grain to the surrounding countries.' He also notes the obverse of this – the profusion of animals, particularly 'an enormous number of sheep'. For two centuries, wool had been by far the most important raw material produced in England for the export as well as the home market. During the fifteenth century the cloth industry and exports flourished in both town and country, and great quantities of wool and cloth were exported, mainly to the Netherlands. Pastoral farming was now more profitable than arable farming, partly because it involved less labour at a time when labourers were in short supply and, consequently, wages were comparatively high. By the end of the century, there was already concern at the encroachment by flocks of sheep onto the old arable fields, which destroyed villages and employment. As Thomas More put it, 'sheep . . . have become so great devourers . . . that they eat up . . . the very men themselves'.

Few settlements had been 'devoured' in this way before the end of the century. In the South and East there remained a dense network of roads and tracks connecting thousands of villages to one another and the major towns. In the North, it is true, there were wide tracts of very sparsely populated hills, moorland and forest, and settlements were few, except in pockets of fertile land. Even in the South there were regions of fen, forest and moor, where villages were scarce, but for most of England south of the Trent they were rarely more than a few miles apart.

> *Of English shires our Norfolk seems to yield*
> *Most pleasures and commodities for gain*

wrote a local patriot in the sixteenth century. Norfolk, the homeland of the Paston family for at least 400 years, was one of the most isolated, yet prosperous of southern English counties. It was not on the way to anywhere else; it was surrounded almost entirely by water and 'the air is sharp and piercing', as a seventeenth-century observer noted. Although generally low-lying and nowhere reaching 400 feet above sea-level, the county had very varied terrain and soils.

Norfolk's wealth derived from its vast numbers of sheep and its extensive cloth-manufacture as well as from its rich arable lands. Norwich, Lynn and Yarmouth were all among the top thirty English towns in population and wealth, and there were still many weekly markets held in the county. A network of roads and tracks connected these markets and towns; water-transport, both along the rivers and around the coast, where there were many flourishing havens and fishing-ports, was also important. The great rebuilding of village and town churches in the fifteenth century suggests that there was wealth to spare in spite of the ravages of pestilence and, for some of the period, heavy taxation for war.

Norfolk in the fifteenth century had some 100,000 inhabitants. The majority of these lived in the east and south of the county; and the extreme east and north-east, where most of the Pastons' lands lay, probably still contained some of the most densely populated villages in England. Here, there were few large estates and most of the peasantry had long been free from most forms of service to the lords of the numerous small manors. Their holdings were small and, though these had grown in size as competition for land had diminished, the fertility of the soil, the availability of marsh and wood-pasture, and employment in fishing, shipping and cloth-working allowed many to live on a few acres of arable land. The population of Margaret Paston's Mautby, for instance, was almost certainly much larger than the 66 inhabitants it could boast at the census of 1841. Their houses tended to be grouped in clusters or single farms, often well separated from the parish-church, the heart of most villages, near which, as at Paston, lay the chief manor-house. The bulk of any gentleman's landed property was made up of 'manors' – estates which provided an income to the lord from rents, dues and services of the tenants, both freemen and villeins.

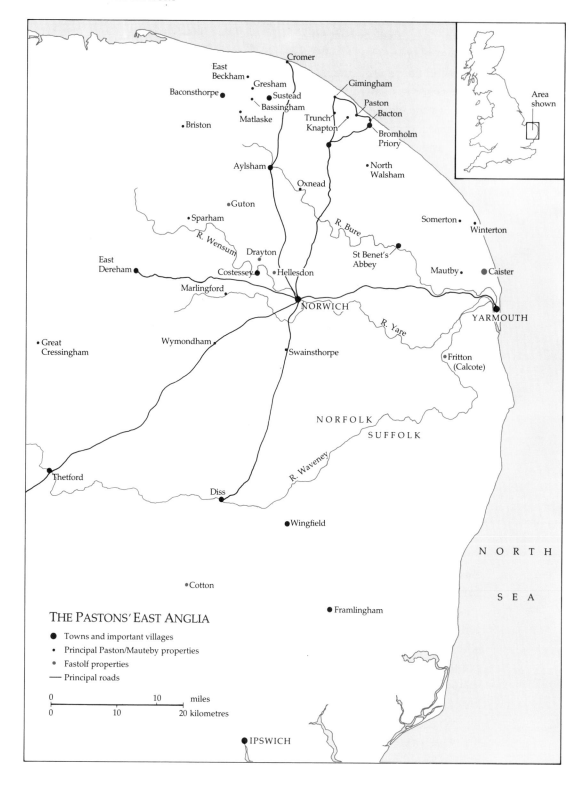

Area
shown

Cromer
East
Beckham
Gresham
Baconsthorpe
Sustead
Bassingham
Briston
Matlaske
Gimingham
Paston
Bacton
Trunch
Knapton
Bromholm
Priory
Aylsham
Oxnead
North
Walsham
Guton
Sparham
R. Bure
Somerton
Winterton
R. Wensum
Drayton
St Benet's
Abbey
Mautby
Caister
East
Dereham
Costessey
Hellesdon
Marlingford
NORWICH
YARMOUTH
R. Yare
Great
Cressingham
Wymondham
Swainsthorpe
Fritton
(Calcote)
NORFOLK
SUFFOLK
R. Waveney
Thetford
Diss
Wingfield
NORTH
Cotton
Framlingham
SEA

THE PASTONS' EAST ANGLIA

● Towns and important villages
• Principal Paston/Mauteby properties
• Fastolf properties
— Principal roads

0                    10         miles
0         10        20 kilometres

IPSWICH

Ownership of a manor implied jurisdiction through a manor-court which fined tenants for breaches of agricultural rules, registered transfers of land and often punished minor crime. Control of the manor-court remained evidence of ownership of the manor, even though its power over the peasantry was declining.

Most of the Norfolk peasantry was now of free status because, in an age of low grain prices and higher wages, it was no longer profitable for manorial lords to grow for the open market and, wherever possible, they leased out their lands to the peasantry. The Pastons, like other medium-sized and small landlords, took some of their rents in kind to sell to the market and they continued to own flocks of sheep, but most of their income came from money-rents. As the need for labour-services disappeared, serfdom (the status of being legally unfree) became an anachronism; claims that men were serfs, such as that made against John Paston in the 1460s, were clearly intended to harrass and to extort money, rather than to enforce the performance of dues and services.

Despite attempts by the government to keep wages at levels which had prevailed before the Black Death, they had risen inexorably. A labourer in 1450, earning perhaps 4d. a day, or a skilled craftsman, earning between 5d. and 8d., could buy twice as much food as his ancestors a hundred years before. In Norfolk there were increasing opportunities for employment in the cloth industry and a variety of other crafts, but there were also many purely agricultural workers who found it more profitable to sell their labour than to squeeze a living from their own small holdings. Of course, the standard of living of such men and their families was not high: living in one or two-room hovels with few amenities and with no cushion against a slump in the cloth trade or against old age and sickness, there was plenty of scope for their richer contemporaries to show benevolence by giving alms. The number of people who waited outside the monasteries and the houses of the King and his nobles for the leavings from their tables shows the continued prevalence of poverty.

Nevertheless, the prospects were good for the energetic and the fortunate. The land available in the form of leases and freeholds allowed them to build up large holdings. Some of these became the husbandmen or 'yeomen' whom the seventeenth-century writer, Thomas Fuller, described as 'gentlemen in ore, whom the next age will see refined'. Others rose from humble origins to make large fortunes in the cloth industry. The Spring family of Lavenham in Suffolk, for example, were peasants who, by the early sixteenth century, had become the richest family in Suffolk; and there was even a villein tenant of Sir John Fastolf at Castlecombe in Wiltshire who was able to leave over £2,000 at his death, mainly from the profits of cloth-making.

## Towns and Townsmen

Of over seven hundred townships in Norfolk and the ten thousand or so in England as a whole, only three per cent would be considered 'towns' in the modern sense. Many of these places would have possessed a successful market. There had been over a hundred markets in thirteenth-century Norfolk, but of these probably fewer than half had survived the fourteenth-century drop in population and many of these were to fade away in the following century. Places such as North Walsham and Aylsham, however, remained the natural markets and economic centres for North-East Norfolk and provided a wide range of services for the neighbouring villages. They were not distinguished from their smaller neighbours by name or legal status. The title 'borough' was reserved for those towns which had been granted charters by their lord or by the King; such charters gave them the right, to a greater or lesser extent, to control their own finances and the activities of their inhabitants. There were several hundred of these boroughs in the country but only four – Norwich, Lynn, Yarmouth and Thetford – in Norfolk. The title did not necessarily imply large size or economic activity; the populous and wealthy village of Lavenham in Suffolk, for instance, was not a borough, whereas there were many boroughs in the West Country and the South which had shrunk to the size of small villages, while still retaining their nominal status.

Most of the substantial towns of fifteenth-century England did, however, have borough status. These included industrial centres, regional markets and a number of ports, such as Lynn, Sandwich and Southampton, which had remained important centres of overseas trade despite the constant growth in London's share of that traffic. They usually contained a wide variety of trades: there were scores of separate crafts in Norwich and well over a hundred in London, ranging from the specialized skills associated with the cloth, leather and metal industries to general wholesale merchants belonging to the grocers' and mercers' guilds and scriveners, or professional writers.

Such boroughs were usually headed by a mayor or by bailiffs elected annually, and many of the larger ones had a governing body modelled on that of London with aldermen and a common council. In most of these towns, real power resided in the hands of the wealthier wholesale merchants who tended to monopolize senior offices and to secure election for their towns to parliament. Men such as Dick Whittington of London, who died in 1423, and Hamo Sutton of Lincoln, Mayor of the Staple at Calais and many times a member of parliament for Linconshire as well as the city of Lincoln, were of national as well as local importance. They sat in parliaments, negotiated with and lent money to kings and ministers, and through membership of the 'Company of the Staple' or the 'Merchant Adventurers', they influenced the nature of overseas trade in wool and cloth, and thus of England's foreign policy.

The author of a treatise on precedence at banquets emphasized that 'The Mayor of London, notable of dignity, and the Mayor of Queenborough are nothing alike in degree' and should not be sat at the same table – an indication of the vast difference between the governing élites of London and those of smaller boroughs. Nevertheless, they shared similar duties and had the same sort of pride in their community. They represented their towns in parliaments, were responsible for their finances, justice and corporate property and, so far as was possible, maintained their independence from the pressures of local

*Opposite: The Crucifixion, from the fourteenth-century Norwich Retable in Norwich Cathedral.*

magnates and the King's officials. English towns, even London, did not have the independence of action possessed by many of the cities of Italy or Germany, but their considerable civic pride was displayed in the increasingly elaborate mayor-making ceremonies and processions, the great guild processions on Corpus Christi day and the expensive pageants put on at the entry of kings and noblemen into the town. It was this pride that spurred the massive rebuilding programmes which characterized many towns in the period.

The bigger towns, like Norwich and York, were often the seats of county government and of dioceses; Quarter Sessions met there regularly and the Assize Judges twice a year. County-dwellers constantly made their way there on business, stimulating the growth of 'service industries' – inns, taverns, attorneys and providers of luxury goods. Some country gentlemen owned or rented houses in towns and lived in them for part of the year, as did the Pastons. Similarly, a good many of the richer citizens owned land outside the town-walls and some would found gentry families on the profits of their trade. Boroughs were social and political communities, many of them physically separated by their walls from the surrounding country. They were governed by their own elected officials. But they were not self-contained entities: often there were areas within the walls which, like the priory at Norwich, were outside civic control.

### Gentlemen of the County

A few boroughs, including Norwich, had followed London in securing exemption from the authority of the sheriff and had become counties themselves, with their own sheriffs. But, in general, it was the county or 'shire' which was the unit of local government and justice in fifteenth-century England. Sheriffs, Justices of the Peace and commissioners were appointed for the county by the Crown; troops were levied and mustered in the county and paid for until they had passed its borders; taxes were usually assessed and always collected on a county basis; and each of the 39 English counties, except Durham and Cheshire, was represented in the House of Commons by two representatives – the 'knights of the shire' – who were chosen in the county court. At such elections, the 'county' came together as a political unit. It was not just the gentry who were involved in these decisions. Substantial freeholders like Warren King of Paston – or, no doubt, old Clement Paston in his day – were members of this wider community as well as the community of their village.

At election time, the 'voices' of freeholders were courted by the lords and gentlemen; at the disputed Norfolk election of 1461, for example, John Paston was alleged to have collected over a thousand men to force his will on the meeting, and it is clear that large numbers of freeholders quite frequently appeared on such occasions.

The county was more than an administrative area. The Pastons usually refer to Norfolk as their 'country' and, certainly among the gentry, there was a sense of belonging to a county that transcended the mere fact of residing in it. This is articulated in John Jenney's letter to John Paston in 1455, in which he fears that 'the shire shall not be called of such worship [honour] as it has been'. The richer peasants who sat on juries in the county, acted as deputies for the sheriff, as constables and bailiffs, and took part in the elections of the county's representatives, were all part of this shire or county; real power, however, was normally exercised by their social superiors.

## Upward Mobility

Although in its essentials, this structure of power and social status remained fairly stable for several centuries, there was much mobility within it. If there were no sons of a marriage, the daughters could inherit the family lands and take them to their husbands' families, just as Margaret took the Mauteby estates to the Pastons. The relation of the 'lineage' to its land was constantly at risk therefore. High mortality meant that noble families often failed in the male line and, as a result, there was always a need for recruitment from below. Sometimes, for example, a 'yeoman', or substantial farmer, would acquire enough land and wealth to begin to live like a gentleman, to educate his sons and to marry them into noble families. But there were other routes into the upper classes. The development of the law as a profession for laymen offered ways of accumulating wealth to those who had the fortune and ability to acquire the requisite training. Much of this wealth would have been used to purchase land, and the Pastons and many of their contemporaries, including the Heydons, Townshends, Wodehouses, Knyvetts and Hobarts all owed their early rise to the successful practice of the law. Trade, too, promised even greater fortunes, part of which was usually invested in the purchase of land and the acquisition, in the following generation at least, of gentry or noble status. Many of the richer London merchants bought estates in the Home

## THE HIERARCHY OF STATUS IN FIFTEENTH-CENTURY ENGLAND

| ECCLESIASTICS | SOCIETY | TOWNSMEN | LAWYERS |
|---|---|---|---|
|  | King |  |  |
| Archbishops | Dukes |  |  |
| Bishops | Marquesses |  |  |
|  | Earls |  |  |
| Mitred abbots | Viscounts |  |  |
|  | Barons | Mayor of London | Judges |
| Other abbots and priors; deans, archdeacons, etc | Knights | Aldermen of London | Serjeants-at-law |
|  | Esquires |  |  |
| Beneficed clergy | Gentlemen | Mayors and aldermen of other towns | Apprentices-at-law |
|  |  | Freemen of boroughs | Attorneys |
| Chaplains, etc | Yeomen | Journeymen craftsmen |  |
|  | Husbandmen | Apprentices |  |
|  | Labourers | Labourers |  |

*In this diagram, yeomen, husbandmen, labourers, apprentices and craftsmen accounted for 90 per cent of the population of rural England.*

Counties but Geoffrey Boleyn, for example, made his pile in London, bought estates in Norfolk, married his children into the nobility and eventually became the great-grandfather of a queen. As Fastolf's career shows, success at war could bring rich rewards in booty, ransoms, lucrative offices and lands and a naturally enhanced rise in social status.

The Church offered career prospects, too, but a bishop was precluded from founding a landed family by his vow of celibacy. The most important means of social improvement, however, was service to the Crown. Office in the Royal Household immediately enhanced one's rank in the social hierarchy – a 'Yeoman of the Chamber', for example, would take precedence equal to an esquire, an 'Esquire of the Chamber' that of a knight. For these men, the opportunities of profiting from royal favour by acquiring grants of land, lucrative offices and heiresses could be very great.

Upward mobility was not regarded with favour by the nobility and gentry, and it was desirable to acquire as quickly as possible some of the blood, as well as the lifestyle, of the class one was entering. Marriages were therefore crucially important for such families – a fact which helps to explain the horror at Margery Paston's mésalliance. It was also a good idea to establish a distinguished ancestry, often fictitious, and to represent it by the adoption of an appropriate coat of arms. By the fifteenth century, 'a gentleman of coat armour' was the phrase used to define the lesser nobility or gentry, and the coat of arms had ceased to have its original function as a rallying symbol on the battlefield – badges on banners and liveries were now used for this purpose. As yet there was no effective control by the College of Heralds (incorporated in 1484) but there was some attempt to avoid duplication. The beginning of royal control of unlicensed arms can be seen by Henry V's decree in 1417 that no one joining the army for the French campaign 'shall assume such coats of arms unless he has or ought to have the same by right of his ancestors or by the gift of some person having sufficient power for this purpose'.

The desire to maintain the social hierarchy and to indicate the gradations of status within it is exemplified by the 'Sumptuary Laws' of the fourteenth and fifteenth centuries. These tried to ensure that the social status of men and women could be recognized from the clothes they wore. No labourer, for example, was allowed to wear cloth worth more than 2s. a yard; no one below the rank of gentleman was allowed to wear a doublet padded with wool; no one below the rank of lord was to wear any jacket, gown or cloak which did not 'cover his privy members and buttocks'. Such acts were rarely enforced, as the preambles complain, but they do show what status-indicators were seen as most significant; they also illustrate how the ranks in differing societies and professions, including the Court, the law and urban society, were equated. In 1463, for instance, Esquires of the Body to the King and sons of barons, together with mayors and ex-mayors of London, were permitted to wear much the same things as knights; mayors and aldermen of other towns could dress like esquires and gentlemen with incomes of £40 and more; the servants of gentlemen and above were equated with owners of land worth 40s. a year.

Nevertheless, the permanent acceptance of a family into the gentry depended on its

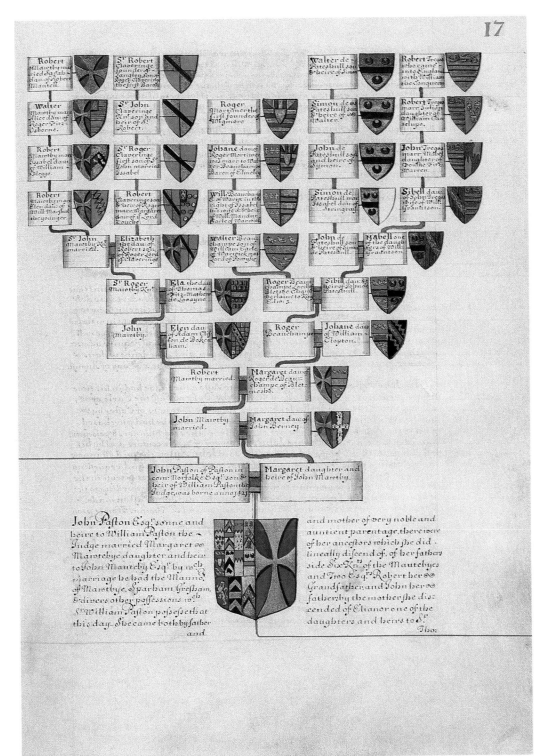

The Mauteby family treee, to the time of Margaret's marriage to John Paston, 1436/40.

possession of landed property. Thus, 'nouveaux riches' like William Paston I or Sir John Fastolf invested heavily in land in order to give themselves power and prestige in their region and to hand on an 'inheritance' to their heirs. Such acquisitions often brought troubles with them. The law governing the ownership and transmission of freehold land, and the legal actions available to those claiming rights in it, had become very complex indeed by the fifteenth century; and since there was no form of central registration, it was difficult to obtain and secure title, particularly of purchased land. Fastolf and Paston were careful purchasers; they had extensive searches made, but both of them later found claimants to some of the lands they had bought, which involved them or their successors in protracted litigation. Fastolf's rights to the manors of Bradwell, Beighton, Titchwell and Dedham were challenged in the 1440s and, after his death, the Pastons spent twenty years defending their rights to these and other parts of his inheritance. As a judge, William Paston was too powerful to be challenged in his lifetime but the rights of his widow and son to Oxnead and Gresham had to be defended stoutly after his death. Indeed, the disputes over the inheritances left by William Paston and John Fastolf form one of the main themes of the letters printed here.

Such disputes were not easily resolved. Deeds, wills and other documents had to be searched for, witnesses collected, and pedigrees constructed. William Worcester spent much of his time as Fastolf's agent delving for evidence to back up his title to disputed

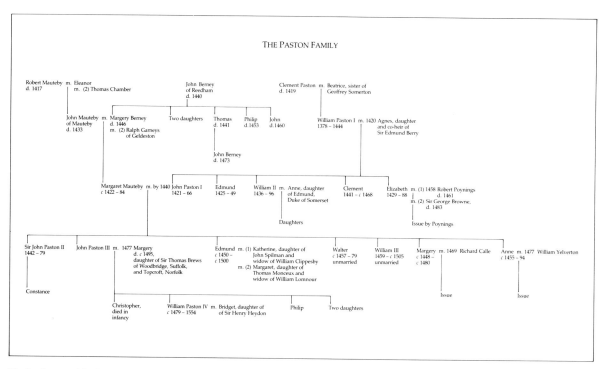

*The family tree of the Pastons.*

manors. Similarly, the Pastons sought evidence from a variety of sources in their dispute with the Duke of Suffolk over Hellesdon. But even more important than evidence was influence. Litigation over land normally took place in the Court of Common pleas or before the Justices of Assize; much of the process was dependent upon the sheriff and decisions were made by juries of the county. Sheriffs and jurors, however, were open to pressure from magnates and courtiers and those who could call upon their patronage. Pressure or 'maintenance' by a lord and corrupt behaviour by a sheriff were widely recognized as evils and their prevalence is clear enough from the Paston correspondence. If an opponent were a man of power, particularly a lord, litigation was generally considered pointless; like John Paston in 1449, the only remedy was to seek the 'grace' of one's opponent or to find an even greater lord to put pressure on him. The ordinary courts were not effective in such situations; only Parliament, the Council or the Court of Chancery could bring the direct power of the King to bear and were unaffected by malleable juries or biased sheriffs. But the success of these institutions depended very heavily upon the authority of the King and this, in turn, upon the political situation, as Sir John Paston found in his negotiations over Caister in 1469. In any case, their role was not to produce a final verdict on the rights of the case but to keep the peace and to settle the matter to the reasonable satisfaction of both sides. Indeed, this was the main function of much litigation in the fifteenth century: there was a strong desire to find a 'means' or compromise, often by agreed arbitration, which would not only save money but, more importantly, would save face. Above all it was his 'honour' – his reputation and the acknowledgment by others of his status – that made the gentleman. And he realized that this could be lost by open defeat in the law-courts as much as by defeat in battle.

## King and Country

Village, borough and county provided a sense of identity for most people but there was also a sense of 'Englishness' which transcended local particularism. 'The English,' wrote an Italian observer in around 1500, 'are great lovers of themselves and of everything belonging to them; they think that there are no other men than themselves, and no other world but England; and whenever they see a handsome foreigner they say that he looks like an Englishman'. This sense of national identity had been stimulated by the long years of war with France and perhaps inflamed by the final loss of the English King's French possessions. After 1453 only Calais and the Channel Islands were left as English possessions on the other side of the Channel. Within the British Isles, too, the boundaries of the English kingdom had hardened. Serious attempts to conquer Scotland had stopped long ago although there was constant tension on the still ill-defined borders. Wales was firmly a part of the Kingdom, although it was administered separately from the rest of the country. In Ireland, however, effective control was mainly limited to the 'Pale' around Dublin, although the English King claimed lordship over the whole island.

The loss of French territory coincided with the end of the French language as the natural medium of the upper classes. Although educated men and women of the late fifteenth and sixteenth centuries would have been expected to know French, they would have known it as a foreign, taught language – much as they knew Latin. English was now, for all classes, the natural language of the written as well as the spoken word. It was a rapidly changing language. William Caxton wrote in 1490 that 'certainly our language now used varies far from that which was used when I was born [about 70 years previously]'. Variations in dialect persisted – 'Lo, what should a man in these days now write, "eggs" or "eyren" [northern and southern forms of the word]?', asked Caxton. Spelling, too remained very arbitrary, although a more standard written English was developing, based on the forms used around London. Caxton, for example, expected his South-Eastern vocabulary and grammar to be readable by any 'clerk or noble gentleman', but not by a 'rude uplandish man'.

Language gave an increasing sense of unity to England, but the unity of the 'community of the realm' was symbolized, above all, in the Crown. Although Parliament represented all the 'estates' or classes of the kingdom, it was the King who provided the focus for the community. A magnificent court, frequent expeditions to display his authority and successful foreign wars were all important means to this end. So was propaganda and the fostering of a myth of national greatness. The triumphs of Edward III and Henry V in the Hundred Years War were parts of that myth, taking their place alongside the achievements of King Arthur and 'Brutus', the legendary Trojan hero who was thought to have founded the kingdom of Britain. It was during the reign of Edward IV that Sir Thomas Malory wrote his great version of the Arthurian tales and under Richard III that William Caxton printed them. John Paston III's comparison of the Burgundian Court to the Court of King Arthur illustrates the widespread knowledge of these legends, which were believed by most to be true history. They inspired the virtues of courage, loyalty to a lord and friends, generosity and courteous behaviour. But they also, quite specifically in parts of Malory's work, emphasized the leadership of the King and the evils brought about by disobedience to him: '(Arthur) was the most king and noblest knight of the world . . . and yet might not the Englishmen hold them content with him . . . Alas, this is a great fault of us Englishmen, for there may nothing please us for long.' It was for this emphasis on kingship that the cult of Arthur was encouraged by both Edward IV and Henry VII. Edward named his illegitimate son Arthur, a name almost unknown in fifteenth-century England, and Henry VII went considerably further by giving the same name to his first-born son, who was expected to be the future king. As a result, the ideals of chivalry – although international – became identified with loyalty to the King and a sense of patriotism.

## The Role of Religion

The really international force, and – for the great majority of men and women – the inspiration for ideals and the source of ethics, was religion. The English provinces of Canterbury and York and their subordinate dioceses were part of the 'universal' church of which the Pope was the head. The beliefs, forms of worship, law and institutional structure were generally the same throughout Western Europe. And, because Latin was the liturgical language everywhere, pilgrims like Margery Kempe would have found church services in Italy, Spain, Germany and the Netherlands comfortably familiar, though sermons and confession might have caused some trouble. Margery Kempe had to rely upon a vision of St John to hear her confession when she could find no English-speaking priest in Rome, though she later found a German priest who understood her. The major monastic and mendicant orders had religious houses in most countries, undertaking the same round of services and performing the same social functions. Spiritual influences were equally international: Margery Kempe's visions of the Holy Family and the Saints and her conversations with them were of the same sort as experienced by St Bridget of Sweden and St Joan of Arc.

In England, as in some other countries, kings and parliaments had limited the ability of the Pope's authority to cross the national frontier. Papal 'provisions' [appointments] to English benefices were forbidden without royal licence; the English clergy could not be taxed by the Pope without royal consent; and the subordinate houses of French monasteries in England were seized by the King during the Hundred Years War on the grounds that they were owned by foreigners. Above all, it was the King who nominated the bishops even if the actual appointments were made by papal provision.

Royal involvement in such appointments was inevitable, for bishops were not simply spiritual leaders; they were also holders of large estates and sat in parliaments and in the King's councils as peers of the realm. The Archbishops of Canterbury and York, for example, and the Bishops of Winchester, Durham and Lincoln were some of the greatest lords of the land and behaved accordingly. Cardinal Kemp, Archbishop of Canterbury from 1452 to 1454, and Thomas Bourchier, who succeeded him, had served the King in high office. Others were favourite chaplains of the King or a great lord. William Waynflete, for instance, who played such an important part in the fortunes of the Pastons, had been one of the first fellows of Henry VI's foundation at Eton. Waynflete was then nominated by the King to the wealthy see of Winchester, where he was Bishop from 1447 to 1486. Walter Lyhert, Bishop of Norwich from 1446 to 1472, owed his see to the patronage of William, Duke of Suffolk, whose chaplain he was. Such prelates were often absent from their dioceses – indeed, Cardinal Kemp hardly ever visited York although he held the archbishopric for 26 years. Their dioceses were run by efficient subordinate officers and suffragans, while the bishops themselves served as royal councillors, filled high offices of state or attended parliaments. The abbots of the great monastic houses with large landed estates such as Bury St Edmunds, Westminster and St Albans were also parliamentary lords, though few played a major part in national politics.

In spite of their involvement with the secular world, religious institutions from the parish church to the bishopric and the great monastery had all been founded and endowed to carry out the cure of souls, the daily round of prayer, preaching and caring for the sick and

In this pagent is shewed howe the noble Erle Richard was made knyght
of the Garter at that tyme to his gret worship / And after by marciall
act by hym ful notably and knyghtly acheved in his pore psone. Did
gret hono~ & worship to the noble ordre of knyghtes of the Garter.
As by the pagentes hereafter folowyng more pleynly is shewed.

poor. The emphasis varied with the status of the cleric and the order to which he belonged: there was a place for many sorts of devotion.

Late Medieval religion has been called 'a ritual method of living rather than a set of dogmas'. Although there have been few other times when so many men of such great intellectual gifts have devoted themselves to the study of theological problems and the codification and implementation of the doctrines of the Church, these filtered down only in very diluted form to the devotions of the individual. There is little evidence in the age of the Paston Letters of any considerable dissatisfaction with the beliefs and practices of the Church. The late fourteenth century had witnessed a great crisis in the constitution and confidence of the Church in Western Europe. In England it had found its most notable expression in virulent criticism of the clergy, particularly the religious orders, and in the rapid spread of heretical Lollard ideas – ideas which attacked fundamental practices of the Church, such as the Mass, the adoration of the saints and relics, pilgrimages, confession, and the special nature of the priesthood. By the mid-fifteenth century, however, the structure of the Church had recovered its equilibrium and Lollardy had been extirpated at the universities, where it had begun, and destroyed or driven underground in the country at large. In the late 1420s there had been a major series of Lollard trials in the diocese of Norwich, which resulted in several burnings and a large number of heavy penances, but there are no references to heterodox religion in the Paston Letters. Undoubtedly, Lollardy still existed underground but outwardly, anyway, there seems to have been almost universal acceptance of the dogma, institutions and discipline of the Church, exercised through its structure of courts and officials from the Papal Curia down to the parish.

The parish church was the focus for the devotion of most people. Although his pastoral work was important, the parson's duties revolved around the daily prayers at the Canonical Hours, the ceremony of the Mass and the variety of observances associated with the feast-days of the Church, together with the 'rites of passage' – baptism, marriage, churching and burial. Piety was expressed, above all, in devout observance, and in imagery and ceremony. The great religious feasts, such as Christmas, Palm Sunday, Easter, Corpus Christi, Michaelmas and Hallowmas or All Saints, punctuated the year and gave a focus for the lives of the parishioners of all classes.

The structure of the parish church, with its proliferation of side-chapels, reflected the subsidiary religious groups within the parish. The seigneurial family would have its own place, perhaps its own chapel, within the church, where the tombs of its forebears lay; Margaret Paston asks, for instance, to be buried at Mautby in the aisle in which 'rest the bodies of divers of mine ancestors'. Religious guilds had their own altars at least, with the images of their patron saints, and they might well have had their own chapels as well within the body of the church, where a common act of worship for members living and

*Opposite: Richard Beauchamp, Earl of Warwick, being made a Knight of the Garter after the Battle of Shrewsbury, 1403.*

dead was kept. Such guilds also provided money for the welfare of their members, ensuring that they had a proper funeral. From time to time they would hold feasts, but their prime function was religious. Guilds, like the parish itself, provided a sphere for the communal activities of the laity and clergy together: 'scot-ales' and other fund-raising activities were needed to maintain the fabric and services of the church for which the parishioners were largely responsible. It is clear that, despite having their private chaplain and chapel, the Pastons did attend their parish church, certainly when in Norwich, and were involved in its activities: John Paston paid for substantial rebuilding work at St Peter Hungate in Norwich and the surviving wills of the Pastons and their contemporaries generally leave money for the fabric of the church, and frequently for charitable works

Late medieval religious practices had a strong communal aspect then, but the piety of the period is also characterized by increasing individualism. The account by Agnes Paston of the last hours of Sir John Heveningham, who had been 'to his church and heard three masses . . . and said to his wife that he would go to say a little devotion in his garden' and there died, provides a nice illustration of the contemporary combination of public worship and private devotion. The most obvious 'individualism' in religion is, perhaps, rather less attractive to a later age. The desire of many wealthy testators to have large numbers of masses and prayers said for their souls suggests an overemphasis upon the possibility of purchasing a way through Purgatory: both William and Margaret Paston provide for seven years of daily masses and, compared with some of their contemporaries, this was far from extravagant. But there is another side to such practices. They did provide a continuing reminder of past generations – links with which were particularly tenuous in an age when people lived only for a short time and when few actions were recorded in permanent form.

**Lordship and Local Government**

The formal structure of local government in most of England was based on the county, with its internal divisions of hundreds or wapentakes, each composed of a group of townships, the lowest institutions through which the King's authority was administered. Township, hundred and country were linked to the major central courts of the Crown through the sheriffs and other county officers, such as escheators and coroners, through commissions and through the bi-annual visitations of the justices of assize. But these were not the only sources of power in the regions of England. The informal authority wielded by the lords and lesser landowners cut across this 'official' structure and manipulated it. Such authority derived from wealth, particularly land, the ability to muster large numbers of men, influence with the King and his officers, and a traditional deference towards long-established magnate families.

In East Anglia it was the Dukes of Norfolk who generally claimed deference, deriving from centuries of possession of the most substantial lay estate in the region. Their authority

*Opposite: The Neville family at prayer; a French fifteenth-century illustration.*

straddled the county boundary with Suffolk but, unlike some counties, Norfolk was too big to be dominated by any one magnate for any length of time. Through his retainers, Sir Thomas Tuddenham in the west at Oxburgh and John Heydon in the north-east at Baconsthorpe, William, Duke of Suffolk had come close to dominating the county during the 1440s. Although in 1452 the Duke of Norfolk claimed that 'next the King . . . we will . . . have the principal rule and governance in the shire of which we bear our name', his authority was limited mainly to the east of both counties, where his main estates lay. He rarely had much power in the west of Norfolk where, for much of the century, the leading lords were the successive Lords Scales at Middleton, near Lynn, and the Earl of Oxford, who had acquired the West Norfolk estates of the Howards by marriage.

In North-East Norfolk, the home of the Pastons, no lord had substantial estates, except for the Duchy of Lancaster at Gimingham, which was in the hands of the Crown. Manors and land were widely dispersed in ownership and it was this which enabled William Paston and his son to build up estates in the area. On the other hand, the power of the lords was relatively weak and large bands of loyal tenants could not be mustered at will. John Paston had to work hard to gather enough supporters in his bid to become knight of the shire in 1461, most of them from North-East Norfolk. Despite his wife's opinions that the 'people' of that region were sympathetic to him, they were an isolated and independent-minded breed. The Pastons too seem to have inherited much of the stubbornness and acquisitiveness of their peasant forebears. Such characteristics are to be found in their letters, along with others that are rather more engaging.

### The King's Government

The King was served by a large bureaucracy divided into several major departments, each of which kept elaborate records, and had its own career structure and traditional methods of working. Apart from the Law Courts, the two oldest and most formal departments were the Chancery and the Exchequer: the Chancery issued the King's formal documents, such as grants, appointments to offices and commissions, and the vast numbers of legal and administrative writs issued each year; the Exchequer controlled the receipts and issues of the Crown and audited the accounts of inferior officials. In theory, therefore, all parts of the realm were closely linked to the Crown, although in practice supervision was very weak in the more distant parts of the kingdom, such as the North and the Welsh Marches.

Much of the work of the Chancery and Exchequer was very formal: as with most bureaucracies, any new action needed a warrant from superior authority or a petition from below. Such warrants were provided in the last resort by the King, in whose name most actions of the government were done but, in fact, the King's direct initiative was limited to the fairly small number of matters that directly concerned him, his family and servants, or that were politically or diplomatically important. Initiatives often came from those around the King in his Household, from his Council and the great officers of state, such as the Chancellor and Treasurer, and occasionally from Parliament. Which of these individuals

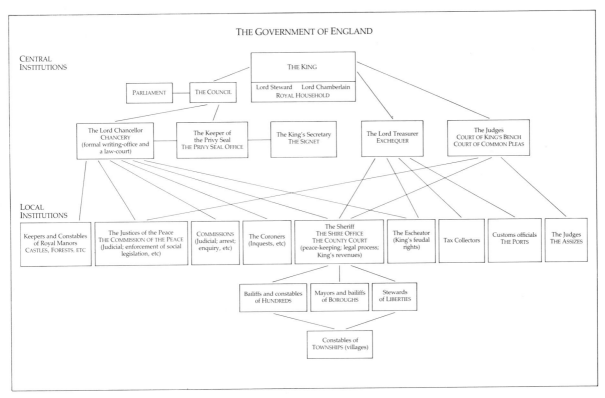

*A simplified diagram showing the structure of fifteenth-century government in England.*

and institutions had most influence depended very much on the personality of the King and the political situation in the realm. Warrants for action, whether sponsored by a councillor or courtier, often began with a request from a subject who desired some office, grant or other favour which needed a royal letter under the Great Seal issued by Chancery or involved expenditure from the Exchequer. If approved by the King, the Keeper of the Privy Seal would be ordered to draw up a warrant on which the Chancery or the Exchequer would take action. As John Paston III found in 1471, royal approval for the issue of letters of pardon was only the first step in the process. On 17 July 1471 he received, through the good offices of one of the King's Household, the King's signature on his bill and 'trusted to have my bill eninsealed by the Chancellor' within a few days; in fact, it was another six months before he received the security of the formal document. At every stage in the process of obtaining Crown action there were people to conciliate and, frequently, to pay: patience, political and personal skills, money and influence, were all needed to get what was wanted if the request were at all out of the ordinary. John Paston had used his acquaintance at Court to take the first vital step, but he was clearly less successful at fighting his way through the thickets of the offices of the Privy Seal and the Chancery. It was this sort of problem that made connections with key figures at all levels so important. A man like

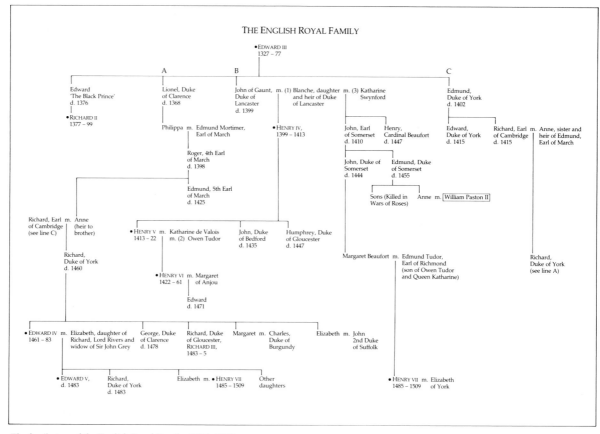

*The family tree of the English Royal Family, 1327–1509.*

Edmund Blake, Clerk of the King's Signet, was very valuable to his fellow Norfolk men in 1450–1 in seeing their petitions through their early stages and in expediting action against the opponents of Fastolf and Paston. Fastolf insisted that he be thanked 'for his friendship to the country'. Even more useful to Fastolf and other Norfolk gentlemen was Hugh Fenne, a senior Exchequer official for twenty-five years before his death in 1476. As Elizabeth Clere pointed out, 'he is very faithful to his friends and may do much with the King and Lords'. But there were other Exchequer clerks whom Fastolf, and John Paston after him, had to wine, dine and pay in order to get their business done.

This is not intended to suggest that those close to the King and his government were particularly corrupt. At all levels and for all purposes in pre-modern societies, presents lubricated official and unofficial action; it was only when demands for 'rewards' were excessive that complaints became widespread. Rewards were not always financial: Fenne and Blake, for instance, would expect their assistance to local friends and relatives to be

*Opposite: Charles the Bold of Burgundy, surrounded by his court and council.*

IE LAV EN PRINS                    BIEN EN AVIENGNE

Rdonnance faitte par mon tres
redoubte s: monseigneur le duc
de bourgoingne xe brabant xc

reciprocated in kind, when possible. The informal contacts of courtiers with the King became even more important during the later part of the century as the King's direct control of his revenue and administration grew; Sir John Paston's desire to stay at Court and maintain links first with the Woodvilles, then with Lord Hastings, is understandable, however much it irritated his mother and brother.

### English Politics in the Fifteenth Century

The politics of the century were deeply affected by the conflicts of the main powers of Western Europe, the Kings of France and the Duke of Burgundy. The Kings of France had been England's rivals for a hundred years, but the rise of the Duchy of Burgundy had brought a new force into West European diplomacy. The Dukes were also rulers of Flanders and much of the Netherlands, and it was these territories which produced much of their wealth. Their links with England were deeply affected by the dependence of Netherlands towns on massive imports of English wool and clothing. Duke Philip of Burgundy had been an ally of England against Charles VII of France up to the Congress of Arras in 1435. Even after that date, the Burgundian Dukes remained the great rivals to the Kings of France, and English support was sought by both sides in their conflicts. This French-Burgundian rivalry played a major part in the English civil wars until 1494, when the invasion of Italy by Charles VIII of France pushed England firmly to the periphery of Western European diplomacy.

The involvement of France and Burgundy in English politics followed Henry V's victory at Agincourt in 1415, when the English established their authority in much of northern France, and where the young King Henry VI was recognised as King from 1422 onwards. Had Henry grown up like his father in temperament, he might have made massive (and probably vain) efforts to recover and extend his possessions in France. Instead, he worked for peace, and this, together with his reliance on a small group of courtiers, estranged many of the nobles and people from him. In 1450 the loss of Normandy to Charles VII of France brought about the downfall of Henry's favourite, the Duke of Suffolk, and the arrival on the political scene of Richard, Duke of York. Richard had a claim to the throne through his Mortimer mother, and consequently divisions of allegiance grew throughout the land. Early conflicts leading to the Battle of St. Albans in 1455, and Blore Heath and Ludford four years later were not, however, caused by rival dynastic claims, but by a struggle to control an increasingly feeble king. But by the time the King's forces had been defeated at Northampton in July 1460, the Duke of York finally claimed the throne. His support among the lords was limited, and he lost his life at the Battle of Wakefield, although a few great lords led by the Nevilles were able to put his son, Edward, Earl of March, on the throne in March 1461.

The first ten years of Edward's reign were by no means easy ones. Lancastrian resistance, organised by Queen Margaret (wife of Henry VI) survived for a number of years, especially in the North. Edward was also very dependent on Richard, Earl of Warwick, whose

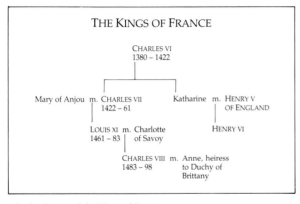

THE KINGS OF FRANCE

CHARLES VI
1380 – 1422

Mary of Anjou m. CHARLES VII        Katharine m. HENRY V
1422 – 61                                        OF ENGLAND

LOUIS XI m. Charlotte              HENRY VI
1461 – 83      of Savoy

CHARLES VIII m. Anne, heiress
1483 – 98        to Duchy of
                     Brittany

*The family tree of the Kings of France.*

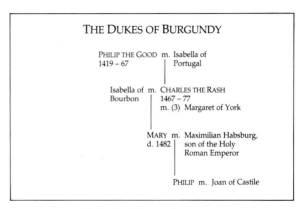

THE DUKES OF BURGUNDY

PHILIP THE GOOD m. Isabella of
1419 – 67              Portugal

Isabella of m. CHARLES THE RASH
Bourbon    |   1467 – 77
           |   m. (3) Margaret of York

MARY m. Maximilian Habsburg,
d. 1482 |   son of the Holy
        |   Roman Emperor

PHILIP m. Joan of Castile

*The family tree of the Dukes of Burgundy.*

boundless ambitions for his Neville faction were not satiated by the great rewards they received. Edward's marriage into the equally clamorous Woodville family introduced new court rivalries. This was an extra source of discontent to the Nevilles and their allies, and they were joined by Edward's brother, the Duke of Clarence.

In 1470 Warwick, Clarence and Queen Margaret forged an unlikely alliance with Louis XI of France and restored the mentally feeble and long-imprisoned Henry VI to the English throne. Louis had hoped thereby to breach the traditional English alliance with the Duke of Burgundy. Edward and his lords fled to Flanders, from where they staged a counter-coup the following year with troops and shipping helpfully supplied by Charles, Duke of Burgundy. In the process, Warwick and his brothers were killed or imprisoned, Henry VI was murdered in the tower and his son died in the Battle of Tewkesbury. There remained no serious rival to Edward, and the last twelve years of his reign were much more secure. He was able to live in great splendour to the end of his life; the first English King, it has been said, to die financially solvent.

The increased personal authority of the King had again exacerbated rivalries at court. Edward was able to dispose of his dangerously 'over-mighty' brother, the Duke of Clarence, by having him drowned in a butt of malmsey wine, but his equally powerful younger brother, Richard Duke of Gloucester, took his opportunity when Edward died unexpectedly in 1483. Gloucester's deposition and murder in the Tower of Edward's two young sons brought a new insecurity to the Yorkist dynasty. Henry Tudor, descended from a younger branch of the House of Lancaster, had been an exile in Brittany since the defeat of the Lancastrians in 1471. With help from the King of France he conquered and killed Richard at Bosworth in 1485.

Henry's grip on the throne was fragile at first, as strong Yorkist feeling survived, even after his judicious marriage to Edward VI's daughter. But with the birth of Prince Arthur in 1486 the blood of Lancaster and York was finally united, although after Arthur's death in 1501 it was his younger brother, Henry, who eventually represented the 'union of the Noble Houses of York and Lancaster.'

# The Paston Letters

During the dispute over the lands of Sir John Fastolf in the 1460s the Pastons were accused of being descended from serfs and thus unable to possess manorial rights. In response they showed before the King's Council large numbers of documents which proved not only that they were free but also that their ancestors had been nobles since soon after the Norman Conquest. In the sixteenth century, when so many gentry families invented Norman ancestries for themselves, this pedigree was elaborated and the Pastons appeared as a knightly family with manors and serfs since the twelfth century. The truth was almost certainly somewhat different. The Paston ancestry cannot be traced with any certainty before about AD 1300, and all of the early members of the family appear to have been peasants, although they were freemen and farmed substantial holdings in the windswept but fertile fields of North Norfolk. It was probably about 1450 that a rival of the Pastons scornfully described what he saw as the shameful origins of the upstart John Paston.

First there was one Clement Paston dwelling in Paston, and he was a good plain husbandman, and lived upon the land he had in Paston and kept a plough there at all times in the year and sometimes at barley-sowing two ploughs. The said Clement went at one plough both winter and summer, and he rode to the mill on bare horseback with his corn under him, and brought home the meal again under him; and he also drove his cart with various corns to sell at Winterton, as a good husbandman ought to do.

Also he had in Paston five or six score acres of land at most, and much of that bond land belonging to Gimingham Hall Manor, together with a little poor water-mill running by means of a little river, apparently there from long ago. He held no other manors or land there nor in any other place.

And he wedded the sister of Geoffrey of Somerton whose true surname is Goneld; she was a bondwoman, to whom it is not unknown if men will enquire – to the Prior of Bromholm and also to Bacton, it is said. As for Geoffrey of Somerton, he was bond also; he was both a pardoner and an attorney; and then was a good world, for he gathered many pence and halfpence, and with them he built a fair chapel at Somerton, as it appears.

Also the said Clement had a son, William, whom he sent to school and he often borrowed money to pay for him. And after that he went to court with the help of Geoffrey Somerton, his uncle, and learned the law, and by that he obtained much profit; and then he was made serjeant-at-law and was afterwards made a justice, being a right cunning man in the law. And he purchased much land in Paston, and . . . with that he has a lordship in Paston, but no manor-house. But by right of this John Paston, son of the said William, claims a manor there, to the great loss of the Duchy of Lancaster [to which Gimingham belonged] . . .

# Good Plain Husbandmen

*A farm labourer holds a simple swing-plough while another whips the oxen.*

The contemptuous account of William Paston's origins describes Clement Paston as a 'good plain husband'; a few decades later, he would have been styled a 'yeoman'. There had always been free peasant-farmers like Clement in East Norfolk and, as land became more available after the Black Death, their numbers and the size of their holdings increased. Clement was typical of those who took advantage of the new opportunities to acquire various pieces of land – some 'bond' (i.e. former villein land), some freehold and some leased – to add to the free holding which his family had held for at least a hundred years.

No doubt, as the Pastons' snobbish critic alleges, Clement did supervise his own ploughing and carry his grain to the mill, getting his hands as dirty as any practical farmer. But, by close supervision of a small labour-force and with none of the conspicuous consumption of the gentleman, he was able to accumulate considerable wealth and to educate his son to a higher social rank.

As can be seen from Agnes Paston's passages with her neighbours over the closed road, such yeomen were self-confident enough not to be cowed by the local gentry. Many were important figures in their local communities: at county level, they acted as jurors and helped to elect the 'knights of the shire' to parliament; they also served under the sheriff in lesser county offices, such as constables of hundreds; and in their own townships they were the constables and bailiffs, as well as the parish church-wardens. As such, they ran their villages as their descendants were to continue to do for centuries. When the Pastons speak of the feeling of the 'country' or of the 'people', it is men like Clement, as much as the gentry, whose views they are representing.

*An unwilling beast is pulled and cajoled to market, while in the background, farmers haggle over the price of livestock.*

In spite of the jeering tone, there is no reason to doubt the essential truth of this account. Geoffrey of Somerton, whether or not of servile origin, was an active and successful attorney in Norfolk around the end of the fourteenth century and, apparently being childless, it would have been natural for him to help in the upbringing of his sister's son, particularly if he were an intelligent and ambitious boy, as William Paston undoubtedly was. Where William got his early education is unknown – possibly at nearby Bromholm Priory, with which he maintained a close connection throughout his life, but as an adolescent he proceeded to one of the Inns of Court – probably the Inner Temple, where his son was to be educated. Here he began a long and successful career in the law which took him, as serjeant-at-law and eventually judge, to heights undreamt of by his father or uncle. Clement's will is typical of the period, although shorter than many.

The Will of Clement Paston. [translated from Latin]     15 June 1419

In the name of God, Amen. I, Clement Paston of Paston, whole in mind and memory, this present Thursday in the Feast of Corpus Christi in the year of Our Lord 1419 and the 7th year of the reign of King Henry the 5th after the Conquest [i.e. the fifth Henry since 1066], make my testament in this form.

First, I leave my soul to Almighty God, the Blessed Mary, the Blessed Margaret and all the saints, my body to be buried in the parish church of St. Margaret, Paston, between the south door of the same church and the tomb of Beatrice, late my wife,

Item, I leave to the vicar of the said church for my tithes and other things owed to him if they be not paid 3s.4d. Item, to the light of the Blessed Margaret in the chancel of the said church before the image of the Blessed Margaret 7 pounds of wax. Item, to the light upon the roodloft of the same church 12d. Item, to the repairing and improvement of the same church and its ornaments 3s.4d.

Item, to the vicar of the church of Bacton for tithes and other things owed by me to him, if they be not paid, 2s. Item, to the improvement of the church of Trunch 12d. Item to the improvement of the church of Mundesley 6d. Item to the prior and convent of Bromholm 6s.8d.

The residue of all my goods I give and bequeath to Margery, formerly the wife of John Bakton, my sister, and to William Paston, my son, for them to pay my debts, amend any extortions and injuries, if I have perpetrated any, and to make true restitution on this part. What remains they shall spend in works of charity and piety for my soul and the souls of the said Beatrice and all my ancestors, parents and benefactors and all deceased believers. I constitute and ordain the said Margery and William my executors of this testament; to do all and singular other things whatsoever which pertain to the executors of this testament.

In witness of which I have placed my seal to these present writings . . .

# Wills

*St Margaret's Church, Paston, Norfolk. Clement Paston asked to be buried between the north door and his wife's grave.*

The fifteenth-century will was primarily a religious document, whose purpose was to ease the testator's soul of any earthly burdens and to prepare him for the after-life. Like most other wills of the time, Clement Paston's was made close to his death and begins with the disposal of the testator's soul and body, the payment of any debts, especially those to the Church, and several bequests of money 'to pious uses'. Often there would follow orders for prayers and masses which, it was hoped, would expedite the soul through Purgatory. After this, the testator would dispose of his worldly goods and lands.

The executors appointed in the will usually included the wife, if she survived, or, in Clement's case, his son. They had to 'prove' the will before the appropriate Church Court, which had jurisdiction over probate matters, and then carry out its provisions under the Court's supervision. Most wills were proved quickly and administered within a year or so, but a deathbed will disposing of large amounts of property, such as Sir John Fastolf's, could produce long years of litigation and its original provisions could be considerably modified.

Testators would dispose of their goods freely in most respects, and of much of their landed estate too, but the courts would in practice ensure that wives and under-age children were provided for. Married women could make wills only with the consent of their husbands but widows were as free as men and their wills, like Margaret Paston's, are often lengthy and revealing. It is unfortunate that so few wills have survived; John Paston I's, in particular, would have told much about the family's relationships and his attitude to his property.

William appears to have been Clement's only surviving child and inherited all his lands in Paston and its neighbourhood. He must by that time have had a substantial income from his legal practice and, at the age of forty-two years he added to his wealth by marrying Agnes, the daughter and eventual co-heiress of Sir Edmund Berry. William settled upon her the recently purchased manor and house of Oxnead, which was to be one of the main Paston seats for the next three hundred years. He had also purchased another substantial manor-house and estate at Gresham to add to the family house at Paston and a residence in Norwich. Agnes bore him a number of children, of whom five reached adulthood.

The eldest of these was John, born in 1421, who was given an education superior to most of his contemporaries, being sent to Trinity Hall, Cambridge, (he also appears to have been resident for a time at Peterhouse) before following in his father's footsteps to the Inner Temple. But he was still at Cambridge when his parents seized upon the chance of increasing the family fortunes and status by marrying him to Margaret Mauteby, the young heiress of a distinguished local family. Agnes reported to her husband on the first meeting of the young people.

---

Agnes Paston to William Paston            April 1436/40
Paston

Dear Husband

I recommend me to you etc. Blessed be God, I send you good tidings of the coming and bringing home of the gentlewoman that you know of from Reedham this same night according to the appointment that you made there yourself.

And as for the first acquaintance between John Paston and the said gentlewoman, she made him gentle cheer in gentle wise [gave him a warm welcome] and said he was verily your son. And so I hope that there shall need no great treaty between them.

The parson of Stockton told me if you would buy her a gown her mother would give thereto a goodly fur. The gown needs to be had, and of colour it should be a goodly blue or else a bright sanguine [blood-red].

I pray you buy for me two pipes of gold [reels of gold thread]. Your stews [fishponds] do well.

The Holy Trinity have you in governance.

Written at Paston in haste . . . for default of a good secretary,

Yours, Agnes Paston.

Margaret Paston was born in the early 1420s and, since heiresses tended to be married off young, she was probably not much more than twelve – the minimum age for a binding marriage – when she married John. The Mauteby lands were a few miles south of Paston, mostly around the village of Mautby near Yarmouth: it was to be some years before John and Margaret got the whole estate, as both her mother and grandmother had remarried and held part of it, but the marriage was immediately profitable in terms of status and friendship. Through her Berney mother, Margaret was related to most of the leading families of eastern Norfolk, including the powerful Sir John Fastolf at Caister. After her marriage Margaret remained in touch with her mother and sometimes visited her at the house of her new husband, Ralph Garneys, at Geldeston in South Norfolk. As was normal at this period, however, she also refers to William and Agnes Paston as her father and mother, as she does in the following letter written to John, who had now moved from Cambridge to the Inner Temple. Margaret was clearly pregnant for the first time (her eldest son, John, was born in 1442) and is gently humorous about its effects on her figure.

---

Margaret Paston to John Paston                    14 December 1441
Oxnead

Right reverent and worshipful husband, I recommend me to you, desiring heartily to hear of your welfare . . . praying you to understand that my mother sent to my father at London for a gown cloth of musterdevillers [a grey woollen cloth] to make a gown for me . . . I pray you, if it be not bought, that you will vouchsafe to buy it and send it home as soon as you may, for I have no gown to wear this winter but my black and my green . . . and that is so cumbrous that I am weary of it. As for the girdle that my father promised me, I spoke to him of it a little before he went to London last, and he said to me that the fault was in you, that you would not think thereupon to have it made; but I suppose that is not so: he said it but for an excuse. I pray you, if you will take it upon you, that you will vouchsafe to have it made before you come home for I had never more need of it than now; for I have grown so slim that I cannot be girt into any girdle I have except one.

   Elizabeth Peverel has been sick 15 or 16 weeks with the sciatica but she has sent my mother word by Kate that she would come here when my time comes from God, though she should have to be wheeled in a barrow. John Damme was here and my mother discovered me [my pregnancy] to him and he said, by his troth, that he was not more glad of anything he had heard for a twelvemonth than of this. I may no longer live by my craft [deception], for I am discovered of all men that see me . . . I pray that you will wear the ring with the image of St. Margaret that I sent you for a remembrance till you come home; you have left me such a remembrance that makes me to think upon you both day and night when I would sleep.

# Fifteenth-Century Fashions

The Sumptuary Act of 1463, which attempted to maintain a strict relationship between social status and sartorial standards, was more concerned with men's than with women's clothing. Although the clothes that Edmund ordered would not have breached the statute, it is likely that both he and his older brothers displayed the fashions.that are criticized in the Act and which moralists saw as a sign of national decadence:

> You proud gallants heartless
> With your high caps witless
> And your short gowns thriftless
> Have brought this land in great heaviness
>
> . . .
>
> With your long piked shoes . . .
> And with your long hair into your eyes.

Standard male dress comprised a linen shirt and drawers under a tunic or doublet, and hose tied to the latter by 'points' or laces. Over this would be a cloak, often with slashed sleeves and a hood flung over the shoulder. On the head would probably be a tall bonnet or a small, basin-shaped hat. Although John Paston had wanted his doublet made of fine worsted 'for the honour of Norfolk', the materials preferred by courtiers were imported cloths, including silks, velvets and furs. Bright colours, often patterned, were common.

Many of these features had characterized the young aristocracy of the late fourteenth century. Chaucer's Squire typifies the young gallant of that period, with his curled hair, doublet embroidered with 'fresh flowers' and his short gown with long, wide sleeves. In the early years of the fifteenth century there was a trend towards a greater austerity of appearance but, by the time of the Paston Letters, cloaks were shortening yet again and waists becoming tighter, creating an emphasis on the buttocks and loins. Long hair was back in fashion and shoes, which had shortened early in the century, became increasingly 'piked' [long, with toes curling up]. It was this look which became the butt of moralists – 'every good man truly such shape loathes,' wrote Peter Idley. And the Act of 1463 forbade short cloaks and long pikes for all but the highest. It is unlikely that the Act had any effect, however, since the fashion was universal in the courts of France and Burgundy, as well as England. Changing fashion, rather than statutes or sermons, produced the looser and bulkier clothes of the late 1470s.

*Large padded hoods, wide shoulders and slim legs were fashionable for men at the court of Burgundy in the 1450s.*

*Brass rubbings show the tall pill-box caps with butterfly veils and the tight-bodiced dresses which were fashionable in the 1470s and 1480s.*

Although many women made their own clothes at home, just as Margaret Paston presumably intended to make up her 'cloth of musterdevillers', there were tailors in all towns selling more elaborate outer garments. The art of tailoring had made great strides over the previous hundred years and, by the fifteenth century, fashion was less constrained by technical limitations.

In Margaret's time, conventional lady's wear comprised a short-sleeved under-dress – the kirtle – which was worn over a linen shirt and gartered hose and under a long gown. This often had very large, loose sleeves and was fastened with a girdle. Henry VI was affronted by the bare bosoms of women at the Court, which suggests that the low-cut dresses of the late fourteenth century remained in vogue in such circles. But the moralists reserved their fiercest criticism for the very extravagant head-dresses: confections of hair, wire, padding and veils.

Fashion changed considerably during the fifteenth century and Margery Brews's dresses in the 1480s would have produced a slimmer silhouette, while her head would have been crowned with a 'steeple' or with the more elaborate 'butterfly' head-dress. The most valued dress materials were imported fine cloths, silks and velvets, with fur being used for lining or trimming – understandably, considering the temperature of most

houses in winter. The Sumptuary Act of 1463 attempted to restrict the use of such materials to the upper classes, partly in order to differentiate status by appearance and partly to protect the English cloth industry.
But it is unlikely that the Act was very effective.

*The finely embroidered cloth worn by this lady, in a detail from a fifteenth-century tapestry, is a sign of her social status.*

For the next few years John was much in London. None of his letters survives but there are several of Margaret's from this period. In September 1443, when she wrote to him at the Inner Temple, she and Agnes were deeply worried about his health. Judging from the phrase 'the time is come', Margaret was pregnant again.

Margaret Paston to John Paston                    28 September 1443
Oxnead

Right worshipful husband, I recommend me to you, heartily desiring to hear of your welfare, thanking God for your mending of the great dis-ease that you have had. And I thank you for the letter that you sent me, for, by my troth, my mother and I were not at ease from the time that we knew of your sickness till we knew verily of your mending. My mother promised another image of wax of the weight of yourself to Our Lady of Walsingham and she sent 4 nobles to the 4 orders of friars at Norwich to pray for you; and I have promised pilgrimages to be made for you to Walsingham and to St. Leonard's [Priory, Norwich]. By my troth, I never had so heavy a season from the time that I knew of your sickness until I knew of your amending, and still my heart is not at great ease, nor shall be until I know that you are truly well.

Your father and mine was this day a week ago at Beccles . . . My father Garneys sent me word that he should be here the next week and my uncle also, and play here with their hawks; and they would have me home with them but, so God help me, I shall excuse myself from going thither if I may, for I suppose that I shall have tidings more readily from you here than I should there.

I shall send my mother a token that she gave me, for I suppose the time is come that I should send for her if I keep the promise that I have made – I suppose that I have told you what it was.

I pray you heartily that you will vouchsafe to send me a letter as hastily as you may, if writing be no disease to you, and that you will vouchsafe to send me word how your sore does. I would rather you were at home now, if it were to your ease and if your sore might be as well looked to here as it is where you are, than have a gown, though it were of scarlet. I pray you, if your sore be whole and that you may endure to ride, that when my father comes to London you ask leave to come home when the horse shall be sent home again, for I hope that you would be kept as tenderly here as you are in London.

I may have no leisure to write half a quarter as much as I should say to you if I might speak with you. I thank you that you vouchsafed to remember my girdle and that you wrote to me at the time, for I suppose that writing was none ease for you. Almighty God have you in his keeping and send you health. . .

When Margaret wrote her next surviving letter – probably in the following year – she was staying at Geldeston and looking after Agnes's younger children as well as her own – her second son, also John, was probably born early in 1444. Her main concern was shortage of money but she was also able to pass on some gossip about John Heydon, their neighbour at Baconsthorpe, a rising lawyer who was to appear to John and Margaret as their main local rival for the next twenty years. Heydon clearly suspected the parentage of his wife's baby and his marital troubles were to continue, as a later letter shows.

Margaret Paston to John Paston                  [? July 1444]
Geldeston

Right reverent and worshipful husband, I recommend me to you, desiring heartily to hear of your welfare, thanking you for your letter and for the things you sent me therewith. And touching John Eastgate, he neither came nor sent hither yet, wherefore I suppose I must borrow money shortly unless you come home soon; for I suppose I shall have none from him, so God help me. I have but four shillings and I owe near as much money as comes to the aforesaid sum. I have done your errands to my mother and my uncle, and as for the feoffees of Stokesby, my uncle says that there are no more than he wrote to you about, so far as he knows . . . I pray that you will vouchsafe to buy for me such laces as I send you examples of in this letter and one piece of black lace. As for the caps that you sent me for the children, they are too little for them. I pray you buy them finer caps and larger than those were. Also I pray that you will vouchsafe to recommend me to my father and mother and tell her that all her children are in good health, blessed be God.

    Heydon's wife had a child on St Peter's Day [29 June]. I heard say that her husband will have nothing to do with her nor with her child that she had last neither. I heard say that he said that if she came in his presence to make her excuse, he would cut off her nose to make her be known for what she is; and if her child come in his presence he said he would kill it. He will not be entreated to have her again in no wise, as I heard say.

# Currency and Incomes

## CURRENCY

The basic unit was the penny: in accounts the units of the shilling (12d.) and the pound (20s.) were used, together with the mark of 13s.4d. (⅔ of a pound).

The coinage did not correspond directly with this system. The silver penny had been the basic coin for centuries and 4d. and 2d. pieces (the groat and half-groat) circulated, together with half- and quarter-pennies. Until 1464 the higher value coins, struck in gold, consisted of the noble of 6s.8d. and the half and quarter noble. In 1464–5, however, there was a major reconstitution of the gold coinage; after some false starts this produced a noble or 'royal' of 10s., a half-noble of 5s. and a 'farthing' of 2s.6d., while retaining the 6s.8d. coin, which was now called an 'angel'. The royal was soon discontinued but was revived under Henry VII when, for the first time, a pound coin, the 'sovereign', was struck.

*Above: The 'Ryal' or 'Rose Noble' was first struck in 1465; it was so called because of the Yorkist rose stamped on both sides. Left: The obverse of the 'Gold Sovereign' depicts the King enthroned. Below: A fine profile of Henry VII shown on a shilling piece from his reign.*

## INCOMES AND PRICES

It is impossible to provide exact modern equivalents for the incomes and prices which appear in the Paston Letters. The following are intended only to provide the scale of incomes and average of prices found in the correspondence and in other contemporary sources.

## LANDED INCOME

The Dukes of York, Buckingham and the Earl of Warwick – the wealthiest of the great lords – net landed incomes of between £4,000 and £6,000.

Minimum income for a J.P. – £20 p.a. from land.

Minimum income to vote at a county election – 40s. p.a. from land.

John Paston's 1451 tax assessment – £66 p.a. from land.

## OTHER WAGES

Agricultural labourer – about 4d. a day.
Building worker – about 5d. to 6d. a day.
Soldiers' wages:
    a knight – 2s. a day
    a man-at-arms – 1s. a day
    an archer – 6d. a day.

## COSTS AND PRICES

Building:
    Caister Castle – £6,000
    Emneth, Cambridgeshire – £1,333.6s.8d.
    A one-bay cottage in Devon – £3.4s.

Comestibles:
    Wheat – 5s.8d. a quarter
    Oats – 2–3s. a quarter
    Salt – 5d. a bushel
    Eggs – 5d. a hundred
    Pepper – 2s. a pound
    Sugar – 1s.6d. a pound
    Raisins – 3d. a pound
    Candles – 1d. a pound
    Milk – 1d. a gallon
    Beer – 1d. a gallon
    Red wine – 10d. a gallon.

Animals:
    Cattle – 9–11s. each
    Sheep – 1–2s. each
    Pigs – 2s.–3s.6d. each.

William Paston died on 14 August 1444. By his will he made provision from his lands for his younger sons and left Paston, Oxnead and other lands to his wife for her lifetime. As she now also regained control of her own inheritance John Paston, as heir, had immediate possession of less than half of the lands his father had enjoyed, and was apparently far from satisfied with his share. During the 1440s, however, most of the Mauteby inheritance came to John and Margaret on the death of Margaret's mother and grandmother and it was this which provided the bulk of their income, although they seem to have resided at the Paston manor of Gresham or in Norwich. John, however, was often in London where he may have begun to practise the law.

The marriage of Elizabeth, John's only surviving sister, became a subject of some family concern from soon after her father's death, when she was about sixteen years old. Probably in 1446 the family came close to finalising a match with a young Suffolk lawyer, John Clopton, son of William Clopton of Long Melford: he was, perhaps, a fellow-member of John's Inn. Negotiations got as far as drawing up a draft marriage settlement but whether because of differences over the property settlement or because of a change of mind among the parties, the marriage did not take place and Elizabeth's disposal was to be a running theme through the correspondence for another thirteen years.

John Paston's status in the county and his legal training brought him appointment to the commission of the peace in Norfolk in December 1447 but he was left off when the commission was renewed in May 1448. This was probably because he had by now become embroiled in a major dispute over some of his property and had thus fallen foul of the dominant political figure in the region and the country, William, Duke of Suffolk. For the next three years he was to need all his legal expertise, the assistance of family and friends, and a fortunate turn in national politics to hold on to parts of his paternal inheritance. A long-running claim to Oxnead by a certain Friar Hauteyne surfaced during these years and caused some troubles to Agnes and her sons, but much more serious was the challenge to the Pastons' ownership of Gresham. This manor had been bought by William Paston in 1426 but there was enough obscurity in the title to allow the Wiltshire peer, Lord Moleyns, inspired, it was thought, by John Heydon, to lay claim to it. On 17 February 1448 he forcibly entered upon the house and manor and began to collect the rents from the tenants.

It was impossible for John to bring a successful legal suit against a man so powerful and well-connected as Lord Moleyns, and so he petitioned him for redress and sought the mediation of the much-respected Bishop Waynflete of Winchester, who was to play an important part in the Pastons' lives for the next thirty years.

Moleyns would not, however, return the manor, so in October 1448 Paston took the law into his own hands and re-entered the property, apparently without resistance. But Moleyns's men stayed nearby and the situation remained tense. James Gloys, the Pastons' chaplain, reported scornfully on the attitude of Margaret's uncle, Philip Berney.

James Gloys to John Paston                               3 December 1448
Norwich

. . . If it please you to hear of my Master Berney, he was at Gresham with my mistress . . . the same day that we distrained James Rokysson. I had met a little before with Pertrych [Moleyns's servant] and he threatened me and said that we should not long keep the distress [goods they had seized]; and therefore my mistress made us don our jacks and sallets [protective jackets and helmets]. My master Berney came in and the Parson of Oxnead with him, and saw us in our jacks, and he went as pale as any herd [? shepherd] and would right fain have been away. So my mistress had him to dine and while they were at dinner Harry Colles told my mistress openly among us all that, at the time that Pertrych entered again upon Gresham his master was at Cawston on his way to you, and there it was told him that Pertrych had put you out and all your men . . . and that caused him to come no further that time. And my Master Berney confirmed all this and said that it was so.

When they had eaten he had much haste to be away, so my mistress desired and prayed him that he would come again before long, and so with much praying he promised her that he would if he might. And Harry Colles stood there beside and said to my fellowship 'What should my master do here?', quoth he, 'let your master send for his kinsmen at Mautby for they have nothing that they might lose.' And so they rode away. And within a week after my Master Berney sent Davy to my mistress that she would hold his master excused, for he had hurt his own horse and had ordered Davy to saddle another horse; and he stood by and made water while the horse was saddled and as Davy tried to saddle the horse, he kicked behind and took his master on the hip such a stroke that a man may never trust him after, and broke his hip . . .

So my mistress was right sorry and thought that this story had been true, but I know well that it was not so. It happened that I rode the next day to Norwich and I rode unto my mistress, your mother, and she asked me after my Master Berney and I told her how he was hurt. And she asked the parson of Oxnead if he were hurt and he said no; for Davy lay with him the night before and told him that he was hale and merry . . .

I beseech you . . . that you will not reveal this letter, for if my mistress knew that I sent you such a letter I would never be able to look upon her nor to stay in her sight.

It was inevitable that Moleyns would respond to Paston's action, and on 28 January 1449, while John was in London, a large force of his Wiltshire retainers, together with some local men, forcibly removed Margaret and her servants from the house. In a petition which John Paston put to parliament during the summer he described, perhaps with some exaggeration, what had happened and asked the King and Lords to restore him his property.

Petition of John Paston to Parliament                    Summer 1449
Winchester

To the King, our Sovereign Lord, and to the right wise and discreet Lords assembled in this present parliament.

Your humble liege man beseeches meekly that, whereas he and others enfeoffed to his use [his trustees] have been peaceably possessed of the manor of Gresham in the County of Norfolk for 20 years and more, till the 17th day of February in the 26th year of your noble reign, when Robert, Lord Moleyns, entered in to the said manor. And howbeit that the said John Paston after the said entry sued to the said Lord Moleyns and his council in the most lowly manner that he could, daily from the time of the said entry to the Feast of Michaelmas next following, . . . and no answer had but delays, which caused your said beseecher the 6th day of October last past to inhabit a mansion within the said township. He kept there possession until the 28th day of January last past, when the said Lord Moleyns sent to the said mansion a riotous people to the number of a thousand persons . . . arrayed in manner of war, with cuirasses, briganders and jacks [types of body armour], salletts [helmets], glaives [spears], bows . . . guns, pans with fire, long crooks to drag down houses . . . and long trees with which they broke up the gates and doors, and so came into the mansion, the wife of your beseecher at that time being therein, and twelve persons with her. The which twelve persons they drove out of the said mansion and mined down the wall of the chamber wherein the wife of your beseecher was, and bore her out at the gates; and cut asunder the posts of the houses and let them fall and broke up all the chambers and coffers within the said mansion and rifled . . . and bore away all the stuff . . . to the value of £200, to the great and outrageous hurt of your said beseecher . . . And still various of the said misdoers and riotous people unknown, contrary to your laws, daily keep the said manor with force . . . and lie in wait for various of the friends, tenants and servants of your said beseecher . . .

Margaret was given shelter by the Pastons' friend, John Damme, at his nearby house at Sustead. From there she reported on her negotiations with Moleyns's men.

Margaret Paston to John Paston                    15 February 1449
Sustead

Right worshipful husband . . . The Lord's men had a letter on Thursday last : what tidings they had I know not but . . . I hear say they will abide here still till their lord comes . . . I sent Katherine [with a message to them], for I could get no man to do it, and sent with her James Halman and Harry Holt; and she desired of Barrow to have an answer to her message . . . And he made her great cheer and them that were with her, and said that he desired for to speak with me if it should be no displeasure to me; and Katherine said that she supposed that I desired not to speak with him . . .

   And after noon they came hither and sent in to me to know if they might speak with me, and they abided still without the gates. And I came out to them and spoke with them outside, and prayed them that they would hold me excused that I brought them not in to the place. I said in as much as they were not well willing to the good man of the place I would not take it upon me to bring them to the gentlewoman. They said I did right and then we walked forth and I desired an answer of them for what I had sent to them for . . . I conceived well by them that they were weary of what they had done . . . I said to Barrow that he should have compassion on you and other that were disseised [dispossessed] of their livelode in as much as he had been disseised himself; and he said he was, and told me that he had sued to my Lord of Suffolk divers times and would do till he may get his goods again . . . And he said that he would never blame my Lord of Suffolk for the entry on his livelode for he said my said Lord of Suffolk was set therupon by the information of a false shrew; and I said to him that the matter between my Lord Moleyns and you is in like manner. Much other language we had which would take long leisure in writing . . .

   I hear say that you and John Damme are sore threatened always and they say that, even though you are at London, you shall be met with there just as well as here; and therefore I pray you heartily beware how you walk there and have a good fellowship with you when you walk out. The Lord Moleyns has a company of scoundrels with him that care not what they do, and such men are most to be dreaded . . . I pray you heartily that you will send me word how you do, and how you speed in your matters, for, by my troth, I cannot be well at ease in my heart, nor shall be till I hear tidings how you do . . . Here dare no man say a good word for you in this country. God amend it.

# Gentlemen's Houses

*The Great Hall at Haddon Hall, Derbyshire, shows the improvements made by the Vernon family in the fourteenth and fifteenth centuries.*

what the eventual reconstruction was like, but it was almost certainly more complex and comfortable than the old house had been. The hall still formed the core of most manor-houses, but it was partitioned by a screen and a passage from the service-rooms; such as kitchen, buttery and pantry. Off the other end of the hall, more 'chambers' were added, (including a chapel at Mautby), where the family ate, slept and received visitors.

New houses, such as Caister and Oxburgh, shared this basic pattern, but they were built increasingly around one or more courts, allowing a proliferation of chambers along the lines of the great royal and baronial houses, such as Windsor and Framlingham. At Caister there were more than 25 chambers, occupied by senior servants as well as by family and guests. Even in the fifteenth century, many gentlemen's houses continued to be constructed with defence in mind. Although they could not resist siege-engines or guns, their moats, ramparts and massive gate-towers with drawbridges were reasonably effective against assault by a neighbour or robbers. Nevertheless, the size of the new windows, the elaborate external decoration and the increasing use of brick rather than stone indicate that both the fortified manor-house and 'the unique combination of fortress and personal residence' that was the medieval castle were giving way to the country house.

Apart from Caister and some fragments of Gresham, none of the Paston houses of the fifteenth century survives. Their fate is shared by thousands of manor-houses of the period which were abandoned or totally rebuilt during the following centuries. Most manor-houses in Norfolk were probably still timber-framed rather than built of brick. They would have been set in a courtyard with a garden and farm-buildings attached, and surrounded by ditches, walls, fences and banks. New fashions in design and materials were certainly available and, when money was to hand, extensive rebuilding would have been undertaken. Margaret Paston comments to her husband in the 1450s on 'your work at Mautby', and reports that the thatcher had finished his work on the hall but that nothing else would be completed that year 'but the gables of the chamber and the chapel windows'. There is nothing to tell us

*The remains of Baconsthorpe Castle, Norfolk, built in the second half of the fifteenth century by the Pastons' rivals, the Heydons.*

Margaret left Sustead for fear of further violence and moved to Norwich. Late in February she wrote of what was happening at Gresham and also about the friar's claim to Oxnead. John's brother, Edmund, had just died in London, making John his executor.

---

Margaret Paston to John Paston                  2 April 1449
Norwich

Right worshipful husband . . . My cousin [Elizabeth] Clere dined with me this day, and she told me that Heydon was with her sister lately, and he told her that he had a letter from Lord Moleyns, and showed her the letter, which prayed him that he would say to his friends and well-willers in this country that he thanks them for their goodwill and for what they have done for him.

The friar who claims Oxnead was in this town yesterday and today and was lodged at Beri's and this afternoon he rode but I know not whither. He said plainly that he will have Oxnead and that he has my Lord of Suffolk's good lordship and he will be his good lord in this matter. There was a person warned my mother within the past two days that she should beware, for they said plainly she was like to be served [treated] as you were served at Gresham within right short time . . .

My mother prays you that you will send my brother, William, at Cambridge . . . [books] . . . of my brother, Edmund's, which my said brother promised my mother the last time he spoke with her, that he should have sent to my brother.

---

She continued through the spring and summer to report the local news and the advice she had received. The dominance of the Duke of Suffolk in the country as a whole was reflected in the control he exercised in East Anglia through his retainers, Sir Thomas Tuddenham of Oxborough and John Heydon of Baconsthorpe. Heydon was also counsel to Lord Moleyns which made the Paston's ambition to recover Gresham even more difficult to attain.

---

Margaret Paston to John Paston                      May 1449
Norwich

. . . Sundry folk have said to me that they think verily unless you have my Lord of Suffolk's good lordship, while the world is as it is, you can never live in peace. Therefore I pray you with all my heart that you will do your part to have his good lordship and his love to the easing of all the matters that you have to do, and in easing of my heart also; for, by my troth, I am afraid otherwise for both these matters that you have in hand now and others that are not done yet, unless he will . . . be your good lord . . .

---

In the summer John followed the Court and Parliament to Winchester, where he put his petition in to the parliament. Petitions and legal actions, however, had little effect. Moleyns's men remained at Gresham – although the threat to Oxnead seems to have faded out. But the political scene was changing. The rapid crumbling of the English position in Normandy during the latter half of 1449 had weakened the power of the Duke of Suffolk and, during the second session of the parliament that met in November 1449, he was impeached: he was murdered on the way into exile early in May 1450. A letter from William Lomnour which, he says, he had 'washed with sorrowful tears', recounted some of the details of Suffolk's death as they were known in London.

---

William Lomnour to John Paston                              5 May 1450
Norwich

. . . On the Thursday before [30 April] the Duke of Suffolk came to the coast of Kent near Dover with his two ships and a little pinnace, which pinnace he sent with certain letters to certain of his trusted men in Calais, to know how he should be received. And from them that were in the pinnace the master of the Nicholas had knowledge of the Duke's coming, and [the master] . . . sent forth his boat to know who they were. And there met with him a ship called the Nicholas of the Tower, with other ships waiting for him . . . and they said he must speak with their master. And so he, with 2 or 3 of his men, went forth with them in their boat to the Nicholas; and when he came there the Master bade him 'Welcome, traitor'. And so he was on the Nicholas till Saturday following . . . And some say he was tried after their fashion upon the articles of his impeachment and found guilty etc . . . And in the sight of all his men he was drawn out of the great ship into a boat, and there was an axe and a stock, and one of the lewdest of the ship bade him lay down his head, and he should be dealt with fairly and die on a sword. And he took a rusty sword and smote off his head within half a dozen strokes, and they took away his gown of russet and his doublet of mailed velvet and laid his body on the sands of Dover. And some say that his head was set on a pole by it . . . I know nothing more, but if the procedure were erroneous let his counsel try to reverse it . . .

# The Dukes of Suffolk

The Dukes of Suffolk – the perennial opponents of the Pastons – were descended from a fourteenth-century Hull merchant, and they were never allowed to forget their humble origins. For four generations, however, they had married into noble families and by marriage, royal grant and purchase, they had acquired large estates, mainly in East Anglia. Here, their main seat was their castle, with its associated college of priests, at Wingfield.

William, the 4th Earl and 1st Duke, had spent many years as one of the leading English captains in France. After his defeat by Joan of Arc at Orleans and his subsequent capture, he turned from war to politics: as Steward of the Royal Household from 1433 to 1447 and then as Lord Great Chamberlain. Having made himself indispensable to the young King, he dominated foreign and domestic affairs during the 1440s. He arranged the marriage of Henry with Margaret of Anjou, but his policy of peace with France whereby he ceded the provinces of Maine and Anjou and his control of royal patronage, which made him very rich, estranged both lords and commons. In East Anglia, the control exercised by him and his followers was bitterly resented by Sir John Fastolf and John Paston. William was created Duke of Suffolk in 1448, but when Normandy was overrun by the French in 1449-50, he was impeached in parliament and murdered by sailors on his way to exile.

In 1430 William married Alice, widow of his comrade-in-arms, the Earl of Salisbury, and daughter of Thomas Chaucer of Ewelme in Oxfordshire (son of the poet). They made their main residence at Ewelme, where they founded a college of priests and the almshouses which still survive. Their only surviving son, John, was not born until 1442 and his formidable mother continued to play an important part in the affairs of East Anglia – and of the Pastons – until her death in 1475. John married Edward IV's sister, but he showed none of the political skills or ambition of his father and, judging by some of the references to him in the Paston Letters, was not regarded with much respect. He died in 1491 and, although seven of his sons reached adulthood, the royal blood they had inherited from their mother made them objects of suspicion to the Tudor kings. By 1540 the De La Poles were no more.

THE SUFFOLKS

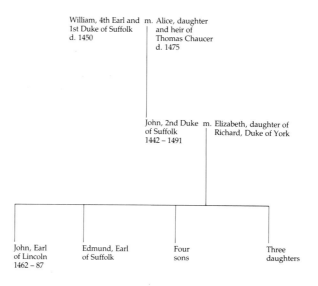

*The family tree of the Dukes of Suffolk.*

It is unlikely that the Pastons grieved greatly for the murdered Duke. The political situation was now turning in their favour and they had the support of their kinsman, Sir John Fastolf, who, though mainly resident in London, had also suffered from the dominance of the Duke of Suffolk and his followers in East Anglia. He kept in close touch with what was going on in the county of Norfolk and particularly at his splendid new house at Caister through an extensive and sometimes querulous correspondence with his main local servants.

Sir John Fastolf to Thomas Howes                27 May 1450
London

Trusty and well-beloved friend, I greet you well . . . And I pray you send me word who dare be so [fool]hardy to kick against you in my rights. And say to them on my behalf that they shall be quit [dealt with] as far as law and reason will. And if they will not dread nor obey that, then they shall be quit by Blackbeard or Whitebeard, that is to say, by God or the Devil. And therefore I charge you send me word whether such as have been my adversaries before this time continue still in their wilfulness.

Item, I hear oft times many strange reports of the governance of my place at Caister and other places, as in making profit from my chattels, my wines, the keeping of my wardrobe and clothes, my coneys [rabbits] at Hellesdon and in my lands. I pray you heartily, as my full trust is in you, to help reform it, and that you suffer no vicious man to abide at my place of Caister but only well governed and diligent, as you will answer for it.

Almighty God keep you.

John Fastolf, knight.

# Caister Castle

*Caister Castle, Norfolk, one of the first brick-built castles in England, was built for Sir John Fastolf and then inherited by the Pastons.*

Sir John Fastolf used his great wealth to purchase large estates and vast amounts of plate and other luxury goods. But, like other captains who had done well out of the Hundred Years War, the building of a great new house, on the site of his ancestral manor-house at Caister, was the clearest assertion of his new wealth and power. This took over 20 years and cost more than £6,000; although it was inhabited by 1446, it was not until 1454 that Sir John came to live there permanently.

The castle differed from most other great houses of the fifteenth century in that it was built of brick and, with its slender tower and prominent moat, it resembles some of the castles of the Rhineland, rather than those familiar to Fastolf from England and France.

It was also very easy to defend, as the 1469 siege showed, and was clearly seen as a fortress protecting the exposed coast north of Yarmouth. Nevertheless, Fastolf's inventory and the surviving ruins illustrate that its internal structure was 'modern' with a multiplicity of chambers and elaborate furnishings. For Fastolf, and later for the Pastons, it was the jewel of the estates, demonstrating by its massiveness and by its domination of the countryside the power of its owner. It is no wonder that the Duke of Norfolk, and the King himself, thought it more suitable for a great lord. In a later age, however, it was old-fashioned and uncomfortable; the Pastons rarely seem to have resided there after the fifteenth century and had sold it by 1669.

It was about this time, or possibly a year or two earlier, that negotiations began for a marriage between John's sister, Elizabeth, and Fastolf's stepson, Stephen Scrope. Scrope was a fifty-year-old widower with a daughter by an earlier marriage and had himself admitted that he was 'disfigured in my person and shall be while I live'. He was by no means a splendid match, except for the connection with Fastolf, and difficulties about property settlements as well as doubts about the suitability of such a marriage caused the negotiations to drag on for some time. Letters to John from his mother and from the close family friend, Elizabeth Clere of Ormesby, suggest rather differing views about the desirability of the match and they describe some of the pressures upon Elizabeth, now about twenty years of age and clearly mistrusted by her mother who feared, perhaps, a relationship with a low-born household servant.

---

Agnes Paston to John Paston                                              June 144[?]
Oxnead

Son, I greet you well with God's blessing and mine. And I let you know that my cousin Clere wrote to me that she spoke with Scrope after he had been with me at Norwich and told her what cheer I had made him, and he said to her he liked well the cheer I had made him. He had such words to my cousin Clere that unless you made him good cheer and gave him words of comfort at London he would speak no more of the matter.

My cousin Clere thinks that it were a folly to forsake him unless you knew another as good or better; and I have assayed [tested] your sister and I found her never so willing to anyone as she is to him, if it be so that his lands stand clear . . . Sir Harry Inglose is right busy about Scrope for one of his daughters . . .

---

Elizabeth Clere to John Paston                    29 June 144[?]

Trusty and well beloved cousin . . . Cousin, I let you know that Scrope has
been in this country to see your sister and he has spoken with my cousin,
your mother, and she desires of him that he should show you the indentures
made between the knight that has married his daughter and him, to see
whether Scrope, if he were married and fortuned to have children, if those
children should inherit his land or his daughter who is married . . .

   Scrope said to me that if he be married and have a son and heir, his
daughter that is married shall have of his livelode fifty marks and no more.
And therefore, cousin, it seems to me that he were good for my cousin, your
sister, unless you might get her a better. And if you can get a better, I would
advise you to labour it in as short time as you rightly may, for she was never
in so great sorrow as she is nowadays; for she may not speak with any man,
whoever comes, and may not see nor speak with my man nor with servants
of her mother, without her mother suggesting that she is behaving otherwise
than she means to. And since Easter she has been mostly beaten once or twice
a week and sometimes twice in one day, and her head broken in 2 or 3 places.

   Wherefore, cousin, she has sent to me in secret by Friar Newton, and prays
that I would send you a letter about her unhappiness, and prays you to be her
good brother, as her trust is in you. And she says that if you may see by his
evidences that his children by her may inherit and she to have reasonable
jointure, she has heard so much of his birth and his condition that if you
wish, she will have him whether her mother will or not, notwithstanding she
is told his person [appearance] is simple; for she says men will have the more
respect for her if she submits herself to him as she ought to do.

   Cousin, it is told me there is a goodly man in your Inn, whose father died
lately, and if you think that he were better for her than Scrope then he could
be laboured, but give Scrope a goodly answer, so that he be not put off till you
are sure of a better. For he said when he was with me that unless he has some
comfortable answer from you he will labour no more in this matter, because
he was not able to see your sister, and he said that he ought to have been able
to see her even if she had been better [in rank] than she is; and that caused
him to complain that her mother was not well willing, and so I have informed
my cousin, your mother.

   Wherefore, cousin, think on this matter, for sorrow oft-times causes
women to behave otherwise than they should do, and if she were in that case
I am sure you would be sorry.

   Cousin, I pray you burn this letter so that neither your men nor other men
see it; for if my cousin, your mother, knew that I had sent you this letter, she
would never love me. I write no more to you at this time, but the Holy Ghost
have you in his keeping . . .

The story of Elizabeth's 'courtships' and eventual marriage had several chapters still to come, but during 1450-1 the main theme of the correspondence is the political situation in England and in East Anglia in particular, and its implications for the Pastons and their friends.

During the summer of 1450 – following the murder of the Duke of Suffolk – there was a rebellion of Kentishmen under Jack Cade. They captured London briefly and murdered the Treasurer of England. A letter written many years later by one of Fastolf's servants gives a vivid insight into the character of Cade's Rebellion.

---

John Payn to John Paston                                        1465

. . . Please it your good and gracious mastership tenderly to consider the great losses and hurts that your poor petitioner has had since the Commons of Kent came to the Blackheath, that is fifteen years past, when my master, Sir John Fastolf . . . commanded me to take a man and 2 of the best horses that were in his stable with him, to ride to the Commons of Kent to get the articles [demands for reform] that they came for. And so I did; and as soon as I came to Blackheath the Captain had the commons seize me . . . and I was brought before the Captain of Kent. And the Captain demanded of me what was the cause of my coming thither, and I said that I came there to have cheer with my wife's brothers and others that were my allies and gossips that were present there. And then one of those that were there said to the Captain that I was one of Sir John Fastolf's men . . . and then the Captain had treason cried upon me through all the field and brought me to 4 parts of the field with a herald of the Duke of Exeter before me in the Duke of Exeter's coat of arms . . . proclaiming openly by the said herald that I was sent from the greatest traitor that was in England or in France to spy on their power and habiliments of war [weapons] . . . And moreover he said that the said Sir John Fastolf had furnished his place [in Southwark] with the old soldiers [returned] from Normandy and habiliments of war to destroy the commons of Kent when they should come to Southwark; and therefore he said plainly that I should lose my head.

And so forthwith I was taken and led to the Captain's tent and an axe and a block were brought forth to have smitten off my head. And then my Master Poynings, your brother [in-law], with other of my friends, came and prevented the Captain and said plainly that there should die a hundred or two if I died; and so by that means my life was saved at that time. And then I was made to swear to the Captain and commons that I would go to Southwark and array myself in the best way I could and come again to help them; and so I got the articles and brought them to my master, and that day cost me amongst the commons more than 27s . . .

# Jack Cade's Rebellion

'The law serveth of nought else in these days but for to do wrong . . . [the King's] false council has lost his law, his merchandise is lost, his common people is destroyed, the sea is lost, France is lost, and the King himself is so set that he may not pay for his meat and drink.' So reads one of the numerous 'articles' of the Kentish rebels which Fastolf sent John Payn to collect in June 1450. About 10 June the rebels had arrived at Blackheath, already led by Jack Cade, who took the name of Mortimer, presumably to claim connection with the family of the Duke of York. Cade's actual origins are obscure, but even hostile chroniclers admit that he was 'witty and subtle' in his speech, and his efficient control of a large unorganized army suggests that he was a natural leader of men.

Kent had been seething with discontent for several months; earlier in 1450 there had been risings led by men who had taken the names of 'Bluebeard' and 'Queen of the Fairies'. These were part of a long tradition of unruliness in the county which went back to the Peasants' Revolt of 1381. Kent's proximity to London and the Continent, its large number of free peasants, the prevalence of cloth-working in the Weald, and its generally advanced economy all explain the county's tendency to rebel. But unlike 1381 – when the demands of the rebels were of a fundamental social nature, including the end of villeinage and lordship – Cade's rebels in 1450 were mostly concerned with misgovernment, both central and local, and their main demands pressed for the punishment of traitors and for the King to 'take about his noble person' the Duke of York and the other great lords of the land.

The King's response was to march on Blackheath with a large army, but after the rebels had retreated into Kent and cut up a pursuing force, the royal army disintegrated and the King returned to Kenilworth. News then came in of risings in other parts of Southern England, especially in Wiltshire where Bishop Ayscough of Salisbury was dragged from his altar by his own tenants and murdered. The rebels returned to encamp at Southwark in early July and on 4 July Cade entered London and beheaded Lord Say, Treasurer of England and the leading figure in Kent over the previous decade, and his son-in-law, the Sheriff of Kent. The two heads were paraded around London on spears and 'in divers places of the City they put them together, causing them to kiss one another'. Some looting took place, but on 6 July the royal troops who had remained in the Tower, together with some Londoners, attacked the rebels. After a long, indecisive fight on London Bridge, pardons were offered and the rebels dispersed. Cade himself was killed in Kent on 12 July, but otherwise the pardons were honoured.

Cade's Rebellion completed the disintegration of the government begun by the Impeachment of the Duke of Suffolk; in August and September the Dukes of York and Somerset returned to England and a new phase of political conflict began. But Kent remained disturbed for many years: as John Bocking wrote to Paston in 1456, 'the Commons of Kent, as is their wont, are not all well disposed, for there is doing among them, whatever it be.'

*A contemporary copy of one of the petitions of Jack Cade's rebels, now in the British Library.*

In September 1450 the Duke of York arrived home from Ireland, a month after his rival, the Duke of Somerset, had come home from France. Their rivalries were to dominate national politics for the next five years but in 1450 York was the hope of all who had suffered from the dominance of the Duke of Suffolk and the Royal Household. York had great popular support and in East Anglia the alliance of the Duke of Norfolk, his wife's nephew. Sir John Fastolf had been York's councillor and was still close to him, whilst the Pastons had traditionally been followers of the Duke of Norfolk. Hopes were therefore high that the humiliations of the past few years could be reversed. In response to complaints about the offences perpetrated by Suffolk and his men during the previous decade, the new regime sent commissions consisting of groups of lords, knights and judges into various counties, including Norfolk, to enquire into the charges and to try the offenders. But John Paston was prepared to pay for his own commission to deal with his complaints against Lord Moleyns, for reasons he explains in a letter to his agent in London, James Gresham.

---

John Paston to James Gresham                    4 September 1450
Norwich

James Gresham, I pray you labour forth to have an answer to my bill for my special assize and oyer and terminer according to the bill that I delivered to my Lord Chancellor . . . Men talk of a general oyer and terminer being granted to the Duke of Norfolk . . . and men be right glad thereof. Yet, that notwithstanding, labour forth for me. For in a general oyer and terminer a supersedeas [a writ suspending the commission's powers] may dash all, and so it shall not in a special commission. And also, if the justices come at my request, they shall sit as long as I will and so shall they not by the general . . .

And as for that Lord Moleyns has written that he may put the matter in the award [arbitration] of my Lord Chancellor [Cardinal Kemp, Archbishop of York] and in whatsoever judge he will take to him etc. (which offer, as I suppose, shall be told to you to make you cease your labour), then let it be answered and my Lord Chancellor informed thus: the matter was in treaty by the assent of Lord Moleyns between his counsel and mine assembled at London 16 different days, for the most part with a serjeant-at-law and six or seven able apprentices; at which time the Lord Moleyns's title was clearly showed and answered, in so much that his own counsel said they could no further in the matter . . . And also my Lord Chancellor should understand that the Lord Moleyns's men took and bore away more than 200 worth of my goods and chattels . . . And if he were disposed to do right, my counsel think he should restore that, for that needs no discussion or treaty . . . The manor is so decayed by the Lord Moleyns's occupation, that, where it was worth to me 50 marks a year clear, I could not now make it worth 20.

# The Dukes of Norfolk

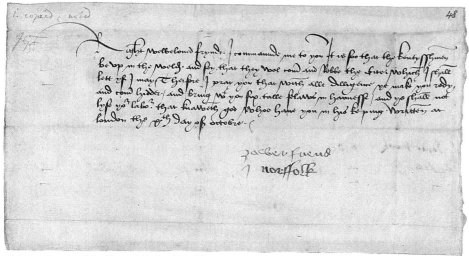

*A letter, signed by John Howard, Duke of Norfolk, to John Paston III, 1483.*

The Mowbrays, Dukes of Norfolk and Earls Marshal held lands in many parts of England and Wales, but it was in East Anglia that their prestige was greatest. Except when the Duke of Suffolk dominated affairs in the 1440s, they represented the single most important focus of power in East Anglia. The 3rd Duke claimed that after the King he should have 'the principal rule and governance through all the shire of which we bear the name' and although neither he nor his son was strong or politically skilful enough to wield absolute power in the region, their attitudes and interests could never be ignored by the gentry of the two counties. The Pastons' connection with the Mowbrays went back to the early career of William I, and, despite periods of tension, particularly during the dispute over Caister, the relationship was not totally broken until the death of the 4th Duke in 1476. He was succeeded by his only child, the young Anne Mowbray, who was married to Edward IV's second son. Anne died while a child, and Framlingham and the East Anglian estates were eventually inherited by the Howards, descendants of the 2nd Duke's sister.

## THE DUKES OF NORFOLK

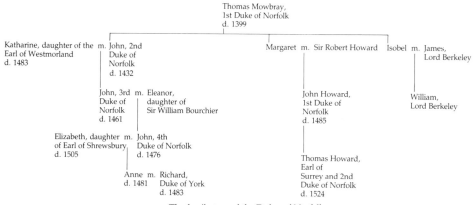

*The family tree of the Dukes of Norfolk.*

In October William Wayte, clerk to Judge William Yelverton, who was a friend of Fastolf and John Paston, wrote to the latter to report on the effects on the Court of the Duke of York's arrival. He advised on the organising of demonstrations to prevent Tuddenham, Heydon and the rest from gaining the favour of the Duke when he came to Norfolk. He also suggested the election of reliable members to the parliament which had just been summoned. Sir William Oldhall, chamberlain to the Duke of York, and a very powerful figure who was to be Speaker of the parliament that met in November, was originally a Norfolk man and probably known to the Pastons.

William Wayte to John Paston                          6 October 1450
London

Sir, if it please you, I was in my Lord of York's house and I heard much more than my master wrote to you about; I heard many things in Fleet Street. But Sir, my Lord [of York] was with the King and he so presented the matter that all the King's Household was and is afraid right sore; and my said Lord has presented a bill to the King and desired many things which are much after the desire of the common people; and all is upon justice and to put all those that are indicted under arrest without surety or bail, and to be tried by law . . .

Sir, Burley, Young and Josse labour sore for Heydon and Tuddenham to Sir William Oldhall and proffer more than two thousand pounds to have his good lordship; and therefore there is no other remedy but to let men of Swaffham [in West Norfolk] be warned to meet with my said Lord on Friday next coming at Pickenham on horseback in the most goodly wise and put some bill unto my Lord against Sir Thomas Tuddenham, Heydon and Prentice, and cry out upon them; and let all the women of the same town be there also and cry out upon them also and call them extortioners, and pray my Lord that he will do sharp execution upon them [punish them severely]. And my Master counsels you that you should move the Mayor and all the aldermen with all their commoners to ride to meet my Lord . . . For, Sir, unless my Lord hear some foul tales of them and some hideous noise and cry, by my faith they are like to come to grace . . .

Sir, labour you to be knight of the shire, and speak to Master [Sir Miles] Stapleton also that he be one. Sir, all Swaffham, if they be warned, will give you their voices. Sir, speak with Thomas Denys and take his good advice herein . . . Sir, labour you to the Mayor that John Damme or William Jenney be burgess for the City of Norwich: tell them that he may be it as well as Young is for Bristol or the Recorder is for London and as the Recorder of Coventry is for Coventry, and so it is in many places in England. Also, Sir, think on Yarmouth, that you arrange that John Jenney or Lomnour or some good man be burgess for Yarmouth. Arrange that the Jenneys be in the parliament, for they can speak well . . .

**W**ayte may have been the source for James Gresham's stories of encounters between Yelverton and John Heydon in London and another between Heydon and one of Yelverton's judicial colleagues.

---

James Gresham to John Paston                    [October 1450]
London

Please you to understand that I arrived at London the Wednesday evening after parting from you . . . Heydon was with my Master Yelverton, and asked him to let him see the records of his indictments, and asked him if he were indicted of felony; and my Master Yelverton told him he was. And thereupon H. said 'Sir, you will record that I was never a thief' . . . H. hopes to have the world better to his intent than it is now. For I am told that, rather than he should fail to have a sheriff to his intent this year, he would spend £1000.

   This communication between them was on Monday last passed, and on Tuesday H. met with Master Markham, and he told H. on his part how that he lived ungoodly in putting away his wife and keeping another etc. And therewith he turned pale colour and said he lived only as God was pleased with, and did no wrong to any person. And thereupon Master Markham reminded him how he behaved against men of [the Inns of] Court, and named you and Jenney; and H. said, so far as the people who looted you and the action itself were concerned, he was not privy to it, for he was at that time in London; and as touching the Lord Moleyns's title, he said firmly that his title was better than yours . . .

---

**B**y mid-October the Dukes of York and Norfolk had met to decide who should be knights of the shire for Norfolk and Suffolk in the coming parliament. Such pressures were difficult to resist, but in the event only one of their two choices in each shire was elected.

---

The Duke of Norfolk to John Paston                    16 October 1450
Bury St. Edmunds

Right trusty and well beloved, we greet you well. And forasmuch as our uncle of York and we have fully appointed and agreed of such 2 persons for to be knights of the shire of Norfolk as our said uncle and we think convenient and necessary for the welfare of the said shire, we therefore pray you in our said uncle's name and ours both, as you desire to stand in the favour of our good lordship, that you make no labour contrary to our desire . . .

The parliament that met in November 1450 was dominated by York and his allies. There was an attempt to reform the government by dismissing members of the King's Household and 'resuming' crown lands which had been given away over the past twenty years. Paston, Fastolf and their friends had high hopes of winning their legal cases and seeing their enemies punished. Tuddenham, Heydon, and many others of the affinity of the Duke of Suffolk were indicted on charges of extortion and other crimes before judicial commissions in Norfolk and Suffolk, and Lord Moleyns and his men were charged with the forcible seizure of Gresham and the looting of its contents. Continued pressure and 'labouring' were necessary, however, as is shown by the careful preparations made by Fastolf for a session of the commission at Lynn in January 1451. Lord Scales of Middleton near Lynn, was a veteran soldier and a member of the judicial commission. It was feared that he might be amenable to the 'labouring' of Tuddenham and Heydon.

---

Sir John Fastolf to Thomas Howys                    20 December 1450
London

Right trusty friend . . . I understand that the Lord Scales will be at Lynn this Christmas and at the oyer and terminer held there, and Sir Thomas Tuddenham and Heydon will appear, at which I am well content; and it is likely that great labour and special pursuit will be made to the Lord Scales to maintain the said Tuddenham and Heydon in all he can or may, and thus I have heard it said. For which reason such persons as have found themselves sore grieved by extortion, as I have been, and have process [a legal action] or will have process before the commissioners, must most effectually labour to my Lord of Oxford and to my brother, Justice Yelverton, that they will, as far as justice, reason and conscience do allow, ensure that justice may be equally administered, and not to withdraw their support from the poor people . . .
For it is clear that by excessive extortions they have lived in misery and great poverty for many years so that the most part of the commoners have little or nothing to maintain their living and households, nor to pay the king's taxes, nor their rents and services to the lords whose tenants they are, as is shown daily to all the world, which is too pitiful to think of. And when the said poor people have been by such injuries overlaid and undone, the gentlemen that have their livelode among them must needs be greatly diminished and hindered in their profits and living . . .

Item, forasmuch as you will have to deal at Lynn with my matters concerning Titchwell and other places, I will that you arrange for good friends within Flegge that may be jurors, to wait upon you there at Lynn, together with other such trusty men that you can get to speed my process. And do them good cheer and spend upon them what is necessary. I commit this to be dealt with at your discretion.

Proceedings on most of the actions were adjourned from Lynn to a session to be held at Walsingham in early May. In the intervening period, the Duke of York began to lose his hold on the government to the Duke of Somerset in alliance with the Chancellor, Cardinal Kemp, and there were frequent rumours in Norfolk that Tuddenham and Heydon would regain power. John Paston, however, felt confident enough to re-enter Gresham, apparently without resistance, although the house was not fit to live in and it proved impossible to regain much of their stolen goods. Paston continued to pursue claims to the manor and for damages against Moleyns, but his servants found many problems.

Margaret was still active in her husband's interests, although she remained worried about the possibility of Lord Moleyns taking further action. With John mainly in London during this period, she was his representative in Norfolk.

---

Margaret Paston to John Paston                         15 March 1451
Norwich

Right worshipful husband . . . It is said here that the King will come to this country and that Sir Thomas Tuddenham and Heydon are well cherished with him. And also it is said that they shall have as great rule in this country as ever they had, and many more folks are sorry therefore than merry. Sir Thomas Tuddenham's men and Heydon's sow this seed all about the country, that their masters shall come home in haste in prosperity and be as well at ease as ever they were. As for your desire that I should enquire where any stuff of yours is, I do not know how to do this, for if anyone were seen to have some of your stuff and we had it from him, others who have more thereof would beware and rid themselves of it. I suppose John Osbern will tell you when you come home a good means to know where much of it is. James Gloys is again to Gresham and I suppose John Damme will tell you what he has done there. Your tenants would fain that some of your men should abide among them, for they are in great unsureness what to do: the boasting is so great on the other party that it makes the tenants sore afraid that you will not enjoy it [Gresham Manor] . . . I was told that Lord Moleyns was likely to have a day against you at Thetford at the next assize . . . it is good to be aware of their falsehood.

I pray you that you will send me word in haste whether you will have red for your livery as you were intending. And also I pray you that you will have bought two good hats for your sons, for I can get none in this town. More tidings I can not send you yet.

---

# Livery and Maintenance

*Knights armed with swords and lances. Shields, tabards and trappings display their coats of arms.*

'I pray you . . . bring such company of tall men as you may,' wrote John Howard, Duke of Norfolk, to John Paston before the Battle of Bosworth, '. . . (and) ordain them jackets of my livery'. The advantage of 'livery' or uniform on the battlefield is obvious, but its use was much wider than that. Livery was the outward sign of its wearer's allegiance to a particular master. It might take the form of a hood or cap, but more commonly it consisted of a jacket of particular colour or design, such as the dark blue and tawny in which the Duke of Norfolk's 200 men were dressed when they joined the King in 1469. Livery might well include the badge of the lord, such as the Duke's white lion or the white bear with ragged staff worn by the Earl of Warwick's 600-strong retinue when he arrived in London in 1458. Or it might be a chain, such as the famous 'double S' worn by retainers of the Duchy of Lancaster. The wearing of livery had long been recognized as perilous to the peace of the country, since liveried retinues provided private armies which could overawe a region and perhaps become a menace to the King himself. As a result, various statutes had tried to restrict their usage, and those of Edward IV forbade anyone 'to give any such livery or sign or retain any person other than his menial

servant . . . or man learned in the law'.

Livery was often associated with 'maintenance', the use of illicit pressure on judges, juries and officials to pervert the course of justice. Such practices were widespread in the Norfolk of the Pastons. In 1450 Sir Thomas Tuddenham, John Heydon and other followers of the late Duke of Suffolk were accused of conspiring with the Duke fifteen years earlier to 'maintain one another in all matters in Norfolk and Suffolk'. But the practice did not cease with the statutes against liveries, as the Paston correspondence clearly shows. It stemmed from the King himself, who needed the retinues of friendly magnates during the civil wars and to form the nucleus of royal armies, such as that of 1475. It was not until the more settled Tudor age that it became impossible for great lords to call out liveried retainers in their own interest.

Every gentleman from the King downwards wanted his servants to be recognized. The annual or bi-annual kitting-out must have provided a substantial market for the clothiers of Norfolk and Suffolk, and Margaret Paston found in 1460 that, if the order were left too late, it might be impossible to obtain enough cloth for her husband's score of servants.

John returned to Norfolk in time for the sessions of the commision of oyer and terminer at Walsingham in May, where he was to act for Fastolf, as well as for himself. A full report of the proceedings before the judges was sent by Thomas Howes to Sir John Fastolf, which, though, of course, one-sided, throws light upon the various pressures which affected fifteenth-century litigation.

Thomas Howes to Sir John Fastolf                    9 May 1451
Caister

Right reverent and worshipful master . . . The more special cause of my writing at this time is to give you a relation of the untrue behaviour of this oyer and terminer by the partiality of the judges of it. For when the counsel of the City of Norwich, of the town of Swaffham, yours, my master [Sir Henry] Ingloses, Paston's and many other plaintiffs had put in and declared, both by writing and by word of mouth, before the judges many lawful points, the judges, by their wilfulness, might not find it in their hearts to give not as much as a beck [nod] nor a twinkling of their eye towards them but took it to derision, God reform such partiality. And because Prisot thought that if the sessions of the oyer and terminer had been held at Norwich as they had begun, it would not so quickly pass after the intent of Tuddenham and Heydon and their fellows, as it would otherwise do in another place, he adjourned to Walsingham, where they have greatest rule [influence], there to be held on Tuesday, the 4th day of May.

Knowing this, my Master Yelverton, Jenney and others might well understand how the governance of the oyer and terminer would proceed, for it [Walsingham] was the most partial place of all the shire; and there were summoned all their friends, knights, and esquires and gentlemen who would in no wise do other than they wished. And the said Tuddenham, Heydon and other oppressors of their set came down there, as I understand, with 400 horse and more. And, considering how their well-willers were there assembled at their instance it would have been right dangerous and frightening for any of the plaintiffs to have been present, for there was not one of the plaintiffs nor complainants there but your right faithful and trusty well-willer, John Paston. And my Master Yelverton spoke full discreetly and controlled the said Prisot who, sitting in the Guildhall of Norwich, said these words to the Mayor and Commonalty: 'Ah, Sir Mayor and your brethren, as to the process of your complaints, we will put them in continuance [adjourn them], but in all other we will proceed'. Which words Yelverton thought right partial. And besides this the said Prisot would suffer no man that was learned to speak for the plaintiffs, but took it as a poison, and took them by the nose [interrupted] at every third word, which might well be seen as open partiality . . .

Lord Moleyns was acquitted but proceedings continued against his men and for recovery of damages. A report from Paston's servant, John Osbern, on negotiations with the sheriff, John Jermyn, shows that pressures and bribes were not all on one side. Paston had left a gift with the under-sheriff for his master, but, though John Jermyn seemed to be acting scrupulously, Osbern was sceptical about his motives.

John Osbern to John Paston                                27 May 1451
Norwich

Please it your mastership to know that I have spoken with the sheriff at his place, showing him that, as for what was left with his under-sheriff, it is your will that he should send a man for it; for you would be glad he should take it, even if it were more. He thanked you and said that his under-sheriff was at London, and that he himself had not deserved it: if he had he would take it . . . Then he said that he would do for you what he may, except that he must acquit the Lord Moleyns's men, in so much as the King has written to him to show favour to the Lord Moleyns and his men and, as he says, the indictment belongs to the King and not to you and Lord Moleyns is a great lord . . . It seems to me that it would do good if you would get a commandment of the King to the sheriff to show you favour and to impanell gentlemen [as jurors] and not to favour such riots etc. For he reminded you that he sent you the letter that the King sent him and you had said that a man could get such a letter for a noble. I reminded him of the promises that he had made to Tymperley, and said that if he would make you very true promise you would reward him as much as he would desire . . . Then he said that he never took money from any of them: there was proferred him at Walsingham for the Lord Moleyns 20 nobles, but he had not taken a penny . . . And then he said that if he might do any thing for you, then he will take your money with a good will, and other promise I could not have of him but that he will do for you all that he may except for the indictments. I conceive verily he has made promise to do his part that they be acquitted, but I suppose that he has made no other promise against you for the livelode [the land]. He is looking for a great bribe, but he is not to be trusted unless he has no choice . . .

It is unlikely that Paston received much satisfaction from his legal actions other than a confirmation of his right to Gresham which was to remain a valuable Paston property for centuries. Its house, however, does not appear to have been rebuilt, although John's son may have contemplated this in the 1470s. For the next few years the Pastons seem to have resided mainly in Norwich; Agnes Paston, of course, retained her house at Paston and lived there, as well as in Norwich, with her younger children. About 1451 she was quarrelling with her neighbours over her attempt to block a roadway there. She and her husband had obtained a royal licence to do this in order to round off their property and had given some land to the village in exchange, but their neighbours were not satisfied with the bargain. Agnes's status clearly did not prevent the local farmers and their wives from openly expressing their anger, as she reported in several letters to her son.

---

Agnes Paston to John Paston                                    [circa 1451]
Paston

On Thursday the wall was made a yard high, and a good while before evening it rained so sore that they were fain to heel the wall [they had to lay it on its side] and leave work. And the water has fallen so sore that it stands under the wall a foot deep towards Ball's land. And on Friday, after the Mass, someone came from the Church and shoved down all that was there, and trod on the wall and broke some, and went over it; but I cannot yet know who it was . . .

---

Agnes Paston to John Paston                          November [circa 1451]
Paston

I greet you well and let you know that Warin Harman on Sunday after All Hallows day after evensong, said openly in the churchyard that he knew well that if the wall were put down, even though he were a hundred miles away from Paston, I would say that he did it and he should bear the blame; and said 'tell it here who so will, though it should cost me 20 nobles it shall be put down again'. And the said Warin's wife said with a loud voice 'All the devils of hell draw her soul to hell for the way that she has made' . . . And John Marchall said that there was a respectable woman came by for watering and found the way stopped and asked him who had stopped the way, and he said 'those that had power to give it', and asked her what was freer than a gift; and she said that she had seen the day when the men of Paston would not have suffered it . . .

Matters at Paston are unlikely to have been in the forefront of the minds of John and Margaret at this period. John continued to be much in London in the early 1450s and Margaret kept him informed of local news. Now living at Norwich, the social centre of the region, where gentry, merchants and senior clergy mixed, she was able to provide more extensive information. Unfortunately few of her letters survive from these years. In one that does she tells of dining out at the house of the wealthy merchant, Robert Toppes, whose brother-in-law, John Knyvett, was involved in a major law-suit with Sir Andrew Ogard. Margaret was also worried about the prevalence of disease and hoped that treacle, a popular remedy for many ailments, would be beneficial.

---

Margaret Paston to John Paston                                    1 July 1451
Norwich

. . . I was at Toppes's at dinner on St. Peter's Day: my Lady Felbrigge and other gentlewomen desired to have had you there. They said they would all have been the merrier if you had been there. My cousin Toppes has much worry till she hear good tidings of her brother's [John Knyvett] matter. She told me that they were to keep a day [appear in Court] on Monday next coming between her brother and Sir Andrew Ogard and Wyndham. I pray you send me word how they sped, and how you sped in your matters also. Also I pray you heartily that you will send me a pot of treacle in haste; for I have been right ill at ease, and your daughter also, since you rode hence, and one of the tallest young men of this parish lies sick and has a great fever. How he shall do God knows. I have sent my Uncle Berney the pot of treacle that you bought for him.

Sir Henry Inglose is passed to God this night, whose soul God assoil, and was carried forth this day at 9 of the clock to St. Faith's [Priory], and there shall be buried. If you desire to buy any of his stuff I pray you send me word thereof in haste and I shall speak to Robert Inglose and to Witchingham thereof: I suppose that they are executors.

I pray you trust not the sheriff for any fair language.

---

# The Fifteenth-Century Diet

*A king dines in the banqueting hall with the lord and lady of the manor. They are entertained by two musicians.*

Many of the staple fifteenth-century foodstuffs were produced by the household in its gardens, kitchens, bakehouse and brewery or were purchased locally, like the 'horse-load of herrings' bought for 4s.6d. by Margaret in the early 1450s. Imported food and drink, on the other hand, like wine and the dates, sugar, pepper, cloves, maces, ginger, cinnamon, almonds and rice whose London price Margaret asked her son to enquire about in 1471, or the figs and raisins anticipated by the young William at Eton in 1479, were expensive luxuries. They provided the necessary flavourings for the gentleman's table – almonds, in particular, were heavily used in the concoctions described in recipe books and in accounts of great banquets. One of the simpler recipes is for 'doucettes', where 'almond-milk' is mixed with eggs, saffron, salt and honey and laid in a thin crust with marrow-bones. Oranges, lemons and dried fruits were seen as much healthier eating than the raw fruit seasonally available in England: 'Beware of salads, green foods and raw fruits' was a typical warning. Wine was traditionally shipped from Bordeaux, but the sweet wines of the Mediterranean were particularly prized.

Even in a gentleman's household, however, far more was spent each year on bread, ale, meat and fish than on imported delicacies. The dinner given by John Paston to the courtiers in 1469 is unlikely to have provided the elaborate 'messes' of noble banquets. It probably resembled, rather, the 'feast for a franklin' [yeoman] suggested in a fifteenth-century treatise. This began with grapes and cherries, and was followed by several courses, each containing many dishes: the first course included brawn and mustard, bacon and peas, stewed beef, boiled chicken, roast pork, goose or game, baked meats and custard; next came a 'sotelte' [an elaborate design, mainly in sugar] of the Annunciation; two more 'courses' followed, and the feast ended with fritters, apples, pears, spiced cakes, jellies, wafers and cheese.

About a gallon of ale, 'a natural drink for an Englishman', was consumed by each household every day. Only the poorest would go without meat (and fish in Lent) although the lower classes would rely more on salted meat and herrings, with peas and beans, for their pottages. For most, then, the diet consisted largely of meat and grain products; vegetables, except onions, were not widely eaten. As a result, skin diseases, such as Chaucer's Summoner's 'whelks white . . . and knobs sitting on his cheek', were very common and, considering the state of medieval sanitation and kitchen hygiene, so undoubtedly was food-poisoning.

The political situation in the country at large remained tense for the next three years. There was violence on a large scale in the West Country and, in February 1452, the Duke of York attempted to overthrow the dominance at Court of the Duke of Somerset. He was forced to accept a settlement and to send away his forces with the result that the next eighteen months saw Somerset and Cardinal Kemp fully in control of government.

In Norfolk, too, there were many disputes among the gentry, a number of which figure large in the Paston correspondence of these years. In one such episode John Paston claimed that he was attacked at Norwich Cathedral by Charles Nowell, a servant of the Duke of Norfolk, 'he smiting at me while one of his fellows held my arms at my back.' To deal with such disorders a strong sheriff was needed, for not only was the sheriff the King's chief representative in the county, but he and his subordinates were responsible for policing and for executing all writs and empanelling juries. He was appointed annually, officially by the King on the advice of his officers, but in practice a variety of outside influences were brought to bear on the choice for private as well as for public reasons, as the following letter – written in 1452 or 1453, just before the sheriffs were to be chosen – illustrates. Witchingham did not want a kinsman chosen as sheriff because in law kinship, unlike friendship, gave an assumption of bias.

---

Edmund Witchingham to John Paston                    October 1452/3
Framlingham

Right reverend and trusty cousin . . . I came home by way of my Lord of Oxford and told him of the great labour of Sir Thomas Tuddenham and Heydon for sheriffs of our shire, and named the persons whom they laboured for. My lord agreed not to two of them: he said not much about the knight, but I felt that he would labour for William Dorward, my nephew. And I answered, 'Sir, he may not help me in my matter, for he has wedded my niece' . . . And before I came to Framlingham my Lord of Norfolk had written for Sir Robert Conyers, taking a promise from him to be ruled in all matters as my Lord of Norfolk shall advise him: and as for the under-sheriff you shall advise thereof.

# Crime and Criminal Justice

*Villagers were often attacked by criminals or by rival peasants.*

Margaret Paston's complaint that the roads to London were infested by robbers was echoed many times during the fifteenth century. For the weakening of the King's control in the 1450s and the 1460s had brought a breakdown of order in many areas. As the chronicler, John Harding lamented:

> *In every shire, with jacks and saletts clean*
> *Misrule doth rise and maketh neighbours war.*

Sir John Fortescue, William Paston's judicial colleague, boasting of the greater courage of English criminals, claimed that 'here be more men hanged in England in a year for robbery and manslaughter than there be hanged in France for such crimes in seven years'. But it was not just violent crime that commanded the death penalty; if the goods stolen were worth more than 1s., simple theft was a felony punishable by hanging, although most criminals escaped this penalty.

Policing – the responsibility of the sheriff and the local constables – was inefficient; and though numerous 'presentments' of offenders were made by local juries, even those who were eventually arrested were often acquitted by juries when tried before the Assize Judges, the Commission of the Peace or a special commission.

Sometimes, no doubt, the evidence really was insufficient to convict; sometimes the jury was bribed or threatened; but most acquittals resulted from the jury's reluctance to impose death for a crime with which they might have some sympathy, such as a minor theft or a murderous brawl. Juries were more prepared to convict professional criminals like the robbers who haunted the routes to London across the heaths of South-West Norfolk and Suffolk – in 1454, for instance, a gang of Yorkshiremen robbed merchants of large amounts of cloth, silk, jewels and money at Icklingham Heath in West Suffolk – but such men were hard to catch.

Even if arrested and convicted, a criminal might claim 'benefit of clergy' if he could read a few words of Latin, or he might receive one of the thousands of pardons issued by the kings of this period. Despite the inefficiency of criminal justice, the writings of John Fortescue show that the right to a jury trial was already seen as one of the glories of the English legal system. 'I would prefer twenty guilty men to escape', he writes, 'than one innocent to be condemned unjustly.' It is the ease with which many avoided the consequences of their crimes that helps to explain the prevalence of disorder in the fifteenth century.

Politics did not, of course, exclude constant concern with family affairs, particularly the marriage of Elizabeth. And John and Margaret appear to have been undertaking some building, perhaps at Norwich or Mautby.

Margaret Paston to John Paston                    January [? 1453]
Norwich

. . . Thomas Howes has provided 4 dormants [large beams] for the withdrawing chamber and the malthouse and the brewery, of which he has bought three and the fourth, that will be the longest and greatest, he will have from Hellesdon, which, he says, my Master Fastolf will give me because my chamber will be made with it. As for the laying of the said dormants, they will be laid this next week, because of the malthouse, and as for the rest, I think it will abide until you come home, because I cannot yet be provided with posts and boards.

I have taken the measure in the drawing chamber, where you want your coffers and desk to be set for the while; and there is no space beside the bed, even though the bed were removed to the door, to set both your board [writing-table] and your coffers and to have space to go and sit beside it. Wherefore I have arranged that you shall have the same drawing chamber as you had before, where you shall lie by yourself; and when your gear is removed out of your little house, the door shall be locked and your bags laid in one of the great coffers, so that they shall be safe, I trust . . .

My mother prays you to remember my sister and to do your part faithfully before you come home to help to get her a good marriage. It seems by my mother's language that she would never so fain to have been rid of her as now. It was told here that [William] Knyvett, the heir, is able to marry: both his wife and child are dead, as it was told here. Wherefore she would that you should inquire whether it is so or not, and what his livelode is, and if you think it is possible, let him be spoken with about it.

I pray you that you be not chary of writing letters to me between this and when you come home. If I might I would have one every day from you

. . .

# Domestic Furnishings and Heirlooms

*A small cupboard, used as a sideboard.*

*A bronze pot for cooking vegetables and small quantities of meat and stews.*

The surviving inventory of Sir John Fastolf's property at Caister gives an insight into the luxurious lifestyle of a rich fifteenth-century gentleman, with its vast quantity of gold and silver plate, of tapestries, arrases and clothes. Much of this was in store, but the visitor to Caister in the 1450s would certainly have wondered at the colour of the arrases which hung in the Hall and Chambers, with their intricate designs of 'a giant bearing a leg of a bear', of 'the siege of Falaise', or of 'three archers shooting a duck'. He would have been dazzled, too, by the gold ewers, silver platters, salt-cellars in the form of towers 'all gilt with roses', and the gilt gallon-pots enamelled with Fastolf's shield. If the visitor had penetrated into Fastolf's chamber, he would have admired the bed-hangings of arras around the feather-bed and the '6 white cushions'. Fastolf would hardly have donned his cloth-of-gold gown for an ordinary visitor but he might have worn his blue velvet gown, trimmed with fur, to go to the chapel which was stocked with half a dozen rich vestments, a variety of church-plate and books.

The visitor would have been less impressed by the furniture, of which little was mentioned in the inventory except two chairs in the Hall and a folding-table and two chairs in Fastolf's chamber. With the exception of beds and their accoutrements, household furniture was still fairly limited and often not valuable enough to be listed in inventories and wills, although there are references to cupboards and chests, in which clothes, napery and

documents were stored. There would also have been many valuable candelabra and candlesticks.

Few would have rivalled Fastolf's great quantities of valuables but the Pastons certainly possessed much plate, which could be pledged or sold in emergencies. Margaret Paston was able to leave a number of splendid pieces of silver and gilt to her children; she also possessed a garnish of pewter vessels which she left to her daughter, together with 'two pairs of my finest sheets', curtains and brass pots. Four years later, her sister-in-law, Elizabeth Poynings, lists large amounts of plate, jewels, clothes, napery and other household goods, including 7 great coffers, 6 chests, 2 cabinets, 6 joined stools, 5 little joined stools, a little table 2 yards long and a round table; all was to be kept for her daughter's marriage, except 'such stuff as cannot be kept from the moths'. Further down the social scale, 'the best service' would have been made from pewter rather than silver; further down still, implements would have been of earthenware or wood, and the napery of coarse cloth rather than fine linen.

*A steel-bladed serving-knife, with an elaborately enamelled handle, for preparing food at the table during a special banquet.*

Possibly in the same year Margaret wrote again to her husband in connection with another possible marriage for Elizabeth: it is not known who this potential husband was.

Margaret Paston to John Paston                                   January [?1453]
Norwich

. . . I spoke yesterday with my sister, and she told me that she was sorry that she might not speak with you before you left; and she desired, if it please you, that you should give the gentleman that you know of such language that he might feel that you will be well-willing to the matter that you know of. For she told me that he has said before this time that he thought that you have set little store by it; wherefore she prays you that you will be her good brother and that you might have a full answer at this time, whether it be yea or nay. For her mother has said to her since you rode hence that she has no liking for it, but that it shall come to nothing . . . and has such language to her that she thinks it right strange and is right weary therof; wherefore she desires the more to have it brought to a conclusion. She says that her full trust is in you and what you do therein she will agree to . . .

In April 1453 the inhabitants of Norwich were excited by a visit from Queen Margaret.

Margaret Paston to John Paston                                   20 April 1453
Norwich

. . . As for tidings, the Queen came into this town on Tuesday last past in the afternoon; and she sent by [Thomas] Sharnburne for my cousin, Elizabeth Clere, to come to her; and she durst not disobey her commandment and came to her. And when she came into the Queen's presence the Queen made right much of her and desired her to have a husband, which you shall know more about hereafter. But as for that, he is never nearer than he was before. The Queen was right well pleased with her answer, and reported of her in the best wise, and said, by her troth, she had seen no gentlewoman that she liked better than her since she came into Norfolk . . .

I pray you that you will buy me a gift for Whitsuntide, that I might have something for my neck. When the Queen was here I borrowed my cousin, Elizabeth Clere's necklace, for I durst not for shame go with my beads among so many fresh [gaily attired] gentlewomen as were here at that time . . .

In the autumn of 1453 there was a new national crisis, produced by the King's falling insane and by the birth of the long-awaited heir to the throne. The King's madness seemed likely to be permanent and, since the young prince would not be of age to govern for at least fifteen years, decisions had to be taken about the government of the realm during that period. Conflicts, similar to those that had occurred during the childhood of Henry VI himself, arose between the claims of the Lords and those of the King's closest kinsman, now the Queen, who was determined to protect the interests of her son. Parliament met early in 1454 at a time of great tension, which is well portrayed in a newsletter sent to the Duke of Norfolk and his council. This illustrates the ways in which news of great political events would have reached the East Anglian gentry.

---

John Stodeley to the Duke of Norfolk                 19 January 1454
London

As for tidings, please you to know that at the Prince's coming to Windsor, the Duke of Buckingham took him in his arms and presented him to the King in goodly wise, beseeching the King to bless him; and the King gave no kind of answer. Nevertheless the Duke still stayed with the Prince by the King, and when he could have no answer, the Queen came in and took the Prince in her arms and presented him in the like form as the Duke had done, desiring that he should bless it; but all their labour was in vain, for they departed thence having received no answer or expression, saving only that once he looked on the Prince and cast down his eyes again, without any more.

Item, the Cardinal [Kemp] has charged and commanded all his servants to be ready with bows and arrows, sword and buckler, crossbows and all other habiliments of war that they can obtain to wait upon the safeguard of his person.

Item, the Earl of Wiltshire and the Lord Bonville have caused it to be cried at Taunton in Somersetshire that every man who is able and willing to go with them and serve them shall have 6d. every day as long as he abides with them.

Item, the Duke of Exeter in his own person has been at Tuxford beside Doncaster in the north country and there the Lord Egremond met him and the two are sworn together [to be allies], and the Duke has come home again . . .

Item, the Queen has made a bill of five articles, desiring them to be granted: the first is that she desires the whole rule of the land . . .

Item, the Duke of York will be at London next Friday night, as his own men tell with certainty, and he will come with his household retinue, well attired and likely men. And the Earl of March comes with him, but he will have another fellowship of good men that will be at London before him . . .

---

# King Henry VI

*Henry VI (1421–1471), third Lancastrian King of England.*

The only child of the great King Henry V and the French princess, Katharine, was born at Windsor on 6 December 1421, two months after John Paston. A year later, on the deaths of his father and maternal grandfather, Charles VI of France, he became titular king of both countries. The young King was brought up first by his mother and nurses and then, from the age of seven, by Richard Beauchamp, Earl of Warwick, regarded as the most cultured nobleman of his day. Warwick received orders, notionally from the King himself, to teach him 'good manners, letters, language, good breeding and courtoisie' [the skills and behaviour of chivalric life] and was given full power to 'chastise us reasonably from time to time according to his good advice and discretion.' Despite this careful education, he displayed from early on none of the political or military interests of his father. Chroniclers point to signs even in infancy of his future piety, as when he cried uncontrollably when forced to travel on a Sunday. His interests as an adult were focused on religion and education, chiefly displayed in his intense concern for his collegiate foundations at Eton and Cambridge.

As the English position in France declined, Henry became associated with the policy of securing a peaceful settlement with Charles VII of France; this was strengthened by his marriage in 1445 to Margaret of Anjou. Domestically, though not a cypher, he was much under the influence of the Duke of Suffolk and his household. Even in the 1440s, some of his subjects saw him as 'not steadfast of wit as other kings have been' and as having 'a child's face'. Perhaps this is the other side of the piety and simplicity described by his chaplain, John Blacman, for whom he was 'a man simple and upright, altogether fearing the Lord God and departing from evil'.

After his bout of insanity from July 1453 to December 1454, he became increasingly ineffective in worldly affairs, and control of the government fell into the hands of his wife. His role seems to have been largely passive during the campaigns of 1460-64. During the next six years he was imprisoned in the Tower and, when released and restored by the Earl of Warwick in 1470, he was 'as a man amazed and utterly dulled with troubles and adversities.' He was killed by the Yorkists after their victory at Tewkesbury. Over the next thirty years he was popularly revered as a saint and, although Henry VII's attempts to have him formally canonized failed, his image appears quite frequently among those of saintly kings on church walls and rood-screens.

Parliament made the Duke of York 'Protector of the Realm', to rule with a council of lords until the King recovered or the Prince came of age: Cardinal Kemp died in March 1454 and York's ally, the Earl of Salisbury, was made Chancellor; the Duke of Somerset remained imprisoned in the Tower. As in 1450, the political situation was turning in favour of the Pastons and Sir John Fastolf, with whom John Paston became increasingly intimate during the 1450s. Particularly after Fastolf had come to spend his last years at Caister in September 1454, Paston was his most trusted councillor and man of business. He and Thomas Howes acquired from the Crown on Fastolf's behalf the 'wardship' of Sir John's young relative, Thomas Fastolf of Cowhaw in Suffolk. Such wardships, which included custody of the lands and the right to sell the marriage of the young heir, were valuable, and the Fastolf wardship led to much litigation, often alluded to in the correspondence of the next years.

Fastolf's secretary and Thomas Howes's nephew by marriage, William Worcester [alias Botoner], became friendly with the Pastons after his master's removal to Norfolk, although their friendship was not to survive the disputes over Fastolf's will. A loyal, if sometimes critical servant, England's first real antiquarian scholar was a man of insatiable curiosity and a wry sense of humour.

---

William Worcester to John Paston    2 September [? 1454]
Caister

After due recommendation with my simple service preceding, please your mastership to know that, as to the matter that you desire me to carry forth to the uttermost, I shall do so with a good will, if my master will permit it . . .

And whereas you are pleased to write or call me Master Worcester, I pray you to forget that name of mastership, for I am not awarded any certain improvement by my master, but shall have wages of household in common 'as long as it shall please us'. As either Worcester or Botoner I have 5s. a year, all costs borne, to help pay for the bonnets that I lose. I told my master so this week and he said to me yesterday that he wished me to be a priest, if I had been so disposed, so to have given me as a living a benefice, that another such as the Bishop must give; and so I endure among the needy 'as a slave at the plough'.

Forgive me, I write to make you laugh; and Our Lord bring my master into a better mood for the sake of others as well as me.

I pray you not to be displeased with your servant for being so long, as my master delayed him.

Your, W. Worcester.

By late in 1454 John's younger brother, William, was in London training for the law, no doubt also at the Inner Temple. He was now a new source of news and, like the rest of the family, became involved in the problem of his sister's marriage. Lord Grey of Ruthin had already approached John Paston, proposing a marriage for Elizabeth with a gentleman 'of £300 livelode'. John's reply had been cautious and William's report suggests that the caution was justified.

William Paston to John Paston                    6 September 1454
London

Right worshipful brother . . . Billing, the serjeant, has been in his country and he came to London this week: he sent for me and asked me how I fared. I told him that here is pestilence and said I felt the better that he was in good health, for it was noised that he was dead. He took my arm and asked how my sister did, and I answered 'well, never better'. He said that he was with Lord Grey and they talked of a gentleman who is ward to my Lord – I remember that he said it was Harry Grey that they talked of – and my Lord said 'I was busy within this few days to have married him to a gentlewoman in Norfolk that will have 400 marks to her marriage . . . for 400 marks would do me ease' . . . These words had my Lord to Billing, as he told me, and he understood that my Lord laboured for his own avail, and counselled to bid her be cautious; and I thanked him for his good counsel.

I sent you an answer to your letter about Sir John Fastolf's coming home, according to what he told me himself; nevertheless, he stayed longer than he said himself that he would do. He told me that when he is in Norfolk he would bring to a conclusion the matter between Scrope and my sister. Many wish that it should not conclude, for they say that it is an unlikely marriage. In case Cressener is talked of any more, he is accounted a gentlemanly man and a worshipful. You know better than me that he is worshipful. At the reverence of God draw to some conclusion: it is time.

My Lord Chancellor has not come here since I came to London, nor my Lord of York. My Lord of Canterbury [Thomas Bourchier] has received his cross and I was with him in the King's Chamber when he made his homage. I told Harry Wilton the demeaning between the King and him: it were too long to write.

. . . Here is great pestilence. I purpose to flee into the country. Much more things I would write to you but I lack leisure.

I pray you recommend me to my sister and my cousin Clere.

By your brother, William Paston.

# The Inns of Court and Legal Education

'I suppose that in all Christendom are not so many pleaders, attorneys and men of law as be in England only', wrote William Caxton in 1475. When the young Edmund Paston began his legal training at Clifford's Inn, his mother wrote to advise him 'to think once a day of your father's counsel to learn the law; for he said many times that whoever should dwell at Paston should have need to know how to defend himself.' To the west of London, between the City and the Law-Courts at Westminster, a series of 'Inns' had grown up, where by the fifteenth century more than a thousand members were involved in the lengthy process of learning the Common Law of England. Clifford's Inn was one of the 'Inns of Chancery', where elementary legal education was obtained. Boys would go there after an early grounding in Latin and perhaps, like some of the Pastons, after a spell at University. They would learn the numerous forms of writ (in Latin) which initiated legal actions and also the various ways of pleading in the courts in English and Law-French.

Most 'lawyers' were attorneys, responsible for ensuring that the elaborate legal process was carried out correctly, but those, like the Pastons, who wished to practise in the superior branch of the profession and to plead in the King's courts, proceeded at the age of about twenty as an 'apprentice-at-law' at one of the four Inns of Court – Lincoln's Inn, Gray's Inn, and the Inner and Middle Temple. There again learning was by 'mooting' – exercises based on more difficult cases – and by attendance at the Courts during term-time and at 'Readings' or lectures by senior members of the society during the vacations. Finally, they might become 'utter barristers' qualified to plead in most of the courts. The best among these, like William Paston, would be appointed as 'serjeants-at-law', men at the peak of their profession and from whom the judges were chosen.

The Inns of Court were also 'a kind of academy of all the manners that the nobles learn', where young men could learn music, singing and dancing and 'all games proper for nobles'. Many boys from prosperous families were sent there for a general education and, with money available and the fleshpots of London on the doorstep, it is no wonder that indiscipline and violence were almost as common as at the universities.

Many used their legal qualifications to become officials of the courts or to administer the estates of or act as councillors for the King or great nobles. John Paston and his brothers all seem to have spent some time at an Inn, and William and John almost certainly became professional lawyers. John does not appear to have pressed his own sons to follow that career but both John II and John III knew enough law to manage their own very involved affairs.

The great central law courts of the King – the King's Bench, Common Pleas, Chancery and Exchequer – all sat around the walls of Westminster Hall. Since there were no substantial partitions, the noise of ushers and criers summoning juries and litigants, of barristers pleading cases, of chattering spectators and students from the Inns of Court, and of attorneys and their clerks running from one court to another, must have been, at the very least, distracting. The satirical poem, 'London Lickpenny', describes the poor man seeking justice in Westminster Hall, thrusting through the press of people and losing his hood in the process, puzzled by the cries of the clerks, kneeling before judges and lawyers asking for their assistance, before being told to depart. 'For lack of money,' he complains, 'I could not speed'.

Most of the activity of the courts in law-terms was formal, and involved the entering of writs and answers. These were recorded in Latin, but pleading took place in French – albeit a French very different from that spoken in France. Of the thousands of cases begun in the central courts each year, however, comparatively few reached the stage of pleading in court and even fewer were decided at Westminster. Jury verdicts were needed for most civil actions and these were usually taken at the Assize courts in the county of origin. Such juries, like the sheriffs who empanelled them, were heavily 'laboured' by both parties. As Fastolf instructed his servant in 1451, 'labour to the sheriff for the return of such panels [of jurors] as will speak for me, and be not ashamed, for great labour will be made by Wentworth's [his opponent] party'.

Where possible, however, it was desirable not to proceed to trial but rather to make a 'means', as the Pastons were frequently advised to do in their controversies with the Dukes – to compromise through mediation or to let the case be settled by arbitration. Issuing a writ often had the object of forcing the adversary to come to a settlement in order to avoid expense and bad feeling. This is the main reason why such a small proportion of the cases that are recorded on the plea rolls of the courts ever came to a verdict.

*The Court of the King's Bench in Westminster Hall. Judges on the bench are dealing with criminals while the clerks write the rolls of the proceedings. The accused, in chains, stand at the bar.*

John Paston's advice and assistance was becoming increasingly essential to the ageing Sir John Fastolf and, although the marriage of Elizabeth and Scrope was clearly not going to take place, there were other possible matches which might bring the two families closer together: Sir John's enthusiasm for the idea reflects the close relations between the two men by the mid-1450s.

Sir John Fastolf to John Paston                    11 November 1454
Caister

Worshipful and right well-beloved cousin . . . I have received a letter at this time from John Bocking, with a copy of the letters patent concerning the wardship [of Thomas Fastolf] that you know of, by which I understand that you have both wrought and helped by your great wisdom to bring this matter about, as I desired your friendship and good advice for the surety of the said ward. For expediting which I thank you right heartily and pray you to continue forth your good labours in the same, in such wise as it shall be made sure in all ways, even though it cost me more of my wealth . . . for now that I have gone so far in the matter I would not have it fail for lack of money but that it should be well proved and taken to a good conclusion . . .

And whereas I have understood of late by certain of your well-wishers that, in case the said ward might be obtained, you desire an alliance might be made between a daughter of yours and the said ward, I was right glad to hear of this motion and shall be right well willing and helping that your blood and mine might increase in alliance. And if it please you that by your wisdom and good conduct you would help bear out this matter substantially against the opposing party contrary and my enemies so that I might have my intent, I assure you that you and I would appoint and accord in such wise that you would hold yourself right pleased both for the increasing of your lineage and of mine. And I pray you beware whom you make of your counsel and mine in this matter, and that it may be well pursued before you come away . . .

A letter from Thomas Howes suggests that this attractive possibility had been a topic of discussion in the Caister household, although it eventually came to nothing – partly, no doubt, because Fastolf never obtained secure custody of the ward.

---

Thomas Howes to John Paston       13 November 1454
Caister

. . . I moved my master out of my own head that if the child were wise [intelligent] then it would be a good marriage between your daughter and him. And, sir, my master was glad when he heard that suggestion, considering that your daughter is descended from him by the mother's side. And, sir, I have enquired after the said child, and there is no doubt that he is a likely boy and of great wit, as I hear by report of sundry persons. And I am credibly informed that Geoffrey Boleyn makes great labour for the marriage of the said child to one of his daughters; I wish him well but you better. Wherefore, sir, labour diligently about this matter, to find means to have the said child, and we shall faithfully do our duty here in like wise, as you shall advise us . . .

---

Letters from Fastolf and his servants figure large in the correspondence during the remainder of the old man's life. Most concern Fastolf's varied legal business and the running of his property but in one letter, at least, certain aspects of his character and his reputation for miserliness are clearly revealed.

---

Sir John Fastolf to John Paston       7 February 1455
Caister

. . . Please you to know that I am told that at a dinner in Norwich at which you and other gentlemen were present, there were certain persons, gentlemen, who uttered scornful language of me, as in this wise, with more: 'Beware, lad, beware and let us go to dinner. Where shall we go? To Sir John Fastolf and there we shall pay well for it'. What their meaning was I know well, and it was to no good intent towards me. Wherefore, cousin, I pray you, as my trust is in you, that you give me knowledge in writing what gentlemen they were that said this and more, and what more gentlemen were present, as you would wish me, and it would be my duty to do for you, in similar wise. And I shall keep your information in this matter secret, and with God's grace so provide for them that they shall not all be well pleased. At such a time a man should know his friends from his foes etc . . .

*This miniature of the White Tower, (Tower of London), with London Bridge supporting wooden-gabled buildings in the background, comes from the Duke of Orleans' book of poems. He wrote it during his imprisonment in the White Tower from 1415 to 1440.*

# London

'London, thou art the flower of cities all', wrote the poet, William Dunbar, at the end of the fifteenth century; and, though the assertion could have been challenged by some of the great cities of the Continent, London was certainly the largest and wealthiest town in Britain. During the fifteenth century, the number of people within the walls of the city was at least five or six times that of any other British town. When people spoke of going to London, they meant a straggle of great houses, streets, buildings and communities which stretched from the Royal Household, the Abbey and the Law Courts at Westminster, via the Inns of Holborn and the Temple, beside the shops, markets, taverns, docks and churches of the City, and past the great fortress of the Tower to the baths and brothels of Southwark.

It was a crowded city, where large merchant houses, often with shops or business premises attached, rubbed shoulders with the hovels of the poor. An Italian observer was amazed by the 52 goldsmiths' shops which lay along Cheapside while the countryman hero of the contemporary satirical ballad, 'London Lickpenny', described the food-sellers offering 'ripe strawberries . . .

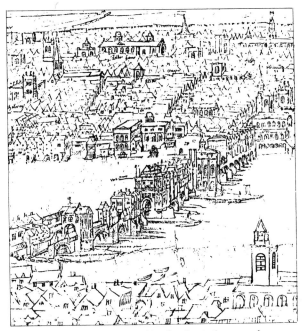

*The first topographical drawing of London, by Anthony van den Wyngaerde, dates from the middle of the sixteenth century.*

ribs of beef and many a pie, hot sheep's feet and mackerel'; the drapers selling cloth and the taverners wine. In Cornhill, among other stolen goods, he finds his own hood for sale, taken from him some hours earlier in the crowd at Westminster. He could not buy it back, however, for here and everywhere in London, 'for lack of money I could not speed'. He was glad to return to the peace of the Kent countryside.

But, though London might frighten the newcomer, there was constant intercourse between the City and the provinces. Most of the Paston men spent much of their lives in London as lawyers or litigants, courtiers, members of parliament – or even in prison. And there were frequent visits there by servants and by the women of the family too. Like other towns, Norwich had based its fifteenth-century charters on London's constitution of Mayor and Aldermen, Sheriffs and Common Councillors. No provincial townsmen, however, could emulate the immense wealth and prestige of the leading London merchants who dominated its aldermanic bench. Precedence books place the Mayor of London on a level with a baron, and aldermen-knights were not uncommon by the late fifteenth century. The mayoral procession from the Guildhall to Westminster on 29 October was one of the great pageants of the year; like the magnificent pageants that greeted the progress of kings, it was an expression of the power of the citizenry. The Italian observer describes the feast given at the mayor-making in the 1490s: over a thousand people were present and it lasted four hours, and there was 'an infinite profusion of victuals and of plate, mostly of gilt'.

As the greatest port and the financial centre of the kingdom, London dominated the wool and cloth export trade, while the proximity of the Court stimulated the production of luxury goods as well as basic manufactures. The numerous craft-guilds were run by their own leaders, but above them were the Mayor and Aldermen who also controlled the large majority of the city's inabitants who were not enfranchised: from the wealthy groups of German and Italian merchants to the apprentices, labourers and criminals. It was among these groups that disorder was always liable to break out, as it did during Cade's Rebellion in 1450, in the attack on the Lombard merchants in 1456 and during the civil strife of 1460–1 and 1471. London may have been a dangerous place, but it was first and foremost the centre of government and the law, of patronage and of luxury.

Fastolf's phrase 'at such a time' may refer to the political change which had occurred in the previous three months which once again diminished the influence and prospects of him and his friends. Around Christmas 1454 the King had recovered his sanity. Edmund Clere, an esquire of the King's Household, recounted the news to his Paston kinsfolk.

---

Edmund Clere to John Paston                                        9 January 1455
Greenwich

Right well beloved cousin, I recommend me to you, letting you know such tidings as we have. Blessed be God, the King is well amended and has been since Christmas, and on St. John's day commanded his almoner to ride to Canterbury with his offering and commanded the secretary to offer at St. Edward's [shrine].

And on the Monday afternoon the Queen came to him and brought my Lord Prince [her son] with her. And then he asked what the Prince's name was and the Queen told him 'Edward': and then he held up his hands and thanked God therefore. And he said he never knew till that time nor understood what was said to him, nor knew where he had been while he was sick until now. And he asked who were the godfathers and the Queen told him and he was well pleased. And she told him that the Cardinal was dead, and he said that he never knew of it till then; and he said that one of the wisest lords in this land was dead. And my Lord of Winchester and [the Prior] of St. John's were with him on the day after Twelfth Day, and he spoke to them as well as he ever did; and when they came out they wept for joy. And he says that he is in charity with all the world, and he would that all the lords were so. And now he says Matins of Our Lady and evensong and hears his Mass devoutly; and Richard shall tell you more tidings by mouth . . .

By your cousin, Edmund Clere.

---

With the King's recovery the Protectorate of the Duke of York came to an end: the Earl of Salisbury lost his post as Chancellor and the Duke of Somerset was released from the Tower. But York and his friends were not prepared to retire into obscurity – such a course would, in any case, have been dangerous, since Somerset was undoubtedly bent on revenge for his humiliations. On 22 May 1455 York and his allies, among whom the Neville Earls of Salisbury and Warwick were most prominent, clashed with the King's forces at St Albans – the first pitched battle of the Wars of the Roses. One of John Paston's kinsmen wrote a succinct report.

---

John Crane to John Paston                                          25 May 1455
Lambeth

. . . As for such tidings as we have here these three lords are dead – the Duke of Somerset, the Earl of Northumberland and Lord Clifford; and as for any other men of name, I know of none, save only [William] Cotton of Cambridgeshire. As for any other lords, many of them are hurt; as for Fillongley [Fastolf's nephew], he lives and fares well as far as I can discover.

And as for any great multitude of people that was there, there was slain at most six score. And as for the lords that were with the King, they and their men were pillaged and spoiled [robbed] of all their harness and horses. As for what rule we shall now have, I do not yet know, save only there are made certain new officers: my Lord of York, Constable of England; my Lord of Warwick is made Captain of Calais; my Lord Bourchier is made Treasurer of England. As yet I have no other tidings.

As for our sovereign lord, thanked be God, he has no great harm.

No more to you at this time, but I pray you send this letter to my Mistress Paston when you have seen it; praying you to remember my sister, Margaret, at the time when she will be made a nun.

---

# Armour

spearmen, the heavily armoured men-at-arms could be decisive in a pitched battle, particularly against less well-protected opponents.

The design and decoration of tilting-armour became more elaborate, increasing in weight and the consequent protection it gave. But battlefield-armour also needed to allow mobility and could not therefore be so all-protective. In any case, even the most powerful armour was of limited effect against firearms and, by the end of the century, the growing accuracy of handguns was gradually making full plate-armour obsolete. When the Earl of Oxford died in 1513, he left in his armoury, besides large numbers of weapons, a valuable suit of armour of his own. But Oxford was an old man whose military memories went back to the Battle of Barnet and his equipment was by now a symbol of status rather than a fighting-man's protection.

*A cavalryman's armour, 1475. A 'sallet' helmet and 'bevor' protect his neck and chin. His horse wears a 'shaffron' head-piece and 'peytral' breast-plate.*

*An armoured knight at prayer – a detail from an early fifteenth-century stained-glass window in a Shropshire church.*

Despite fifteenth-century developments in weaponry, the armoured cavalry soldier, dismounting to fight on foot when necessary, remained a powerful force in Continental warfare. Plate armour improved in quality to such an extent that it could be effective against the cross-bow and the long-bow at all but the shortest range. As the shield disappeared from the battlefield, vulnerable spots, such as shoulders and elbows, were protected by articulated plates which allowed free movement of the limbs. The design of armour also changed dramatically during the fifteenth century. The 'sallet', for instance, with its rim protecting the neck, replaced the globe-shaped, vizored helmet, and a simple belt was now used to carry the sword. Horses, too, were given greater protection and the development of a lance-rest attached to the breast-plate gave greater weight and accuracy to the charge. Used in association with archers and

Four days after the battle, the victorious Duke of York summoned a parliament to meet at Westminster on 9 July. As in 1450, the Duke of Norfolk desired to have loyal followers representing Norfolk and Suffolk in the House of Commons, and he and his wife wrote to the Norfolk gentry asking them to elect Sir Roger Chamberlain and John Howard, the Duke's cousin. Although there was clearly some resentment at this interference with the free choice of the county, Chamberlain and Howard were, in fact, elected on 23 June at the county court which was attended by both Fastolf and Paston. John Paston's name had clearly been canvassed as a possible MP for the county or 'knight of the shire' but he was worried that his reputation would suffer if it were known that he had unsuccessfully challeged the Duke's nominees. His friend, John Jenney, tried to soothe his feelings.

---

John Jenney to John Paston                          24 June 1455
Intwood, Norfolk

My Master Paston, I recommend me to you. And, where you have been informed that I had said to Howard that you laboured to be knight of the shire, I said never so to him. I told my Lord of Norfolk at London that I had laboured divers men for Sir Roger Chamberlain, and they had said to me that they would have him, but not Howard, inasmuch as he had no livelode in the shire, nor acquaintance there; and I had asked whom they would have, and they said they would have you, and thus I told him . . . I could not say that you laboured therein, for I never heard say that you laboured for it, by the faith I vow to God.

  As for the writ of parliament [to elect the MPs] for Norwich I thank you that you will labour therein . . . I pray you that if you think that I will not be successful, that you say that you move it of yourself and not by my desire. Some men hold it right strange to be in this parliament and I think that they are wise men that so do . . .

---

The parliament blamed the Battle of St Albans upon the Duke of Somerset and his allies: in November York was re-appointed Protector and he was to dominate government for the rest of the year. Although he was dismissed from this responsibility in February 1456, he and his allies remained powerful figures in the government of the country for a few more months, until the rivalry between the Queen and the Duke of York began to push the country once again towards open conflict. Paston and Fastolf saw York's influence in affairs as an opportunity to pursue successfully their legal business and most of the correspondence of this period is concerned mainly with such matters. A fairly typical letter from John Bocking, Fastolf's agent in London, gives an idea of the varied nature of the legal processes involved, as well as reporting the whereabouts of some of the great folk. Buckingham's 'uneasiness' may have been due to the new political tensions that were developing.

---

John Bocking to John Paston                                         8 May 1456
Southwark

. . . As to our action of attaint [an action to upset a jury verdict] the Chief Justice has, since this day a week ago, sat at the Guildhall in London with all the lords and all the judges save one from each court. My Master Markham [a judge] rode out of London early yesterday. Notwithstanding, we proceeded upon it and had at the bar Choke, Littleton, Jenney, Illingworth, John Jenney and Dynne [all barristers] and recalled how long drawn-out it had been and the truth of the matter, and how much the parties had been harmed during the time; and we shall have a ruling early next term and not before, for tomorrow the judges sit again in the Town . . . Yesterday we had a great day also in the Exchequer. My Master is much indebted to Haltoft, and we have been assigned there a day next term, and stand upon the law. Our counsel was late in coming but in the end they acquitted themselves well. Our opponents' bill [plea] was thought nothing of by all those who stood at the bar who were of neither party. We are joined in the Common Pleas against Jenney and Howes . . . As for an attachment [an arrest], you may have none unless you or one of you make your oath in your own person before the barons [of the Exchequer]. I would have done it but I could not be admitted. And as for the other process it is advised that by the course of the Exchequer I should take a venire facias [a writ ordering the defendant to appear] against Wentworth, Andrews, Long Bernard and Deyville . . .

    As for tidings . . . the Queen and the Prince are at Tutbury, my Lord of York at Sandal and my Lord of Warwick at Warwick. My Lord of Buckingham rode on Ascension Eve to Writtle nothing well pleased and somewhat uneasy of heart about his purpose . . .

# Parliament

*The Bishop of Norwich with fellow clergy in the Processions of the House of Lords at the opening of Parliament at Westminster, 1512.*

'When all a kingdom gathered is . . . to reform what is amiss' is how a contemporary describes the significance of fifteenth-century parliaments. After 200 years of existence, the institution had come to symbolize the whole nation, and its frequent, though irregular and usually short, sessions were the occasion for great ceremonial as well as for much political and administrative activity. The King, who could summon and dissolve parliaments at will, needed them primarily to obtain grants of taxes from the Commons. Even after 1453, when there were fewer expensive foreign wars and consequently less need for taxes, parliament remained because it was only 'by authority of parliament' that the law of the land could be changed.

Statutes could originate from a petition by an individual or group, or they could be formulated by the King and Council; but all needed the agreement of King, Lords and Commons, which represented 'the assent of the whole realm'. Parliaments could also receive petitions, such as that of John Paston in 1449, concerning matters with which the inferior courts could not effectively deal. For Parliament was also the King's highest court and, as such, was the scene of great events like the Impeachment of the Duke of Suffolk in 1450 and the claim to the throne of Richard, Duke of York, in 1460.

On such occasions it was the Lords who made the major decisions. During the fifteenth century the two houses became clearly distinguished, and the rights and procedures of each more clearly defined. The Lords, 'the Upper House', which was presided over by the Chancellor, contained about 100 members, more or less equally divided between 'Temporal' (including earls and barons) and 'Spiritual' peers (bishops and abbots). The Commons was larger and grew in numbers during this period. There were 74 representatives from the counties ('knights of the shire') and about 200 borough representatives ('burgesses'). The Speaker, who presided, was almost always drawn from the knights of the shire and was usually nominated by the King. Little is known of the internal proceedings of the Commons, but a satirist's picture from the beginning of the century suggests that members were not markedly different from those of later times: 'some were chatterers . . . some slumbered and said little . . . some would take no decision for fear of their master . . . some were pompous and dull . . . and some went with the majority whichever way it went.' For most members, a session of parliament was just an occasional episode in their lives; for some, it may already have become a step in a career at Court, administration or the Law.

*Overleaf: Henry VI's Parliament with the Lords to the left of the kneeling King, and the Commons below them; from the fifteenth-century foundation charter of King's College, Cambridge.*

Kennuis setus rex et fundatur

Et nous le pmoins ayt

rammus pueut

tuum vbeuum quam ipa
musturam dirigentes ac pp
et pontificis sancti Nichi
muniulata se continue ob
gum perpetuum de vuo Cen
uati sigilli mi ac Johanneu
ville mr Cantebi per meta
rettore mpus collegy Johan
ammouend psecuimus cr
bus sumus roshis pratis pat
uaffis m erdem ius spect

...bus collegy...

Dei gra...

prioribz duabz marchionibz comitibus baronibus Iustic vicecomitibus p...
que regnantium et regnoz gubernacio procuratur ac subditoz consulitur comnio...
comuniunt officia et mutuose sibi extent Nam potestas militans nisi fiat...
animi et sapiencie plus invaluit illic floruit eminencius militia secularis et ab...
lie eminentissime respexerit et sicut vitis abundans multos in vina Domini...
mater et illustri virorum in lege divina et humana omnibusque scienciis liberalibz mirabilit nutrit et...
ipsam tanto arduius velle sui semmus fructum differre quanto se cognouerit alimentis proprius...
festo in hanc lucem primo editi sumus extirpacionem heresum et eorum qui quasi totum respergunt...
Augmentum cleri decorem sacrosancte matris ecclie cuius ministeria personis suis ydoneis comitt...
modum scolaribz seu pluribus vel paucioribz prout casus euenerit secundum ipsius collegy facultate...
...seth Scch ipsi et Johannem Langton universitatis predicte cancellarios sub certis modo et forma in...
...dis in dictis hiis ipsis patentibz specificatis duximus exigens Ac realiter et in facto tenore dictarum lit...
keby et Willm Hattecliff scolares residuos eiusdem collegy per nos electos et ad hoc assumptos secund...
...us et ordinauimus Ac cum dicta nob cancellario magn et scolares universitatis predicte quibus super...
...stamentum fforestarii prequisitus cui finis aucramentum parmagnus vestre vocat palfrey silver vel...
magister Johannes Somerseth adtunc tenuit ad terminum vite sue ex concessione ipsa eidem Johann...

By 1456 Fastolf had settled upon his plan to found a college of priests at Caister and to endow it richly from his estates. For this a licence had to be obtained from the crown and Fastolf hoped to get this cheaply in reward for his long service and for joining the King as 'founder'. Bishop Waynflete, whose assistance was hoped for, was to be involved with the project for the next twenty years.

---

Sir John Fastolf to John Paston                    18 November 1456
[Caister]

. . . And whereas I late wrote to you in a letter delivered by Henry Hanson for the foundation of my college, I am sore set upon it. And that is the cause I write now, to remind you again to move my Lords of Canterbury and Winchester for the licence to be obtained that I might have the amortising [right to grant land to a religious body] without a great fine, in recompense of my long service continued and done to the King and to his noble father, whom God assoil, and which has never yet been paid for or rewarded. And now, since I have ordained to make the King founder and ever to be prayed for and for his right noble progenitors, his father and uncles, I think I should not be denied of my desire, but rather it should be remembered and sped.

Wherefore, as I wrote to you, I pray you for the better speeding of it, to make you and me known to a chaplain of my Lord of Canterbury, who may in your absence remember me like wise to my Lord Chancellor [Bishop Waynflete]: for seeing the King's disposition, and his also, to the edifying of God's service, there might be no better time to move it.

My Lord of Norfolk is removed from Framlingham on foot to go to Walsingham, and I wait daily for him to come hither.

---

Family matters remain an important theme of the correspondence, and emerge more frequently in the later 1450s. William Paston was now an active young lawyer and more continuously in London than his elder brother. He was clearly asked to keep an eye on his nephews, John's two elder sons, who were now being educated in London – perhaps at an Inn of Chancery. Elizabeth's marriage was still a subject of interest and so was that of John's elder daughter, Margery.

---

William Paston to Margaret Paston                    August [? 1456-8]
London

Right heartily and well beloved sister, I recommend me etc. And I have received your letters. And as for my nephews, they both learn right well, and their gowns and their gear shall be made for them according to the intent of your letter and all other things that are needed for their profit, to the extent of my power. And, sister, God thank you for your labour for me in the gathering of my money. And I pray you, as soon as you receive it, send it hither by some trusty man . . . My sister and brother both recommend them to you, and I may say to you privately she is upon point of marriage, if my mother and brother set themselves in friendly and steadfast manner on it, as I know well that you would if it lay in your power as it does in theirs. I pray you do your part to help it on. It would be long to write to you all the manner in which this matter has been treated, and therefore I have spoken to William Worcester and to Wydewell to tell it you wholly as it is. I know right well your good labour may do much: send me word what you hear about this as hastily as you may.

Item, Howard spoke of a marriage between his son and my niece, Margery, your daughter: it would be well that such matters were not slothfully laboured for it would be worshipful etc. Send me word, and God have you in his keeping.

By your brother, William Paston.

Item, I send you a letter directed to Wollysby. I pray you let it be delivered to him as hastily as you may; and if you come to this country I am like to see you, and we shall make right merry, I trust.

---

# The Education of Girls

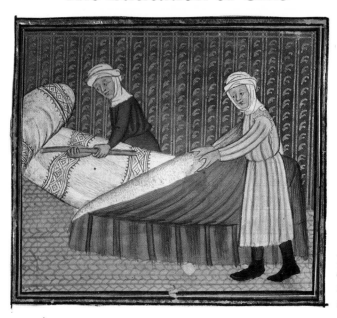

*Two women making a bed; one is using a stick to tuck the stitched coverlet under the bolster.*

The French author of *The Book of the Knight of La Tour Landry*, translated into English more than once in the fifteenth century and printed by Caxton, wrote his treatise, he says, 'to stir and turn [his daughters] to goodness and worship', to 'be humble and courteous to great and small', to 'keep her body undefiled and in cleanness' and to be 'humble, courteous and serviceable unto her husband', and finally, 'to learn them to read'. Another verse treatise on the same theme adds that the well brought-up woman should not haunt taverns or attend wrestling matches, and gives practical instruction on how to manage a household, servants and disobedient children – 'take a smart rod and beat them'. Since, with the exception of nuns, a woman's life was to be spent as part or head of a household, such rules of social behaviour and managerial skills were essential and they parallel the practical skills that were taught to boys.

A lady would also be expected to be able to read, she was probably taught at first by a domestic chaplain or clerk. In England, unlike France, there were few schools to which such girls could go on to learn Latin grammar and the practice of writing.

Nunneries provided teaching for some girls: in 1416 the daughter of the Earl of Suffolk spent twelve weeks at Bruisyard Convent and a brother of the house was paid for teaching her; but neither in this case nor in those of the many other girls who spent some time at nunneries is there much evidence of what they were taught. Skills thought most necessary for well-born girls could be taught by their mothers or by a mistress specially employed for the purpose, as Katherine Swynford served the daughters of John of Gaunt, her future husband. Like their brothers, however, many were sent to other households to finish their education in service: Anne, daughter of John Paston I, spent time as a young girl in the household of Lady Calthorpe, one of the leading figures in Norfolk society; but her aunt, Elizabeth, appears to have remained mainly at home until she went to Lady Pole's household in her late twenties – Agnes perhaps did not trust her away from home. Such girls would learn the elaborate manners necessary to hold a place in polite society and such social accomplishments as music and dancing, riding, archery and, of course, needlework. The more essential details of married life were learned less from treatise than from the example of mother and kinsfolk or by trial and error. These tasks included: the management of a household and perhaps of an estate; the dealing with officials and lawyers; acting as doctor and nurse for family and neighbours; and serving and managing husband and children. Whether or not Margaret Paston could write, she was, in these respects, a well-educated woman.

After some time at Cambridge Agnes's youngest son, Clement, was also being educated in London, probably at an Inn of Chancery, whilst his sister, Elizabeth, was now a member of the household of Lady Pole. A list of 'errands' to be done for Agnes, perhaps intended for William or John, included some advice for Clement's schoolmaster. A letter to John, perhaps somewhat later, shows Agnes in a rather gentler maternal role.

---

Agnes Paston to [?William Paston]                                    28 January 1458

To pray Greenfield to send me faithfully word by writing how Clement Paston has done his duty in learning. And if he has not done well and will not amend, pray him that he will truly belash him till he will amend; and so did the last master, and the best he ever had, at Cambridge. And tell Greenfield that if he will take it upon him to bring him into good rule and learning, so that I may verily know that he does his duty, I will give him 10 marks for his labour, for I had rather that he [Clement] were fairly buried than that he were lost by default [of discipline].

   Item, to see how many gowns Clement has, and those that are [thread]bare should be raised [the nap teased] . . . Item, to have made for me 6 spoons of 8 oz. of troy weight, well fashioned and double gilt. And tell Elizabeth Paston that she must put herself to work readily as other gentlewomen do, and do somewhat to help herself therewith; pay the Lady Pole 26s. 8d. for her board. And if Greenfield has done well his duty to Clement, or will do his duty, give him the noble.

---

Agnes Paston to John Paston                                          29 October [?]
Norwich

Son, I greet you well, and let you know that, forasmuch as your brother, Clement, lets me know that you faithfully desire my blessing – that blessing that I prayed your father to give you on the last day that ever he spoke and the blessing of all the saints under heaven and mine must come to you at all days and times. And think verily not otherwise but that you have it and shall have it, while I find you kind and willing to the welfare of your father's soul and to the welfare of your brethren.

   By my counsel, dispose yourself as much as you may to have less to do in the world: your father said 'in little business lies much rest'. This world is but a thoroughfare, and full of woe; and when we depart from it we bear right nothing with us but our deeds, good and ill. And no man knows how soon God will call him, and therefore it is good for every creature to be ready. Whom God visits, him He loves . . .

   Our Lord have you in his blessed keeping, body and soul . . .

# The Education of Boys

*Richard Beauchamp, Earl of Warwick, holding the young Henry VI. Henry V appointed this cultivated nobleman as tutor to his son.*

The Pastons' interest in the upbringing and education of their children was probably no different from that of most of their contemporaries, in that they well understood the importance of a child's early years. Just as there are detailed instructions which survive for the education of the young King Henry VI and for Prince Edward, son of Edward IV, William Paston's will provided for the education of his younger sons. They were to spend time at a grammar school, then to study logic and civil law (at a university) before going on to learn the 'law of England' (the Common Law). It was for his widow, Agnes, to see that the instructions were carried out, which is why she asked that her sixteen-year old youngest son, Clement, be 'truly belashed' by his master in London if he did not do well. Agnes, like other parents of the time, saw education as the learning of 'good rule' [behaviour] and social accomplishments as much as an academic discipline.

The Pastons' contemporary, Peter Idley, addressed a long series of verses to his son 'that art yet young and somewhat wild' to teach him virtue and manners as well as encourage learning. His advice included these lines:

> *Let thy tongue not clack a mill . . .*
> *Look to such clothing as thou shalt wear*
> *Keep them as cleanly as thou can*
> *And all the remnant of thy gear*
> *For clothing often maketh man . . .*
> *But go not ever too nice and gay*
> *Leave cutting and jagging of clothes*
> *Fellowship of women and taverns also*
> *Accustom not to swear great oaths.*

Specific skills appropriate to the family's status were also taught, of course. Prince Edward's governor was instructed to ensure that he rose and went to bed early and spent a substantial part of the day at prayers; he was to learn Latin and French, listen to noble stories and, for 'disport', to learn music, dancing and riding. A gentleman's son would undergo a similar training. His command of foreign languages may have been limited, but it was sufficient for most purposes. Equally important were physical skills such as riding and fighting with a gentleman's weapons; hunting and hawking and the lore that surrounded them; dancing, singing and playing on instruments; some knowledge of the law, and, of course, the elements of religion and religious observances. How far each of these was taken would depend on the status and potential career of the boy.

Early training would be in the parents' household. He would then either go to school or to the household of another gentleman or nobleman, or, quite frequently, to both: Thomas Howard, later 2nd Duke of Norfolk, spent a 'sufficient time' at the grammar school at Ipswich, and then entered the King's Household as a 'henchman' – one of a group of young gentlemen who had their own governor and schoolmaster and who learned there the accomplishments of the courtier. But those who went straight from school to university or to the Inns in London did not need to miss out on courtly accomplishments, for at these places, too, there were teachers of courtly skills.

Elizabeth Paston's sojourn in the house of Lady Pole was not only, no doubt, more peaceful than her years with her mother, but more successful in finding her a husband. Late in 1458 she married Robert Poynings, a squire of good family, whose lands were mostly in Kent and Sussex, but who must also have been acquainted with the Pastons through his possession of the manor of Sidestrand, only a few miles away from the village of Paston. Elizabeth's marriage had been a family preoccupation for many years but, although she appears again in the correspondence from time to time, the following rather enigmatic letter to her mother is one of only two from her that survive.

---

Elizabeth Poynings to Agnes Paston                    3 January 1459
London

Right worshipful and my most entirely beloved mother . . . If it pleases you to hear of me and how I do, at the making of this letter I was in good health of body, thanked be Jesus. And as for my master [husband], my 'best-beloved' as you call him, and I must needs call him so now, for I find no cause to do otherwise, and, as I trust to Jesus, shall find none, he is full kind to me and is as busy as he can to make me sure of my jointure, whereof he is bound in a bond of £1000 to you, mother, and to my brother, John, my brother, William, and to Edmund Clere – but they needed no such bond. Wherefore I beseech you, good mother, as our most singular trust is in you, that my master, 'my best beloved', does not fail to receive at the beginning of this term the 100 marks you promised him to the marriage, together with the remnant of the money from my father's will . . . As to my Lady Pole, with whom I sojourned, I would you will be my tender and good mother, that she may be paid for all the costs done to me before my marriage, and also Christopher Hanson, as you wrote unto my brother, John, that they should be. And that it please your good motherhood to give credence to William Worcester. And Jesus for his great mercy save you.

    By your humble daughter,
    Elizabeth Poynings.

---

During 1459 national politics moved towards a new crisis. After the confrontation at Ludford on 12 October 1459 the Duke of York fled to Ireland and his son, with the Earls of Salisbury and Warwick, to Calais. A parliament was summoned to Coventry where the Yorkists were attainted and their lands distributed to the Queen's loyal allies.

The events had serious repercussions in Norfolk, particularly on the Fastolf–Paston circle. The Pastons were clearly seen as friendly to the opponents of the Queen.

---

Friar Brackley to John Paston                        [?November] 1459
[?South] Walsham

Right reverent master and most trusty friend in earth . . . A lewd doctor of Ludgate preached on Sunday a fortnight ago at St. Paul's, charging the people that no man should pray for these lords, the traitors [York and his allies] etc.; and he had little thanks, as he deserved. And for his lewd demeaning his brethren are held in less favour in London . . . The Chancellor is not good to these lords . . . Wyndham, Heydon, Tuddenham, Blake, W. Chamberlain and Wentworth have commissions lately to take traitors and send to the nearest gaol all persons who are favourers and well-willers to the said lords etc. Master Radcliffe and you have none of the commissions directed to you for you are held to be favourable to them. Wyndham and Heydon are named here as the causers of the commissions . . . By my faith, here is a cosy world.

As I have written to you often before this, [what follows is in Latin in the original] 'Make yourselves friends of the Mammon of Unrighteousness', since it is a fact. Judas does not sleep . . . As is said in the psalm 'Trust in the Lord and do good, so shalt thou dwell in the land and be fed; and delight thyself in the Lord, and he shall give thee the desires of thine heart' . . . I pray God, therefore, who created you and me and redeemed us by his precious blood, to preserve you and yours in his grace in prosperity and that he direct you with grace in all your affairs . . .

It is unclear whether Brackley's letter was written shortly before or just after Sir John Fastolf died on 5 November 1459. His death was to usher in twenty years of disputes and litigation which were to make the Pastons one of the great families of Norfolk but were also to cause enormous trouble and distress. John Paston had been the old knight's closest friend and legal adviser for some years. Nevertheless, it was a shock to many, including Fastolf's other legal advisers, Judge William Yelverton and William Jenney, that his last will, made on his deathbed, left to Paston all his great estates on condition that he founded the college at Caister on which the dead knight had set his heart. Paston was also made principal executor, with Thomas Howes. The will was bound to be challenged in both the ecclesiastical courts and the King's courts, and Paston at once took action to secure his position. The escheator, who had the duty of holding an enquiry upon the lands of the deceased, was, as William hoped, friendly, and a return favourable to John Paston's claims was made. The Chancellor, now Bishop Waynflete, was also one of Fastolf's executors. While John carried out the necessary activities in East Anglia, his brother acted as his representative in London and also gave him advice about how to treat William Worcester – advice which it would have been well for John to have heeded.

---

William Paston to John Paston                    12 November 1459
London

. . . On Friday last in the morning Worcester and I had come to London . . . and I spoke to the Lord Chancellor and I found him well disposed in all things and you will find him right profitable to you etc. And he desired me to write you a letter in his name and to entrust you to gather the goods together, and prays you to do this and have all his [Fastolf's] goods out of every place of his and from his own place, wheresoever they were, and lay them secretly where you thought best at your choice, till he speaks with you himself; and he said you will have all the favour he may lawfully give . . .

My Lord Treasurer [the Earl of Wiltshire] speaks fair but yet many advise me to put no trust in him. There is much labour to find title for the King in his [Fastolf's] property. [Richard] Southwell is escheator and he is right well disposed . . . I have spoken with my Lord of Canterbury and Master John Stokes and I find them both right well disposed . . .

As for William Worcester, he trusts verily you would do something reasonable for him and his profit; and I doubt not, if he may verily and faithfully understand you so disposed towards him, you will find him faithful to you in like wise. I understand by him he will never have another master after his old master [Fastolf], and in my opinion it would be a pity if he does not obtain enough from my master, that he should never need service again, considering how my master trusted him and the long years that he has been with him and the many hard journeys he has made for his sake . . .

# Colleges and Chantries

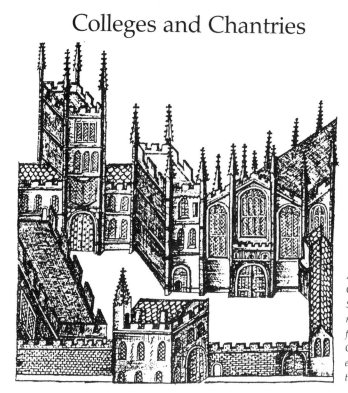

*An engraving of Magdalen College, Oxford, in 1566. Sir John Fastolf's will made provision for the foundation of a college at Caister, but the endowment was later transferred to Magdalen.*

Sir John Fastolf's plan for the foundation of a college of monks or priests at Caister was very much in the religious fashion of his day. All men and women were conscious of the pains of Purgatory and were taught that 'three things helpen souls most out of penance, that is devout praying, alms-giving and mass-singing . . . right as meat and drink comforteth a man when he is feeble, right so the sacrament comforteth and strengtheneth the souls that it is done for'. Even the poorest could hope for the prayers of their families or the communal prayers of their parish on All Souls Day; the rather better-off souls could hope for those of their fellow-members of religious guilds as well; while the rich could leave money for prayers and masses to be said by a priest specially paid for the purpose. Margaret Paston, for example, left a substantial sum for a priest to pray for seven years 'for my soul, the souls of my father and mother, the soul of John Paston, my late husband and for the souls of his ancestors and mine'. The very rich, particularly those like Fastolf who had no direct heir, might try to found a chantry, hospital or college which would be endowed primarily to provide prayers in perpetuity for the founder.

Such institutions abounded in the churches and monasteries of England – there are said to have been over 50 chantries in St Paul's Cathedral alone. But the independent wealthy institutions such as Lord Cromwell's foundation at Tatteshall, which Fastolf may have been trying to emulate, were very expensive. Apart from the landed endowment itself, a licence had to be obtained from the King to grant land into 'mortmain' (to a religious body). Fastolf's kinsman, Henry Fillongley, reported about 1456 that 'they would ask for every 100 marks [value of land] that you would amortize 500 marks'; he therefore suggested a cheaper way of achieving the same end. But Fastolf was 'sore set thereupon' and his last will imposed on his executors the responsibility of carrying out his scheme. As frequently happened, the project succumbed to the disputes that followed his death and the endowment was eventually transferred to William Waynflete's foundation of Magdalen College, Oxford. Given that colleges and chantries were abandoned at the time of the Reformation, it was fortunate perhaps for Sir John's soul that his papers and memory survive today at Magdalen College.

Depositions of important witnesses were taken. Robert Fitzralph, one of Fastolf's gentlemen-servants, gives a version of the making of the last will.

---

Deposition of Robert Fitzralph, esquire        26 November 1459
Caister

. . . I, being in my Master Fastolf's chamber, leaning upon his great bed, at such time as John Paston, esquire, Master John Brackley and Master Clement Felmingham were in communication with my said Master of divers great matters touching his will and certain agreements between my said Master and the said John Paston during the week before my said Master deceased, I heard my said Master and the said John Paston appoint and conclude that the said John Paston should take upon him the rule of my Master's household and of all his livelode in Norfolk and Suffolk during his [Fastolf's] life; and after his decease the said John Paston should cause to be founded a college at Caister of 7 monks or priests, and pay 4000 marks of money at 800 marks a year to my Master's executors till the said sum were paid; and that the said John Paston should have all the livelode that was of my said Master in Norfolk and Suffolk to him and his heirs in fee [in freehold ownership]. And after this said matter had been repeated my Master said these words: 'Cousin, I pray you and require you, let this be settled in all haste without tarrying, for this is my very last will' . . .

---

The death of a relative and such a munificent patron demanded a period of mourning, but Christmas was coming, when all households made merry. John was in London, so Margaret took advice on the proper etiquette from the doyenne of Norfolk ladies, Lady Morley. For the first time the two older sons begin to carry out duties.

---

Margaret Paston to John Paston        24 December 1459

Please you to know that I sent your eldest son to my Lady Morley to have knowledge what sports were used in her house at Christmas next following after the decease of my lord, her husband. And she said that there were no disguisings [acting], nor harping, luting or singing, nor any lewd sports, but just playing at the tables [backgammon] and chess and cards. Such sports she gave her folk leave to play and no other. Your son did his errand right well, as you will hear later. I sent your younger son to Lady Stapleton's and she said the same as Lady Morley, that this had been the practice in places of worship [honourable households] where she had been . . .

The magnificence of the new acquisition, which would transform the standing of the family in the region and, indeed, in the nation, forced the Pastons, as never before, to seek patronage from the great men of the kingdom in order to protect their rights. It inevitably produced envy and resentment, and broke old friendships. A letter from Friar Brackley, who remained a firm and invaluable ally, reports on the demeanour of William Yelverton early in 1460.

> . . . W.Y., the Judge, and his wife were here with their retinue and their horses in our Lady's place etc. on Saturday evening and rode hence on Monday afternoon when some had drunk malmsey and tyre [sweet wines] etc . . . But on Monday, when he had eaten and drunken enough . . . he went on so sore he could not cease till he went to his horse . . . and there was not forgotten any unkindness of my master J.P., your brother . . . And after all these matters he took me to witness that I had said to one of the worthiest of the shire that the said Justice began the trouble at St. Benet's . . . And the Judge went on: 'You should have examined the matter'. And I said 'Sir, it does not belong to me to examine the matter, for I knew well I should not be judge in the matter . . .' And then 'No,' says he strongly, 'you shall not be judge, but if you had owed me as much good will as you did and do to Paston you would then have searched out the cause of my great grief, why I said as I said, etc. But I have seen the day you loved me better than him, for he gave you never cause to love as I have done.' 'Sir,' I say, 'he has given me such cause as I am beholden to him for.' 'Ya,' says he, 'you shall bear witness etc. and the others, Master Clement and W. Shipdham.' To which I: 'As for the witness I shall bear, I shall say and write as I know.' To which he replied: 'I made his testament and I know etc.' To which I said: 'I never saw testament of your making . . .' And he, angrily: 'I know you have a great heart etc., but I assure you that the Lords above at London are informed of you and they shall deal with you well enough' . . .
>
> Then the Prior: [in Latin] 'Lord, it is not reasonable nor befitting your conscience that you should contend with Master Paston or he with you for the goods of the deceased which are only his and not belonging to either of you. I marvel greatly that you were formerly such great friends and are so no more, which I greatly deplore.' To which the Judge: 'There is no man busy to bring us together etc., so that I can only think it is of little importance.' But I know well, in faith, that the Judge, William Wayte, his mawment [plaything] and his boy, James, with their heady and hot language have and do utter daily lewd and harmful slanders etc . . .

A little later in the same year William Paston also had to report on the hostility of some of Fastolf's former servants. By this time John Paston had moved to reside at Caister whilst William was undertaking some of his business at Norwich.

William Paston to John Paston                    2 May 1460
Norwich

. . . I spoke this day with [John] Bocking. He had but few words, but I felt by him he was right evilly disposed to the parson and you, but he had but covert language . . . I understand that this Bocking and Worcester have great trust in their own lewd opinion, whatsoever it is. Bocking told me this day that he stood as well in favour with Master Fastolf three days before he died as any man in England. I said that I supposed not, nor three years before he died . . . It is he that makes William Worcester as assertive as he is.

I would that you had a witness from Robert Inglose, even though he could witness no more than that my Master had his wits, because he was so close to my Master Fastolf. Worcester said at Caister that it would be necessary for you to have good witnesses, as he said it would go hard with you unless your witnesses were sufficient. My cousin Berney can tell you . . .

Item, Arblaster and I spoke together. I felt him right faithfully disposed towards you and he will do much good if he goes to London, for he can labour well among the lords . . . It is full necessary to make yourself strong by lordship and other means . . .

Omnia pro pecunia facta sunt [all things are done for money].

In spite of the opposition to his claims, John Paston seems rapidly to have taken possession of the property and, during the summer, the family seems to have taken up residence at Hellesdon, a Fastolf manor conveniently close to Norwich. After the Battle of Northampton in June 1460 had brought York and the Nevilles to power John's new status in the county was recognised by his being put back on the commission of the peace and, more significantly, his being elected to represent the county in the parliament which met at Westminster in October. Early in that month Friar Brackley wrote to wish him well: at this time the claim to the throne by the Duke of York was not expected and it is the Earl of Warwick who is seen as the leader of the reformers and the potential patron.

---

Friar Brackley to John Paston                                    October 1460
Norwich

Right reverent Sir, after due recommendation. We say in this country that Heydon is for Berkshire in the Commons House, and the Lady of Suffolk has sent up her son and his wife to my Lord of York to ask his favour for a sheriff the next year . . . You have much to do: God speed you. You have many good prayers, from the convent, the city and the country. God save our good lords, Warwick, all his brethren, Salisbury, etc., from all false covetousness and from favouring extortion, so they will flee utterly shame and confusion. God save them and preserve them from treason and poison: let them beware of these for God's pity, for if anything but good comes to my lord of Warwick, farewell you, farewell I and farewell all our friends! For, by my soul, this land would be utterly undone. Their enemies boast that they will use their goods to come into their favour, but God prevent it, and give them grace to know their friends from their enemies and to cherish and prefer their friends and lessen the might of their enemies throughout all the shires of the land . . .

   And I pray you think in this parliament of the text of holy Scripture [in Latin]: 'Whosoever will not do the law of the God and the law of the King, let judgment be executed speedily upon him, whether it be unto death or to banishment or to confiscation of goods or to imprisonment'.

---

# The Friars

*Friars were not allowed to own property, so they received their support by begging and by seeking alms.*

Unlike the monks, the friars, or members of the four 'Mendicant Orders' – the Franciscans (Grey Friars), the Dominicans (Black Friars), the Carmelites (White Friars) and the Augustinians – were expected to mix with the laity. By the fifteenth century their great evangelizing days were past, but they continued to travel the country, seeking alms, preaching sermons and taking confession. The Household Book of a Suffolk lady, Alice de Briene, shows that she entertained friars from various houses every two to three weeks, and it can be assumed that they frequently appeared at Paston and Oxnead too, as well as at Caister, where Friar Brackley, the friend of the Pastons, became Sir John Fastolf's confessor. Most of the friars' convents, however, were in the towns. Norwich had convents of all four orders, and the surviving Black Friars Church, over 200 feet long, indicates the size of the congregations attracted by the more popular preachers, such as John Brackley himself.

In the late fourteenth century, the friars had been violently attacked for their alleged avarice, lechery and hypocrisy: 'friars and fiends be but little asunder', wrote one poet. But they remained popular with most of the laity, being considered not only as pious and learned men but also as worldly enough to understand the sins of the ordinary person. Agnes Paston was a lay sister of the Carmelite Friars in Norwich, and John III's wife, Margery, was buried there. The prayers of a friar and

grounds of a friary were felt to be particularly holy and efficacious. Many of the gentry chose to be buried in such a place, among them John Paston II, who asked rather unexpectedly to be buried in the White Friars' Priory at London 'so that it may cause their prayers the rather to remember my soul'.

*A drawing of a Franciscan friar from a fifteenth-century version of William Langland's Piers Plowman. Langland comments on the friars' alleged vices, particularly their readiness to accept money for giving the sacraments.*

With John in London for the parliament, and with their children still too young to take full responsibility, Margaret became even more essential as her husband's main representative in Norfolk. She lived mainly with the younger children at Hellesdon or Caister: it was from Hellesdon that she wrote in November to report on the successful completion of an inquest on Fastolf's lands and on the honour done her by the Mayor of Norwich in arranging to dine at her home. Rumours of York's claim to the throne had by now reached Norfolk.

---

Margaret Paston to John Paston                           21 October 1460
Hellesdon

. . . This day was held a great day at Acle before the under-sheriff and the under-escheator for the matter of Sir John Fastolf's lands. And my cousin Rookwood and my cousin John Berney of Reedham were there, with divers other gentlemen and worthy men of the country; and the matter is well sped after your intent, blessed be God, as you shall have knowledge in haste.

I suppose that [Thomas] Playter [Fastolf and Paston's agent] will be with you on Sunday or on Monday next coming, if he may. You have many good prayers of the poor people that God should speed you at this parliament, for they live in hope that you should set a way that they might live in better peace in this country than they have done before, and that wool should be provided for so that it should not go out of this land as it has been allowed to do before, and then shall the poor people live better by their working with it . . .

There is great talking in this country of the desire of my Lord of York. The people report full worshipfully of my Lord of Warwick. They have no fear except that he and others should show great favour to those that have been rulers of this country before this time . . .

The Mayor and the Mayoress sent here their dinners this day, and John Damme came with them and they dined here. I am beholden to them, for they have sent to me divers times since you left here. The Mayor says there is no gentleman in Norfolk that he would do more for than he would for you, if it lay in his power . . .

---

# Warwick the Kingmaker and the Nevilles

From the late 1450s to his death in 1471, the Pastons were deeply affected by the ambitions and fortunes of Richard Neville, Earl of Warwick. Warwick had acquired by marriage one of the half-dozen greatest estates in the country, with concentrations of lands and influence in the West Midlands, South Wales and the North which produced a massive income and large reserves of manpower. He used his wealth lavishly to win popular support; one chronicler states that when he was in London, 'six oxen were roasted at breakfast and every tavern was full of his meat, for whoever had any acquaintance in his household could have as much roast as he might carry upon a large dagger'.

It was Warwick's charismatic personality and his military skills – displayed first at St Albans in 1455 and then during his captaincy of Calais in the late 1450s – that attracted men like the Pastons and their friend, Friar Brackley. The Nevilles took the lead in making Edward IV king in early 1461 and obtained great prestige and influence under the new régime; Warwick was well rewarded and his brother, John, was created Earl of Northumberland. A second brother, George, became Chancellor of England. George, whose enthronement as Archbishop of York in 1465 was celebrated with one of the great banquets of the century, was a particularly valuable patron of the Pastons. After Edward's marriage, however, the young King and the Nevilles drifted apart and, in 1467, George was dismissed from his post as Chancellor. The Nevilles' alliance with Edward's discontented brother, Clarence, led to the brief detention of Edward, and 'Re-adeption' of Henry VI in 1470. But Warwick and his brother, John, were killed at the Battle of Barnet in 1471 and, although George remained

*Richard Neville, Earl of Warwick, 'The Kingmaker'.*

Archbishop until his death in 1476, his political power had gone. The great Neville estates were shared by the Dukes of Clarence and Gloucester, the husbands of his daughters, and eventually reverted to the Crown.

## THE NEVILLES

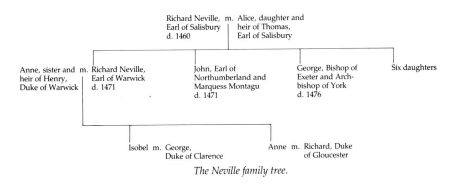

*The Neville family tree.*

The disturbances of the period had made the roads to London more dangerous than usual. John was seeking cloth for himself and his household – new liveries were usually made at Christmas or the New Year – but Margaret found it difficult to carry out his instructions.

Margaret Paston to John Paston                                      25 November 1460
Norwich

Please you to know that my Aunt Mountford has desired me to write to you, beseeching you that you will vouchsafe to borrow for her at London 20 marks for to be paid to Master Poynings . . . the which 20 marks she has delivered to me in gold for you to have at your coming home, for she dare not adventure her money to be brought up to London for fear of robbing; for it is said here that there go many thieves between here and London which causes her to beseech you to obtain the money to discharge the matter and those who are bound for the payment, for she would not have the day [of payment] broken for anything. And she thanks you heartily for the great labour and business that you have had in that matter and in all others touching her and hers, for which, she says, she is bound for ever to be your bede-woman [to pray for you] and ever will be while she lives . . .

    As touching your liveries, there can none be got here of the colour you would have, neither murrey [a dark-red cloth] nor blue nor good russets, underneath 3s. the yard, at the lowest price, and yet there is not enough of one cloth and colour to serve you. And as for providing it from Suffolk, it could not be provided now for this time unless they had had warning at Michaelmas, as I am informed . . .

The next weeks saw the struggle for power reach a climax. On 30 December the Duke of York was defeated and killed by the Queen and her allies at Wakefield. Soon after, the Northerners began to march on London, spreading terror before them, but giving hope to the enemies of the Pastons. Clement Paston, writing from London to his brother, reports on the business he had performed concerning Fastolf's will, but is more concerned to report on news from the North and to encourage his brother to fight for the 'welfare of the South'.

Clement Paston to John Paston                          23 January 1461
London

Right reverent and worshipful brother, I recommend me to you . . . I had Christopher Hanson go to my Lord of Canterbury to tell him what you ordered in your letter . . . but you do well to remember that this lord has many matters to think on, and if it be forgotten the harm is yours.

And my Lord Fitzwalter is ridden northwards, and it is said in my Lord of Canterbury's house that he has captured 200 of Andrew Trollope's men . . . Whatever word you have from the lords that are here it is well done and best for you to see that the country is always ready to come, both footmen and horsemen, when they are sent for; for I have heard say that the further lords will be here sooner than men think – I have heard say within three weeks. You should also come with more men, and cleanlier arrayed, than another man of your country should, for it concerns more your worship and touches you more nearly than other men of that country, and also you are more in favour with my lords here. In this country every man is well willing to go with my lords here and I hope God shall help them, for the people in the North rob and steal, and are prepared to pillage all this country and to give away men's goods and livelode in all the South Country, and that will make for mischief. My lords that are here have as much as they can do to keep down all this country, more than 4 or 5 shires, for they would be up on the men in the North, for it is for the welfare of all the South.

I pray you recommend me to my mother, and tell her that I prayed for her blessing. I pray you excuse me to her that I wrote her no letter, for this was enough to do . . .

The Queen's victory at St Albans on 17 February caused further panic in the South-East and there can be little doubt that the Pastons, like the Duke of Norfolk, welcomed Edward's seizure of the throne on 4 March, as offering them the only chance of salvation from the dreaded Northerners and of maintaining their position in the region against their old rivals, such as Tuddenham and Heydon. None of the Pastons seems to have been present at the second Battle of St Albans or at Edward's great victory at Towton, but their backing, even cautiously, of the winning party seems to have consolidated their position in the shire. Almost at once, however, their right to the heart of their great new possessions was challenged by the Duke of Norfolk. On the pretext of a sale to him by William Yelverton and other of Fastolf's trustees, he entered upon Caister Castle and manor. Much lobbying followed. John's standing was recognised by his being chosen to be knighted at the King's coronation in June.

---

Thomas Playter to John Paston                         May/June 1461
London

. . . Please your mastership to know that the King, because of the siege about Carlisle, changed his day of coronation to be upon the Sunday next after St. John the Baptist [28 June], with the intent to speed northward in all haste; and howbeit that he now has good tidings that Lord Montagu has broken the siege and slain 6000 of the Scots, with two knights, of whom one is Lord Clifford's brother, yet notwithstanding he will still be crowned on the said Sunday.

And John Jenney informed me, and I have truly learned since, you are named to be made a knight at this coronation. Whether you had understanding of this beforehand I know not, but if it pleases you to take the worship upon you, considering the comforting tidings aforesaid, and the gladness and pleasure of all your well-willers and the pain and discomfort of all your ill-willers, it is time that your necessary clothes for that should be provided for; also you should need to hasten to London, for I think the knights will be made the Saturday before the coronation. As much as may be provided for you secretly without cost I shall arrange for you to have, if necessary, before your arrival, trusting for the best; nevertheless, if you are agreeable, you need to send a man before in all haste, that nothing is left to be sought for. William Calthorpe is embilled and Yelverton is embilled – which Markham arranged, for Yelverton looked to be Chief Justice, and Markham thinks to please him thus . . .

Knighthood was an honour but also expensive and demanded a more extravagant life-style. John Paston therefore refused the honour, no doubt on payment of a fine; but in July he was re-appointed to the commission of the peace in Norfolk and elected as knight of the shire to Edward's first parliament which was eventually to meet in November. Not, however, without a struggle, some violence and subsequent litigation. When writs summoning parliaments were issued, the elections of MPs for the counties, the 'knights of the shire', were held at the monthly meeting of the county-court, and only those possessing freehold land worth 40s. a year – the richer peasants and gentry – were permitted a voice. Most elections were uncontested, either because of a general consensus or through overwhelming pressure from a magnate. If there were a contest, however, the sheriff, who presided at the county-court, and made the return, was the key figure. In 1460 the sheriff was John Howard, kinsman and servant of the Duke of Norfolk. His under-sheriff reported the result of the election to John but the doubt implied in his last sentence was justified, as Howard attempted to block his election, causing disorder at the following county-courts.

---

William Price to John Paston                                        19 June 1461
Hethersett

Right worshipful Sir, I recommend me unto you etc. And, Sir, as for the election of the knights of the shire here in Norfolk, in good faith here has been much to-do. Nevertheless, to let you have knowledge of what resulted, my Master Berney, my Master Grey and you had the greatest voice, and I propose, as I will answer to God, to return the due election, that is, according to the majority, you and Master Grey. Nevertheless, I have a master.

---

Although John had refused knighthood and the chance to make a show at Edward's Court, he was well aware of the desirability of having representation and patronage there. Consequently, during the summer of 1461 he sent his eldest son, now nineteen years of age, to the King's Court, to make contacts and friendships which would benefit the whole family. John II, as he will now be called, was eventually to find in the Court a milieu in which he could flourish far more happily than in rural Norfolk or the Inns of Court. But he did not find the early stages of his career there easy, partly because he was kept short of money and had difficulty in carrying out his father's instructions. News of the violence at the county election had reached the Court.

John Paston II to John Paston                    23 August 1461
Lewes

Right reverent and worshipful father . . . I have laboured daily to my Lord of Essex, Treasurer of England, to have moved the King about the manor of Dedham [a Fastolf manor in Essex] . . . every morning before he went to the King, and often have enquired of him whether he had moved the King in these matters. He answered me 'No', saying that it was not the time, and said that he would have liked it to speed as much as I did myself; thus he often delayed me so that in truth I thought to send you word that I felt by him that he was not willing to move the King therein . . . And now of late, reminding him of the same matter, I inquired if he had moved the King's Highness therein; and he answered me that he had felt out and moved the King therein, and repeated the King's answer therein: how that, when he had moved the King concerning the said manor of Dedham, beseeching him to be your good lord therein, considering the good service and true part that you have done and owed to him, and in especial the right you had in it, he said that he would be your good lord therein as he would be to the poorest man in England; he would hold with you in your right, but as for favour, he will not be understood as showing favour more to one man than another, not to anyone in England . . .

I send Pecock home again to you. He is not for me. God send him grace that he may do you good service, but by my estimation that is not likely. You shall have knowledge later how he has behaved here with me. I would, saving your pleasure, that you were rid of him, for he shall never do you profit nor worship.

I suppose you understand that the money that I had of you at London may not last me until the King goes into Wales and comes home again, for I understand that it shall be long before he comes home again. Wherefore I have sent to London to my Uncle Clement to get 100s. from Christopher Hanson, your servant, and to have it sent to me by my servant, and my harness with it, which I left at London to be cleaned. I beseech you not to be displeased with this, for I could borrow none elsewhere, unless I had borrowed it of a stranger or some of my fellows, which I suppose you would not have liked if you had heard of it later. I know where I shall be able to obtain another man in place of Pecock . . .

There is talk here how you and Howard fought together on the shire-day and that one of Howard's men struck you twice with a dagger, and so you would have been hurt but for a good doublet that you had on at that time. Blessed be God that you had it on. I write no more at this time to your good fatherhood, but Almighty God have you in his keeping and send you victory over your enemies and increase in worship to your life's end.

By your servant and elder son,
John Paston.

John's younger brother, Clement, kept an eye on his young nephew's activities: though critical of John II's lack of boldness (he learned quickly), Clement supported his pleas for more money.

Clement Paston to John Paston                     25 August 1461
London

Right reverent and worshipful brother . . . I have spoken with John Russe and Playter spoke with him, too . . . He told us of Howard's behaviour, which made us right sorry till we heard at the end that you came to no harm . . .

I feel from W. Pecock that my nephew is not yet verily acquainted in the King's House, and that he is not as yet taken by the officers of the King's House as being part of it; for the cooks are not ordered to serve him nor the sewer [the officer in charge of the King's dishes etc.] to give him any dishes, for the sewers will take dishes to no men until they are commanded to do so by the Controller. Also he is acquainted with nobody but Wykes [John Wykes, Usher of the King's Chamber], and Wykes had told him that he would bring him to the King, but he has not yet done so. Wherefore it might be best for him to take his leave and come home till you had spoken with somebody to help him forward, for he is not bold enough to put himself forward. But then I considered that if he should now come home the King would think that when he was needed to do him service somewhere, then you would have him home, which would cause him not to be held in favour; and also men would think that he had been put out of the King's service. Also W. Pecock tells me that his money is spent, and not riotously but wisely and with discretion, for the costs are greater in the King's House when he travels than you had thought them to be, as William Pecock can tell you. Therefore we must get for him 100s. at least, as William Pecock says, and yet that will be too little, and I know well that we cannot get 40d. from Christopher Hanson. So I shall have to lend it to him from my own silver. If I knew certainly that it was your intention that he should come home I would send him none; but I shall do what I think would please you best and that, I think, is to send him the silver. Therefore I pray you send me as hastily as you may 5 marks, and the rest, I believe, I shall get from Christopher Hanson and Luket. I pray you send it me as hastily as you may, for I shall leave myself right bare; and I pray you send me a letter how he shall be treated . . .

John Paston's dispute with John Howard at the county election and other complaints from the Duke of Norfolk, perhaps concerned with his attempt to regain Caister, brought John into disfavour at Court. Clement clearly had contacts there other than his nephew.

---

Clement Paston to John Paston       11 October 1461
London

. . . Sir, it was told me by a worshipful man that loves you right well, and you him . . . that on the 11th October the King said 'We have sent two letters of privy seal to Paston by two Yeomen of our Chamber, and he disobeys our writing. But we shall send him another tomorrow, and by God's mercy, if he will not come then he shall die for it. We shall make all other men beware by him [he shall serve as an example] . . .' And therewith he made a great vow that if you do not come at the third command you shall die for it. The man that told me this is as learned a man as any in England; and the same 11th day of October he advised me to send a man to you as hastily as possible to let you have knowledge, and that you should not fail for any excuse, but you should make the man good cheer and come as hastily as you can to the King, for he understands that the King will keep his promise. Notwithstanding, by my advice, if you have this letter before the messenger comes to you, come to the King first, and when you come to him you must be sure of a great excuse. Also, if you come, come in strength, for Howard's wife made boast that if any of her husband's men might get to you your life would not be worth a penny; and Howard has great friendship with the King.

 . . . Also, I understand that the Duke of Norfolk has made a great complaint about you to the King, and my Lord of Suffolk and Howard and Wingfield help every day to speak against you to the King . . .

 My nephew, John, told me also that he supposed that there were proclamations out against you etc. the same day.

---

# Edward IV and His Court

*Edward IV, King of England 1461–70 and 1471–83.*

Edward IV had seized the throne in 1461 with the help of a small group of great lords, the support of London and a military victory over the forces of Henry VI. The first ten years of his reign were punctuated by rebellions and conspiracies. In dealing with these, Edward showed the mixture of firmness and weakness, caution and rashness that characterized his behaviour throughout most of his reign. To the end of his life, this handsome, popular King indulged himself in clothes, food and women, which moralizing chroniclers believed brought him to an early grave. One writer describes him as 'pursuing with no discrimination the married and unmarried, the noble and the lowly, though he took none by force'; when he grew weary of his conquests, as he did with Jane Shore, he passed them on to friends such as Lord Hastings.

Nevertheless, his marriage to Elizabeth Woodville in 1464 was a love-match unprecedented for a medieval English king and it added a new set of rivalries to an already faction-ridden central government. After his recovery of the throne in 1471 and the end of the Neville influence, however, Edward was able to develop a Court and Council more to his personal liking and, though rivalries continued to exist, he and his friends and servants were now the dominant source of power.

Edward's household was large and his Court magnificent. A German visitor described it as 'the most splendid court that one can find in all Christendom' and, even if this was slightly exaggerated, it certainly rivalled those of the King of France and the Duke of Burgundy. Expanding income from land and efficient administration also allowed the King to reward friends and followers, such as the Woodvilles, Lord Hastings, the Chamberlain of the Household, and many lesser men of the Court. For people like the Pastons, such courtiers were worth cultivating, although it was not always easy to pick the winners in the power-game.

In response to these threats John seems to have hurried to London, but when he arrived there he was sent to the Fleet Prison. Margaret again took over the role of local agent. There was still much business resulting from the Fastolf inheritance. Apart from proving the will and making good title to the estates, old Fastolf matters such as the claim on the Duke of Bedford's estate and the Thomas Fastolf wardship still had to be proceeded with.

---

Margaret Paston to John Paston            2 November 1461
[?Caister ]

. . . I received your letter that you sent me by John Holme on Wednesday last past, and I also received another letter on Friday night that you sent me by Nicholas Newman's man, for the which letters I thank you, for I should else have thought that matters had been worse with you than they are or shall be, by the grace of Almighty God. And yet I could not be merry since I had the last letter until this day, when the Mayor sent word to me that he had knowledge for very truth that you were delivered out of the Fleet and that Howard was committed to ward [prison] for divers great complaints that were made to the King about him. It was talked about in Norwich and in divers other places in the country on Saturday last that you were committed to the Fleet and, in good faith, as I heard say, the people were right sorry for it, both in Norwich and in the country. You are much bound to thank God and all those that love you that you have so great love of the people as you have . . .

The parson [Howes] told me that he knew well that Sir William Chamberlain could do you more good in such matters that you spoke of touching my Lord of Bedford than any man can do that lives at this day . . .

I pray you send me word whether you wish me to move from this place for it begins to grow cold staying here . . . My brother [William Paston] and Playter should have been with you before this time, but they wished to wait until this day were past because of the shire-court . . . And the Blessed Trinity have you in his keeping and send you good speed in all your matters and victory over all your enemies.

Margaret also had family concerns and was worried about the state of the Paston household staff, but still had time to give advice about those whom John ought to cultivate.

Margaret Paston to John Paston                    December [? 1461]
[? Caister ]

. . . Please you to know that my aunt is deceased, whose soul God assoil . . . And if it like you to have with you my cousin, William, her son, I think that you would find him a useful man to take care of your household and to buy all manner of stuff needful for it and to see to the rule and good guiding thereof. It has been told me therefore that he has good skill in such things; and if you will that I send for him and speak with him thereof I shall do as you send me word, for in faith it is time to cull out your old officers for divers reasons, partly told me by Daubeney – and I shall tell you more when you come home.

Also it is thought by my cousin, Elizabeth Clere, and the vicar and others that are your friends that it is right necessary for you to have Hugh Fenne to be your friend in your matters; for he is called right faithful and trusty to his friends that trust him, and it is reported that he may do much with the King and Lords and with them that are your adversaries: therefore, if you can have his good will forsake it not. Also, it is thought that the more learned men that you have from your own country for your counsel, the more worshipful it is to you.

Also, if you will be at home this Christmas, it would be well for you to obtain a garnish [set] or two of pewter vessels, 2 basins, 2 ewers and 12 candlesticks, for you have too few of these to serve this place. I am afraid to provide much stuff for this place till we are surer thereof . . .

The Duke of Norfolk had died in November 1461, and the Pastons had clearly regained Caister either shortly before his death or as a consequence of it. The new young Duke, still only seventeen years old, was no immediate threat, but John tried to establish good relations by putting his younger son, John [from now on to be called John III], in the new ducal household, and he remained a servant there for several years, accompanying his lord on expeditions around his estates, to Wales and to the North. His older brother remained in the King's Household, also frequently on the move in these years of rebellion and warfare. He remained short of money.

---

John Paston II to John Paston                          13 March 1462
Stamford

Right reverent and worshipful father, I recommend me to you, beseeching you for your blessing and good fatherhood. May it please you to understand the great expense that I have daily travelling with the King, as the bearer of this can inform you; and how long I am likely to tarry here in this country before I may speak with you again, and how I am ordered to have my horse and harness ready in haste – beseeching you to consider these reasons and so to remember me that I may have such things as I need to do my Master service and pleasure with, trusting in God that it shall be to your worship and to my advantage. In especial I beseech you that I may be sure where to have some money before Easter, either from you or through my Uncle Clement, when it is needed of other matters the bearer hereof can inform you. No more to you at this time but God have you in his keeping.

---

John III accompanied the Duke of Norfolk to the North in December 1462 on the King's campaign against surviving Lancastrian forces. There is certainly no sign of diffidence in the younger John, at this time about eighteen years old and already able to boast about his 'acquaintance' and to offer to mediate with the King on behalf of other East Anglian gentlemen. His older brother was by now back in Norfolk, possibly as a result of his father's unwillingness to continue to finance his activities at Court.

John Paston III to John Paston II            11 December 1462
Newcastle-upon-Tyne

Right worshipful brother, I recommend me to you. Please you to know that this day we had tidings here that the Scots will come into England within 7 days after the writing of this letter to rescue the castles of Alnwick, Dunstanburgh and Bamborough, which castles were besieged from yesterday . . .

The King commanded my Lord of Norfolk to conduct victuals and ordnance out of Newcastle to my Lord of Warwick at Warkworth Castle. And so my Lord of Norfolk commanded Sir John Howard, Sir William Peche . . . and me, Calthorpe, Gorges and others to go forth with the victuals and ordnance to my Lord of Warwick and so we were there with the ordnance and victuals yesterday. The King lies at Durham and my Lord of Norfolk at Newcastle. We have people enough here. In case we abide here I pray you to arrange that I have here more money by Christmas at the latest, for I may not get leave to send home any of my waged men. No man can get leave to go home unless they steal away, and if they were found out they would be sharply punished. Make as merry as you can, for there is no danger approaching yet. If there is any danger I shall send you word, by the Grace of God. I know well that you have more tidings than we have here, but these are true tidings.

Yelverton and Jenney are likely to be greatly punished because they did not come here to the King. They have been noted, and so are John Billingford and Thomas Playter, for which I am right sorry . . . Let them come or send their excuses in writing and I shall arrange that the King shall have knowledge of their excuses; for I am well acquainted with my Lord Hastings and my Lord Dacres, who are now greatest about the King's person; and also I am well acquainted with the younger Mortimer, Ferrers, Haute, Harper, Crowmer and Boswell, all of the King's House.

I pray you let my grandmother and my cousin Clere know that I desired you to let them have knowledge of the tidings in this letter, for I promised to send them tidings. I pray you let my mother have knowledge how I, my fellowship and your servants are at the writing of this letter in good health, blessed be God. I pray you let my father have knowledge of this letter . . . I pray you that you will send me some letter on how you are and of the tidings with you, for it seems long since I had word from my mother and you.

I pray you that this letter may recommend me to my sister, Margery, and to my mistress, Joan Gayne, and to all good masters and fellows in Caister . . . I pray you, in case you speak with my cousin, Margaret Clere, recommend me to her . . .

# The Royal Household

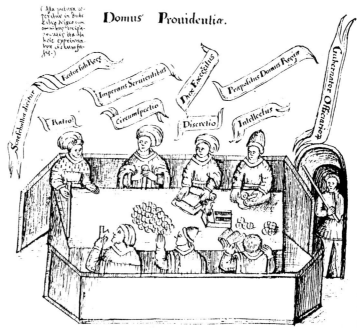

Domus Prouidentia.

*Principal officers of Edward IV's Household: controller, treasurer, steward and cofferer. The engraving is from a contemporary copy of the* Black Book of the Household of Edward IV, *an account of the court's household management.*

The Royal Household, which John Paston II eventually succeeded in joining, was the nerve-centre of national politics and administration, as well as a symbol of royal magnificence for subjects and foreigners. Under Henry VI the Household had been an object of bitter criticism both because it cost so much and because it monopolized political power. Edward IV's accession resulted, however, in an increase of its activity, particularly in its expanding control of royal finance.

The primary purpose of any household organization was to supply the domestic needs of the family, and the King's Household was no exception. An elaborate system of domestic departments supplied and cared for everything from horses to wine and from furs to bread. This was the 'below-stairs' section, presided over by the Lord Steward, with its focus on the Hall, where middling ranks ate, but where the King and his intimates dined only on exceptional occasions. At Westminster, Windsor and the other royal palaces, there was a separate set of rooms off the Hall which, collectively known as the Chamber, formed the normal living quarters for the King, his family and intimates. Here was the Court proper, presided over by the Chamberlain – Lord Hastings – throughout the whole of Edward's reign.

This 'House of Magnificence' was the centre of regal display and, through its proximity to the King, the stage for political intrigue and patronage.

Its members included the King's Secretary, Confessor and Almoner and usually one or more lords, but men of quite low status, such as the Pastons' friend, John Wykes, 'Usher of the Chamber', could acquire great influence through their intimacy with the King.

There were around 500 resident servants of all sorts, nearly all male, though not all travelled with the King, and about another 100 in the Queen's separate ménage. Many others, like the initially unsuccessful John Paston, lived in or near the Court, hoping to be taken on the strength and thus to receive daily rations. A number of attempts were made to cut Household expenses by restricting the number of consumers of the beer, wine, bread and meat bought in every day. In 1445 it was ordered that 'no manner of man that belongs to the King's Court may keep children, dogs or ferrets there', but the human population continued to expand. It was not until Edward IV's Household Ordinance of 1478 that a set of rules laid the foundations for his successors' ability to combine efficiency with the extravagance that was 'the outward and visible sign of royal power'.

His elder brother's return to East Anglia may have been caused partly by his father's need for assistance in imposing his authority upon the Fastolf lands. The scene of action had shifted mainly to Fastolf's Suffolk lands where the rival claimants were William Yelverton, William Jenney, both distinguished lawyers and former friends of the Pastons, and Gilbert Debenham of Wenham, a retainer of the Duke of Norfolk. The dispute led to a number of confrontations: the Pastons' attempt to distrain on Yelverton's property and to occupy the premises at Cotton Hall and elsewhere led to a series of indictments before the Suffolk JPs among whom Jenney was prominent. John and his eldest son and servants were accused of forcible entry, riot and theft. John and several of the servants, among them Richard Calle, now John's senior estate servant, were briefly imprisoned.

---

Richard Calle to John Paston                                    13 October 1462
Norwich

Please your mastership to know that Master John and I, with others, were at Cotton on Friday last and there Jenney had had the manor-court warned to assemble on the same Friday, and he was at Eye at the sessions on the Thursday before: on the Friday morning he was coming to Cotton to hold the court there. And it fortuned that we had entered the place before he came, and he heard of this and turned back to Hoxne [the Bishop of Norwich's Suffolk manor-house], and dined with my Lord of Norwich . . . And so the court was held in your name and the tenants right well pleased thereof, except Thurberne and Agas . . . And Master John was there all day Friday and Saturday till noon and then he took his horse with thirty men and rode to Jenney's place and took there 36 head of cattle, and brought them into Norfolk; and I was left still at Cotton with 12 men with me, because they declared that if we stayed there 2 days we should be put out headfirst. And so we abided there 5 days and kept the place, and I walked about all the lordships and spoke with the farmers and tenants that belong to the manor to understand their attitude and to receive money from them; and I find them right well disposed towards you . . . Saving your better advice, it seems to me that it would be right well done for you to have a letter from my Lord of Canterbury and others to the tenants that it is their will and intent that you should have the rule and governance and receive the money from that and other manors that were Sir John Fastolf's, on whom God have mercy, for I doubt not that if such a letter came down no man would say nay to it . . .

# Prisons

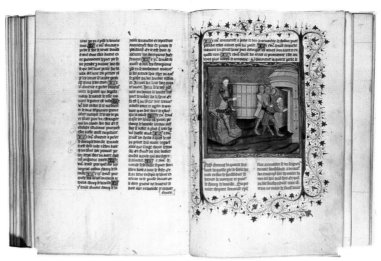

*A miniature from a treatise on war shows a prince ordering a merchant into prison.*

'It is the easiest thing in the world to get a person thrown into prison in this country,' wrote an Italian observer at the end of the fifteenth century. Apart from those serving sentences for the few offences for which prison was a punishment and from those awaiting trial for serious crimes, thousands of people spent time in gaol each year for debt or until they had found the security to answer to a charge. London and Southwark, in particular, had a number of prisons, some royal and others belonging to the City. Apart from the Tower, which was reserved for political prisoners, the most honourable was the Fleet, the royal prison for those accused of trespasses and unpaid debts, where John Paston I's fellow-inmates included Lord Percy, the future Earl of Northumberland, and where he was able to entertain his wife in 1465.

The Londoners' prison, Newgate, was rebuilt at the expense of the wealthy merchant, Richard Whittington, in the 1420s and the ordinances for it throw light on prison life. The best chambers, which had chimneys and privies, were intended for citizens of London; 'the less convenient chambers should be given to outsiders; whilst felons should be confined in basement cells and strongholds.' No prisoner was to be in irons if he owed less than £5 and the Keeper might take a reasonable fee for removing the irons 'as is done in the King's prisons'; 'honest persons' were to be allowed to attend chapel daily and two pairs of prisoners were to be permitted to beg for alms from passers-by; prisoners might buy their victuals and candles where they pleased and use their own beds; the Keeper was not to charge more than 1d. a night for bed, sheets and blankets, not more than a ½d. for a peck of coal and not more than 2d. a gallon for ale.

Cells were allocated according to rank, wealth and the nature of the crime. Accused felons suffered badly in the water-logged cells of castle dungeons; indeed, one prisoner at Norwich complained that his cell was so wet that the pardon he claimed to have received had become illegible. Mortality was inevitably high. The Keeper, if not sufficiently paid, could load a prisoner with chains; one Piers, imprisoned at the suit of John Paston I in 1461, complained that 'I am fettered worse than ever I was and manacled in the hands by day and night for he is afraid of me breaking away.' Even John Pamping, the Pastons' servant, had 'a clog upon his heel' when imprisoned at Ipswich for breach of the peace in 1461. Such behaviour was prompted by the Keeper's financial liability for any escapes.

The Keeper was not given any money with which to pay for food for his prisoners. Indeed, he expected to make a profit from them by selling them food and from the fees that were payable when they were released. The poor had to rely upon their friends and charity for necessities and it was common for fifteenth-century wills to include bequests to the poor prisoners of the nearest gaols.

Soon after John Paston's eldest son came of age he was knighted, but again he did not become established at Court. By May 1463 he was living at home once more and the Vicar of Caister felt it necessary to write to John to reveal the widespread gossip that either the Pastons were in disgrace or that John was too parsimonious to maintain his son at Court. There were already, inevitably, discussions about a possible marriage for the son and heir of such a rich, if troubled inheritance.

---

Robert Cutler, Vicar of Caister, to John Paston                                May 1463
[? Caister]

. . . And on one matter, at the reverence of God, take heed, for in truth, I hear much talking thereof, in Suffolk, Norfolk and Norwich, as well among those that love you as others, and that is about my master, your son, Sir John, why he is at home and not otherwise provided for. Some say that you and he both stand out of the King's good grace and some say that you keep him at home out of niggardliness and will spend nothing on him, and so each man gives his opinion as it pleases him. And I have answered that the main cause is that you are so much away that he is at home for the safeguard of the coast [against Lancastrian raids]. But at the reverence of God, to avoid such gossip, see that he is worshipfully provided for, either in the King's service or in marriage.

---

Sir John's was not the only marriage being discussed by the family during 1463.

---

Margaret Paston to John Paston                                13 November 1463
Caister

. . . Please you to know that I was at Norwich this week to obtain such things as I need for the winter; and I was at my mother's and while I was there there came in one Wroth, a kinsman of Elizabeth Clere, and he saw your daughter and praised her to my mother and said that she was a goodly young woman; and my mother prayed him to get for her a good marriage if he knew any. And he said that he knew one that would have about 300 marks a year, which is the son of Sir John Cley, who is treasurer with my Lady of York, and he is eighteen years of age. If you think this is to be spoken further about, my mother thinks that it should be got for less money now, at this time, than it should be hereafter, either that one or some other good marriage . . .

Relations between John Paston and his son had by this time deteriorated greatly. Presumably Sir John was reluctant to vegetate in Norfolk looking after the estates while his father was busy trying to defend them in London, and thus to miss out on the chance of favour and, indeed, of glory and promotion at Court. In the autumn of 1463 he secretly left home, apparently to make his way to the Court which was now in Yorkshire where the King was organising a further campaign against the Lancastrian rebels. Margaret found her position between father and son uncomfortable.

---

Margaret Paston to Sir John Paston      15 November 1463
Caister

I greet you well, and send you God's blessing and mine, letting you know that I have received a letter from you which you delivered to Master Roger at Lynn, whereby I understand that you think you did not do well in departing hence without my knowledge. Wherefore I let you know that I was right evilly paid through you. Your father thought and still thinks that I was assenting to your departure and that has caused me to have great heaviness. I hope that he will be your good father hereafter, if you behave yourself well and do as you ought towards him; and I charge you upon my blessing that in any thing touching your father that should be to his worship, profit and advantage, you do your duty and diligent labour to its furtherance, if you will have my good will, and that will cause your father to be better father to you.

I was told that you sent him a letter to London. What the contents were I do not know, but, even though he does not take it kindly, I would that you should not fail to write to him again, as humbly as you can, beseeching him to be your good father; and send him such tidings as there are in the country that you are in; and that you look after your expenses better than you have before this time and be your own purse-bearer, for I think you shall find this most profitable to you.

I would you should send me word by some trusty man how you do and how you have shifted for yourself since you departed hence; and do not let your father know of this. I dared not let him know of the last letter that you wrote to me, because he was so displeased with me at that time . . .

I sent your grey horse to Ruston, to the farrier, and he says that he shall never be anything to ride, nor right good to plough or cart. He says he was splayed and his shoulder wrenched from his body. I know not what to do with him.

Your grandmother would fain hear some tidings from you. It would be well if you sent a letter to her about how you are as hastily as you may. And God have you in his keeping and make you a good man and give you grace to do as well as I would that you should do.

Your mother, M. Paston.

Relations between father and son were never fully restored. John had many other worries, which no doubt made his temper worse. His litigation was not proceeding smoothly and, ominously, by early in 1464 his fellow-executor and chief ally, Thomas Howes, parson of Blofield, seemed to be deserting him.

Clement Paston to John Paston                          18 April 1464
London

Please you to know that after I had heard that the parson of Blofield had come to town I went to his inn and he told the messenger to say that he was not within, and I told him to say again that I had come there to him for his own worship and advantage and that I was sorry that I had come so far for him. And after that he sent for me and he could not find me, but I heard about it. And then I wrote him a letter, reciting how he was sworn yesterday to say the truth about all manner of matters concerning Sir John Fastolf . . . and also I bade him remember what manner of men he dealt with, and I rehearsed how untruly they had acted. And notwithstanding this, when I met him in the street and spoke with him I found him quite strangely disposed and his conscience disturbed that you would take the land and give the college only an income of one hundred marks. Nevertheless he could find it in his conscience that the will allowed the college to be founded in another place with only a hundred marks of income, and the rest of the lands be sold, so long as he could pocket the proceeds. So I felt that all his estrangement from you is that he believes that you would part with nothing. And I told him that the contrary is true; for this day he will be examined upon oath to tell the truth about all things that the judge will ask him, which I think will not be good . . .

# Taverns, Inns and Ale-Houses

Taverns, which abounded both in towns and villages, were always suspected as being potential centres of crime and vice; in boroughs, the authorities kept a tight control on them and, at manorial courts, the villagers were asked twice a year to name those who 'continually haunt taverns'. In *Piers Plowman*, William Langland describes a gathering at one of the less salubrious drinking-places in London: among the customers were 'Wat the warrener, with his drunken wife, Tom the Tinker and two of his knaves . . . Clarice, the whore of Cock's Lane, the hangman of Tyburn, Dave the ditcher, with a dozen rogues of porters and pickpockets . . . There was laughter and quarrelling and cries of 'pass the cup round' and they sat and sang till evensong rang.' Taverns were frequently the scenes of drunken violence. A graphic example is recorded in 1450 when, in a Northampton tavern, one Thomas sat drinking and singing with companions until William Cook criticized his singing. Abuse was then exchanged, which led to William striking Thomas on the head with a pitch-fork; Thomas drew his sword and his friend, who was trying to keep the peace, received blows from both the pitch-fork and the sword from which he died.

Not all taverns were of this sort, of course. Many were places where gentlemen could drink fine wine and eat good meals. It was, for instance, at a London tavern, possibly the 'Dolphin', that Thomas Playter, the Pastons' agent, breakfasted with Clement Paston and Richard Calle in 1460 and where he entertained a judge's clerk and others in the hope of expediting business. During the law-terms and in times of parliaments the taverns of London and Westminster were much used for similar 'expense-account' entertaining. Wine, at 6d. to 1s. a gallon, was cheap and surviving accounts suggest that a great deal was drunk.

Ale was, of course, even cheaper. As the staple drink of the people, its quality and price were controlled by appointed officials in towns and villages. Any household of some size, such as Hellesdon and Caister, brewed its own ale, but there were 'alehouses' everywhere, often run by women, where the traditional bunch of leaves or the 'bush' on a pole would indicate the availability of refreshment. Such ale-houses, often at crossroads, served both locals and travellers. On the main roads and in towns, there were any number of inns where travellers like the Pastons could find a bed, food and stabling – though it was advisable to send a servant

*An innkeeper serves wine to customers, one of whom is about to be sick.*

ahead to check the bedding. Statutes attempted to restrict the prices charged by inn-keepers: 1d. for a bed was the norm, with extra payments for food and drink. In London the Pastons seem to have put up most frequently at the 'George' at Paul's Wharf, but the best-known of medieval inns was the 'Tabard' at Southwark. It was here that Chaucer's band of pilgrims found 'the chambers and the stables were wide' and they were 'eased at the best' by a host who was the archetypal inn-keeper. 'Bold of his speech and wise and well-taught', this large 'right merry man' was able to crack jokes with all pilgrims from the Knight to the Cook.

By the same month Sir John was back in Norfolk after the end of the King's winter campaign. His mother interceded for him with her husband.

---

Margaret Paston to John Paston                    6 May 1464
Norwich

Please you to know that on Thursday last there were brought into town many letters of Privy Seal, and one of them was addressed to you and to Hastings and five or six other gentlemen; and another was sent to your son, and endorsed to him alone and signed with the King's own hand; and there were but few of these, so I am told, and also there were more special terms in his than in the others . . . The intent of the writing was that they should be with the King at Leicester the 10th day of May with as many persons defensibly arrayed as they might, according to their degree, and that they should bring with them expenses for two months . . .

I pray you that you vouchsafe to send word in haste how you will that your son should act. Men who are your well-wishers here think that you can do no less than send him forth. As for his behaviour since you departed, in good faith, it has been right good and lowly, and diligent in supervising your servants and other things which I hope you would be pleased with if you had been at home. I hope he will behave in a way to please you hereafter. He desired Arblaster to be a mediator to you on his behalf and was right heavy about his behaviour to you . . . And I beseech you heartily that you vouchsafe to be his good father, for I hope that he is chastened and will be the worthier hereafter . . .

Sir, I would be right glad to hear some good tidings from you.

---

The command to join the King was soon countermanded but it is unclear where Sir John spent the next few months. It would appear that his father, still vexed by litigation on various fronts, which led to another period in the Fleet, had forbidden him to return to the parental home. John's temper did not spare wife or servants, but it was his eldest son who bore the brunt of his father's fury in a long letter of instructions and exhortations.

---

John Paston to Margaret Paston et al.                    15 January 1465

I pray you, see to the good governance of my household and guiding of other things touching my profit and that you, with Daubeney and Richard Calle and other of my friends and servants that can advise you as the matter requires, weekly have a serious discussion of such things that are to be done, or oftener if need be . . . that is to say both for the providing of stuff for my household and for the gathering of my rents and grains, and for setting my servants to work, and for the most sensible means of selling and dispatching my malt, and all other things that need to be done. And when I come home I want no excuse, such that you told my servants to do it, or that Daubeney and Calle excuse themselves that they were so busy they could not attend. For I will have my affairs so guided that if one man may not attend, another shall be commanded to do it . . .

Item, where you desire me that I should take your son to grace, I will for your sake do better, and wish you to know that he shall not be so far out of my favour that I will allow anyone to be responsible for his wrongdoing other than himself. And howbeit that in his presumptuous and indiscreet behaviour he gave both me and you cause of displeasure, and an ill example to other of my servants, and made all men understand that he was weary of abiding in my house, though he was not assured of help in any other place; yet that does not grieve me so much as the fact that I could never feel nor understand him to be sensible nor diligent in helping himself, but only as a drone among bees which labour to get honey in the fields whilst the drone does nothing but take his part of it. And if this might make him know himself better and remind him what time he has wasted, and how he has lived in idleness, and if he could put this behaviour aside hereafter, it might be for the best. But I never yet hear from any place that he has been in of any sensible behaviour or occupation from him. And in the King's house he could put himself forth to be in favour or trust with men of substance that might advance him; nevertheless, as for your house and mine I do not intend him to come there, nor, by my will, to any other, unless he can do something more than look around and make a show and countenance . . .

Item, you should remember that before I ever had [anything] to do with Fastolf's livelode, while I looked after my livelode myself, it [my income] was not only sufficient for my expenses at home and at London and all other    →

expenses, but you also laid up money in my coffers every year, as you know. And I know well that the payment of the expenses that I have through Fastolf's livelode is not so great as the income from the livelode is, even though part of it is in trouble. And then consider that I had nothing from my livelode for my expenses at London this last two months – and you will truly understand that things are not looked after wisely or discreetly. Therefore, I pray you put all your wits together and see to the reform of it. And you might think how you would act if this were yours alone, and so act now . . .

Item, I remember that my hay at Hellesdon was last year used and wasted full recklessly, and it was blamed on my sheep. I pray you see that I am not so treated this year . . .

Item, I am told that you are making no wood either at Caister nor Mautby, at which I marvel; remember that we must have wood to burn another year . . .

Item, Calle sends me word that Thomas Howes is sick and unlikely to recover, and Berney tells me the contrary – wherefore I pray you find out about that and let me have word, for though I am not beholden to him, I would not, for more than he is worth, want him dead . . .

Item, remember well to take heed of your gates by night and day, in case of thieves, for they ride in divers countries with great companies like lords, and ride out of one shire into another.

Item, that Richard Calle bring me up money so that my debts can be paid, and that he come up securely in the company of other men and attorneys.

By April 1465 a major crisis was brewing over another part of the Fastolf inheritance. John, Duke of Suffolk, supported by his formidable mother and, the Pastons thought, inspired by John Heydon, laid claim to the valuable Fastolf manors of Drayton and Hellesdon, both near to Norwich and to Costessey, Suffolk's main manor in the county. In spite of this threat, John apparently still rejected any assistance from his eldest son.

---

Margaret Paston to John Paston                              8 April 1465
Caister

. . . Please you to know that I am sending you a copy of the deed that John Edmonds of Taverham sent to me through Dorlet. He told Dorlet that he had a deed that would help in checking the title that the Duke of Suffolk claims in Drayton. On the deed he sent me, the seal of arms is like the copy I am sending you, and nothing like the Duke of Suffolk's ancestors' arms. The said Edmonds says that if he can find any other thing that may help you in that matter he will do his part to help . . .

Item, there are divers of your tenements at Mautby that have great need of repair, but the tenants are so poor that they have no power to repair them; wherefore, if it please you, I should like the marsh that Brygge had to be kept in your own hand this year, so that the tenants might have rushes to repair their houses with. And also there is windfall wood at the manor that is of no great value, that might help them towards their repairs, if you like to let those that are in most need have it . . .

I understand by John Pamping that you will not let your son be taken into your house nor be helped by you until a year after he was put out of it, which will be about the feast of St. Thomas [probably 7 July but possibly December]. For God's sake, Sir, have pity on him. Remember that it has been a long time since he had anything from you to help him, and he has obeyed you and will do at all times, and will do all that he can or may to have your good fatherhood. And at the reverence of God, be his good father and have a fatherly heart towards him; and I hope that he shall always know himself the better hereafter and be the more careful to avoid such things as should displease you. Pecock shall tell you by mouth of more things than I have time to write to you now. The Blessed Trinity have you in his keeping . . .

---

# Parents and Children

*A man wielding a stick reprimands a boy stealing fruit. From a manuscript in the British Library.*

*Thy father and mother thou shalt honour,*
*This is the precept of God to every man,*

wrote Peter Idley to his son in the 1460s. Parents were obliged by contemporary religious teaching to bring up their children to obey God, the King and themselves in that order, to live good lives and, if possible, to enhance the honour and prosperity of the family. There is no reason to doubt the care taken of their children by all three generations of the Pastons and we should not be too impressed either by the harshness of Agnes to her daughter and youngest son, nor by the exasperation shown by John and Margaret to some of their offspring. Parents were taught that sparing the rod spoiled the child, and there can have been few parents of adolescent children in any age who did not sometimes feel, like John, that his son 'never stood you nor me in profit, ease or help to the value of a groat', or like Margaret that she and her daughter, 'weary of one another'. It is notable that John, Margaret and their children remained a particularly united family throughout the period of the correspondence.

Not all relationships were so good, of course. William II had remained loyal to his older brother, but after John's death he and his mother quarrelled with his nephews over the Paston property. When a father or a mother had remarried, much worse conflict could arise. Towards the end of his long life, Judge Yelverton was involved in a bitter dispute with his oldest son over the disposal of his property. 'That cursed son', he called him, 'the falsest liar and impious against the precept of God to honour his parents'. William Lancaster of Bressingham, Norfolk, also quarrelled with his daughter and heir: when he made his will in 1491, he specified that she was to have none of his lands while her step-mother lived and after her death she should have a part 'with God's blessing and mine' unless she challenged the will, in which case she was to have nothing but 'God's curse and mine'.

Impatience with a parent's longevity could also lead to unfilial actions. Peter Idley is aware of such dangers. It was not uncommon for an elderly parent to make over his lands to his son in return for a pension and houseroom, as Sir Robert Plumpton did in 1515. But Idley deplores the practice:

*For [if] thine heir of that condition is*
*That all thy lands, goods and chattels*
*Everything he claimeth wholly to be his*
*He will gladly part with never a deal*

*. . .*

*And remember sadly in every hour*
*Let never thine heir be thy executor*
*For they never reck how thy soul fares*
*So they may have thy lands and goods.*

The crisis developed rapidly and Margaret moved to Hellesdon to maintain an effective presence there. Over the next six months a series of letters from her to John in London describes the developing crisis.

---

Margaret Paston to John Paston                                       3 May 1465
Caister

. . . Please you to know that I have spoken this week with divers of your tenants of Drayton and comforted them that all will be well hereafter by the grace of God; and I feel well from them that they will be right glad to have again their old master, and so would they all, except one or two that are false shrews. And this next week I purpose to be at Hellesdon on Wednesday or Thursday and to abide there a week or two and to send our men about to gather money at Drayton or Hellesdon; and if you wish I will hold a [manor-]court at Drayton before I leave there . . . Your son will come home tomorrow, as I think, and I shall let you know how he behaves himself hereafter; and I pray you not to believe that I will support or favour him in any lewdness, for I will not. I shall let you know how I find him hereafter . . .

---

Sir John's help was now needed, although Margaret trusted herself, rather than her son, to deal with the most pressing problem since she had the assistance of the two senior Paston servants, Richard Calle and John Daubeney. The Duke of Suffolk's men at Costessey were harrassing the Paston tenants. John Paston was also involved in a dispute with his mother, who has appeared only rarely in the correspondence of the previous ten years. As is shown by some of her surviving draft wills, she was far from happy with her eldest son's attitude to his younger brothers' interests or to his father's memory.

---

Margaret Paston to John Paston                                    10 May 1465
Hellesdon

. . . On Wednesday last Daubeney, Naunton, Wykes and John Love were at Drayton to speak with your tenants there to put them in comfort and to ask money of them also. And Piers Waryn had a plough going on your land at Drayton and your servants took the mares from his plough and brought them to Hellesdon and there they still are. And on the next morning Master Philip [Lipgate, the Duke's servant] and the bailiff of Costessey came to Hellesdon with a great number of people, that is to say eight-score men and more in harness, and there took from the Parson's plough 2 horses, price 4 marks, and 2 horses from Thomas Stermyn's plough, price 40s., saying to them that they were taken because of a plea against them in the hundred court brought by the said Piers for the taking of his plough-beasts; . . . and so they led the beasts forth to Drayton and from Drayton to Costessey.

And the same afternoon the parson of Hellesdon sent his man to Drayton with Stermyn to speak with Master Philip to find out if there was a way of getting back their animals; and Master Philip answered that if they would return the distress taken from Piers Waryn then he would deliver theirs, otherwise not. And he let them plainly know that if you or any of your servants took any distress in Drayton, even of the value of a hen, they would come into Hellesdon and take for it the value of an ox; and if they could not take that value they will break into your tenants' houses in Hellesdon and take as much as they can find therein. And if they are prevented from doing so – which, he said, shall never lie in your power to do, for the Duke of Suffolk is able to keep daily in his house more men than Daubeney has hairs on his head . . . then they will go into any livelode that you have in Norfolk or Suffolk and take a distress just as they would at Hellesdon. And they could get no other answer and so they departed.

Richard Calle asked the Parson and Stermyn if they would take an action for their animals, and the Parson said he was aged and sickly and he did not want to be troubled hereafter: he said that he would rather lose his cattle, for if he did take action he knew he would be indicted and so be vexed by them that he would never have rest from them . . .                              →

Skipwith [a neighbouring lawyer] went with me to the Bishop of Norwich and I let him know of the riotous and evil behaviour of Master Philip . . . My Lord said to me that he much wished that you might have a good conclusion to your affairs, and said, by his troth, that he owed you right good will and would right fain that you were at home: he said to me that it would be a great comfort to your friends and neighbours, and that your presence would do more among them than a hundred of your men should do in your absence . . .

Item, I pray you to send word hastily how you wish me to be guided about this place, for, as I am told, it is likely soon to stand in as great jeopardy as the other has done. On Thursday there were at Drayton Lodge up to 60 persons all day, and I am told that there are sixteen to twenty persons there day and night . . .

Item, I have left John Paston the elder at Caister to keep the place there, as Richard [Calle] can tell you; for I had rather, if it please you, be captainess here than at Caister. I did not intend to abide here more than a day or two when I first came, but I shall abide here until I hear tidings from you . . .

Item, my mother told me that she thinks it right strange that she may not because of you have the profits of Clere's place peaceably: she says it is hers and she has paid most for it and says she will have the profits from it or else she will make more folk speak about it . . . In good faith, I hear much language of the relations between you and her. I would right fain that it were otherwise between you than it is, and so would many more of your friends . . .

# Households and Servants

*The comfortable life of a gentleman in his fortified house. Colourful wool-tapestry hangings provide insulation from the winter weather, and a servant carries in wood for the fire.*

Fifteenth-century England, in town and country, was made up of a large number of 'families', most of them comprising a husband, wife and children with a number of servants proportionate to the social status. Households of great lords mirrored, on a smaller scale, that of the King, and the semi-official *Black Book* of the Royal Household of 1472 listed models of households for different ranks: a Duke's might total 240 people, including 4 knights and 40 esquires and gentlemen, while an ordinary knight should have about 16.

In the greater households there was considerable 'departmentalisation', marked by the physical separation of the kitchen complex, Hall and Chamber; in lesser families, like that of the Pastons, there was much less. In 1422–3 the Earl Marshal (later 2nd Duke of Norfolk), for instance, employed a dozen or so senior officials, such as the treasurer, chamberlain, steward and clerk of the household; about half a dozen others of gentle rank; and some 70 yeomen and 12 grooms of whom some, such as the wardrober, cook, skinner and Laurence Luter, leader of five minstrels, were clearly specialists. The gentlemen must have included the 'Usher of the Chamber' and the Marshal of the Hall', responsible for the smooth running of those departments. Besides these, the Countess had six 'damsels' and another two who looked after the

young heir; chaplains, as well as the outside staff, were paid separately. Sir John Fastolf's household at Caister, on the other hand, numbered about 25 in 1431, during the lifetime of his wife.

No household accounts survive for the Pastons and it is difficult to list their servants at any one time, but John and Margaret may have had a dozen to fifteen indoor servants. These were led by Richard Calle, who was also mainly responsible for the estates, by John Daubeney and by the chaplain, James Gloys, under the general supervision of Margaret and, usually from a distance, of John. Servants generally came from the neighbourhood but Calle, at least, came from Framlingham on the recommendation to John Paston of the Duke.

Service in the household of a gentleman or lord provided status and some security: the more distinguished the household, the higher the status of its servants. For servants did not cater only for the material needs of their masters (and in the case of chaplains like Gloys the spiritual needs as well); they also maintained their social position. Households, like the buildings that housed them, displayed the wealth and status of the family, and the larger ones, like Framlingham, provided an important focus for the political, social and economic activities of their neighbourhoods.

Margaret's consistently respectful mode of address to her husband cannot disguise the fact that she was now responsible for organising the defence of John's property and was clearly far from happy with his handling of their affairs. She was confident enough in her judgements to advise on nominations to public offices.

The Duke of Suffolk's influence among the local officers made it difficult for the Pastons to make any headway: even when writs were obtained to recover the animals that had been seized they could not be served, and Yelverton ['the Judge'] remained a powerful enemy.

---

Margaret Paston to John Paston                          13 May 1465
Hellesdon

. . . if it pleased you I would right fain that John Jenney were put out of the commission of the peace and that my brother, William Lomnour, were set in his stead, for I think it right necessary that there should be such a man in that country that owes you good will . . . If there is any labour for Dr. Aleyn to be made a Justice of the Peace, I pray you, for God's sake let it be prevented, if you may. For he will take too much upon himself if he were . . .

And at the reverence of God, be not slothful in your matters now and make an end of them: arrange to either make or mar them in haste, for this is too horrible a cost and trouble that you have and have had, to endure for long, and it is great heaviness to your friends and well-wishers and great joy and comfort to your enemies. My Lord [Bishop] of Norwich said that he would not abide the sorrow and trouble that you have endured even to win all Sir John Fastolf's property.

I think it right long to wait for tidings till I hear tidings from you.

---

Margaret Paston to John Paston                          24 June 1465
Hellesdon

. . . I sent Richard Charles to speak with the under-sheriff, requiring him that he should serve the writ to recover the sheep and horses that were taken etc. And the under-sheriff said plainly that he would not, nor dare not, serve it, not though I would give him £20 to serve it . . . and so the writ is not yet served . . .

On Friday last John Paston the younger, Wykes and Thomas Honworth were indicted at Dereham, by what means the bearer of this, Crome, can tell you. I sent there Richard Charles, John Seve and three or four other good fellows to do a similar good turn to other folk, but . . . the Judge is so partial towards the other party that I think no matters of yours or any of your men will speed before him until it is otherwise between you than it is now . . .

John Paston encouraged his wife to continue to maintain his position in Hellesdon and Drayton and to comfort his tenants. He had no words of comfort for his son, however.

John Paston to Margaret Paston                                    27 June 1465
London

I recommend me to you and have received a letter from you and another from Richard Calle . . .

Item, as for your son, I let you know that I would that he did well, but I see in him no disposition towards discretion nor self-control as a man of the world ought to have, but he lives only, and always has, as a dissolute man, without any foresight; nor does he busy himself to understand such matters as a man of property needs to understand . . . I can think only that he would dwell again in your house and mine, and there eat and drink and sleep . . . Every poor man that has brought up his children to the age of 12 years expects then to be helped and profited by his children, and every gentleman who has discretion expects that his kin and servants that live under him and at his cost should help him forward. As for your son, you know well he never stood you nor me in ease nor profit nor help to the value of a groat [4d.], saving at Caldecot Hall, when he and his brother kept it for one day against Debenham – and yet it was at 3 times the cost that ever Debenham's sons put him to . . . they keep Cotton at my cost and take the profits of the same. Wherefore give him no favour till you feel what he is and will be.

Item, Calle sends me word that Master Philip has entered into Drayton in my Lord of Suffolk's name, and intends to enter upon Hellesdon, and he asks my advice: which is that you should comfort my tenants and help them till I come home, and let them know I shall not lose it . . . You are a gentlewoman and it is worshipful for you to comfort your tenants; wherefore I would that you should ride to Hellesdon and Drayton and Sparham and stay at Drayton and speak with them and bid them hold with their old master till I come; and say that you have only recently sent me word, and have no answer yet . . .

In July the Duke himself arrived at Costessey and tension mounted. Sir John now came to join his mother at Hellesdon. But to Richard Calle it seemed that only outside help or a compromise settlement could save them.

---

Richard Calle to John Paston           10 July 1465
Hellesdon

Please your mastership to know of the behaviour of Master Philip and the bailiff of Costessey with other of my Lord of Suffolk's men. On Monday last in the afternoon they were at Hellesdon to the number of 300 men, with the intention of entering, even though they said that they did not intend to enter . . . but we, knowing of their coming, prepared for them and were strong enough. We had 60 men in the place and guns and such ordnance that if they had set upon us they would have been destroyed. And my mistress was there inside and my master, Sir John, who got himself as much worship from that day as any gentleman might, and so it is reported by the other party and in all Norwich . . . And Harleston desired to speak at Hellesdon with my master, Sir John, and so he did, and said to him that it would be right for him to ride to my Lord of Suffolk and desired him strongly to do so, and said that it was his duty to do so, inasmuch as my Lord had come to the country; and he said that he would ride with him and bring him to my Lord. And Sir John answered and said to him that when he understood that my Lord was his father's good lord and his, that then he would see his Lordship, and otherwise he had nothing to say to him; and so they parted . . .

Wherefore would you please send word how my mistress and we should act at Hellesdon in all matters, and whether you will that we fetch back the Hellesdon flock, for they have now been driven to Cawston [another manor of the Duke of Suffolk] and there they are on the heath; and my Lord of Suffolk will be at Drayton on Lammas Day [1 August] and keep the court there, so you must seek a remedy for it or it will not do well.

If my Lord of Norfolk would come he would make all well, for they fear him above all things . . . And it seems to me that it would be good to move my Lord [of Norfolk] in the matter, even if you have to give him the profits of Hellesdon and Drayton to keep, and some money besides, for you must seek some other remedy than you do, or else, in my opinion, it will go to the Devil and be destroyed, and that in a very short time. Therefore, at the reverence of God make some agreement with Master Yelverton and those who can do most harm.

I beseech you to pardon me for writing like this, but I have pity to see the tribulation that my mistress has here, and all your friends, also . . .

---

Iohn was pleased with Margaret's actions in the attempted entry and shows some concern about her health and safety, but much of the following letter consists of an attack upon the Duke's claim to the manors and an assertion of his determination not to be forced to justify his title by threats of violence: he was clearly in no mood to take Calle's advice to seek a settlement, even though this had clearly also been the advice of the Bishop of Norwich.

John Paston to Margaret Paston                    13 July 1465
London

I recommend me to you and thank you for your labour and diligence against the unruly fellowship that came before you on Monday last, of which I have heard report by John Hobbs. In good faith you acquit yourself right well and discreetly, and much to your worship and mine, and to the shame of your adversaries . . . John Hobbs tells me that you are unwell, which I do not like to hear. I pray you heartily that you obtain whatever may help you, and do not spare expense; and do not trouble too much over these matters, nor set them so to your heart that you become more ill as a result . . . And in case I do not come home within three weeks, I pray you come to me, and Wykes has promised to keep the place in your absence. Nevertheless, when you do come, set both Hellesdon and Caister in such state as seems best and most secure to you if the war continues. If you have peace send me word.

As for the desire that I should show my title and evidences to the Duke, I think he had bad advice to enter upon my land, trusting I should show him my evidences . . . Inform my Lord of Norwich that it is not to the profit or common well-being of gentlemen that a gentleman should be compelled by entry of a lord to show his evidences or title to his land, and I shall not give such an example of slavery for gentlemen or others . . .

I pray you be as merry with your fellowship as you can . . . If you lack money you must make it from your wool and malt.

Many other letters passed to and fro between Norfolk and London during this summer. John hoped that legal methods and strong defence would still hold off the Duke's threatened entry into Hellesdon, although Drayton seemed increasingly a lost cause. On Lammas Day Margaret tried to hold a court there but was physically prevented from doing so. She had sympathetic treatment from the Judges of Assize sitting at Norwich in early August, but no permanent success.

Margaret Paston to John Paston                    7 August 1465
Hellesdon

. . . Please you to know that on Lammas day I sent Thomas Bonde and James Gloys to hold the [manor-]court at Drayton in your name and to claim your title, for I could get nobody else to keep the court or go there but the said Thomas Bonde, because, I suppose, they were afraid of the people of the Duke of Suffolk that would be there. The said Thomas and James, as they came into the manor court to keep the court, met with the Duke of Suffolk's men, that is to say, Harleston, the parson of Salle, Master Philip and William Yelverton [the son of the judge], who was steward, with some 60 persons or more by estimation, together with the tenants of the same township, some of them having rusty pollaxes and bills. They told them they had come to keep the court in your name and to claim your title. Wherefore the said Harleston without any more words or any occasion given by your men, committed the said Thomas Bonde to the keeping of the new bailiff of Drayton, William Dokett . . . and they led Thomas Bonde to Costessey and bound his arms behind him with whip-cord, like a thief, and would have led him to the Duke of Suffolk if I had not spoken with the judges in the morning before they rode to the shirehouse, and informed them of the riots and assaults they had made upon me and my men: the bailiff of Costessey and all the Duke of Suffolk's counsel were present, and all the learned men of Norfolk, with William Jenney and many people of the country. The judge called the bailiff of Costessey before them all and gave him a great rebuke, commanding the sheriff to see what people they had gathered at Drayton: he afterwards came to Hellesdon to see the people there and was well content with them, afterwards riding to Drayton to see the people there, who had departed before he came . . .

And the judges . . . forthwith commanded the sheriff to deliver the said Bonde without any fine, saying that he ought not to make one. And in good faith I found the judges right gentle and favourable to me in my matters, notwithstanding that the Duke's counsel had made their complaint to them before I came, in the worst way they could, accusing us of great gatherings of people and many riotous things done by me and your men . . .

A lull followed the assizes: perhaps the outbreak of plague at Norwich affected the attitudes of both parties. Margaret hoped to visit her husband in London, but suggested that his return home would do most to stabilize the situation. Margaret remained concerned to make peace between her husband and his mother and Elizabeth Clere.

---

Margaret Paston to John Paston                                    18 August 1465
Hellesdon

. . . Please you to know that the cause that I wrote to you no earlier than I did after the sessions was because Yelverton held sessions at Dereham and Walsingham the week after the assizes, and I wished to have knowledge what labour was made there and to send you word of it. There was great labour made by the bailiff of Costessy and others to have your men indicted at both Dereham and at Walsingham, but I arranged that their intention was prevented on both occasions. Hugh Fenn is in Flegg, . . . if he comes I shall make him good cheer, for I am told by divers folk who have spoken with him since he came to Norfolk that they feel by what he says that he owes you right good will . . .

. . . As for my coming to you, if it please you that I should come, I hope that I shall provide for everything before I come so that it will be safe enough, by the grace of God, till I return. But, at the reverence of God, if you may, arrange to come home yourself, for that will be most profitable to you . . .

Item, my cousin, Elizabeth Clere, is at Ormesby and your mother intends to be at her place at Caister this week, for the pestilence is so strong in Norwich that they dare no longer abide there, God help us. I think by my mother that she would right fain you did well and that you will speed well in your matter. And I think from my cousin Clere, that she would fain have your goodwill . . . She says that she knows well that she has been reported to you otherwise than she has deserved and this has caused you to be otherwise to her than you ought to be. She wept while she said these things to me and told me about divers other things which you shall have knowledge of hereafter

. . .

$B$y late August, John was in no position to leave London. There had been important developments in various of his legal actions, including the examination in the ecclesiastical court of Canterbury of witnesses in his action to prove Sir John Fastolf's will. By the last week of August, John was back in the Fleet Prison, but Margaret felt that things were safe enough at Hellesdon to leave Sir John in charge and to depart on a visit to London, taking her elder daughter, and possibly the younger sons. John III was also left in Norfolk.

---

John Paston III to Margaret Paston          14 September 1465
Norwich

. . . Please you to know that I have sent to my father to have an answer of such matters as I have sent to him for in haste, of which matters the most substantial is about the manor of Cotton, beseeching you to remind him of the same matter, so that I may have an answer in the most hasty wise . . . Also, mother, I beseech you that it might be arranged that I be sent home by the same messenger two pairs of hose, one pair black and another russet, which are already made for me at the hosier with the crooked back next to Black Friars Gate within Ludgate – John Pamping knows him well enough, I suppose. If the black hose is paid for he will send me the russet without payment. I beseech you that this gear is not forgotten, for I have not a useable whole hose. I think they will cost together eight shillings.

My brother and my sister, Anne, and all the garrison of Hellesdon are well, blessed be God, and recommend them to you, each one.

I pray you visit the Rood of the North Door [of St. Paul's] and St. Saviour at Bermondsey, while you abide in London, and let my sister, Margery, go with you to pray that she may have a good husband before she comes home again. And now I pray you to send us some tidings, as you were accustomed to command me to do. And the Holy Trinity have you in his keeping, and my fair mistress of the Fleet.

---

The visit to London seems to have brought John and Margaret closer together emotionally as well as physically, and John's first letter after his wife's departure, though written by his servant, John Pamping, is both more affectionate and more playful than any other of his that survives – at the end it even breaks into doggerel verse.

John Paston to Margaret Paston            20 September 1465
London

My own dear sovereign lady, I recommend me to you, and thank you for the great cheer that you made me here, to my great cost and expense and labour.

No more at this time, except that I pray you that you will send me here two ells of worsted for doublets, to help me this cold winter. Will you enquire where William Paston bought his tippet of fine worsted, which is almost like silk, and if that is much finer than what you can buy me for seven or eight shillings, then buy me a quarter, with the nail [a small strip of cloth] of it for collars, even though it is dearer than the other, for I would make my doublet all worsted for the worship of Norfolk . . . [in spite of the first words of the paragraph the letter is a long one, full of instructions and advice, and ends]

. . .

Item, I shall tell you a tale.
Pamping and I have picked your male [trunk]
And taken out pieces five,
For upon trust of Calle's promise we may not soon thrive.
And if Calle brings us hither twenty pound
You shall have your pieces again, good and round;
Or else, if he will not pay you the value of the pieces there,
To the post you may nail his ear,
Or else do him some other sorrow,
For I will no more for his fault borrow,
And unless the receiving of my livelode is better plied,
He shall have Christ's curse and mine clean tried.
And look you be merry and take no thought
For this rhyme is cunningly wrought.
My Lord Percy and all his house
Recommend them to you, dog, cat and mouse
And wish you had been here still,
For they say you are a good Gill.
No more to you at this time
But God him save that made this rhyme.
Written on the Vigil of St. Mathew by your true and trusty husband,
J.P.

Margaret replied with a very long letter mainly concerning the activities of John III, herself and their servants at the manors of Cotton and Caldecott through which she had passed on her way back from London to Norfolk. As with some other of Margaret's letters, this is annotated by John with summaries of its contents and notes of what he intends to reply.

---

Margaret Paston to John Paston            27 September 1465
[? Hellesdon]

Right worshipful husband, I recommend me to you, desiring heartily to hear of your welfare, thanking you for the great cheer that you made me and the costs that you spent on me. You spent more than I wished that you should do, but as it pleased you to do so, God give me grace to do that which may please you . . .

Item, as for Cotton, I entered on the place on Sunday last and there I stayed until Wednesday last passed. I have left there John Paston the younger, Wykes and twelve other men to receive the profits of the manor and for the day on which the [manor-]court is to be kept I hope there will be more men there to strengthen them, if need be. John Paston has been to see my Lord of Norfolk since we entered the manor and has desired his good lordship to strengthen him with men from his household and others if need be, and he has promised that he would do so . . .

Item, on Saturday last Jenney had proclaimed that a court would be held at Caldecott in his name on Tuesday last, and Debenham on the Sunday following ordered another court to be held on the same Tuesday in his name. And Daubeney had knowledge of this and sent on Sunday night for your elder son to have some men from there [presumably Hellesdon]; and he sent him Wykes and Berney on Monday morning. And as soon as they had come to Caister they sent for men there in that country, and got some sixty men. And Daubeney, Wykes and Berney rode to Caldecott the same Monday at night with their fellowship and hid there secretly so that none of the tenants knew they were there, save Rising's wife and her household, until Tuesday at 10 a.m. . . . And when they had dined Sir Gilbert Debenham came to Caldecott with twenty horse . . . and Wykes saw them coming and he and Berney and two others with them rode out to speak with them. And when Sir Gilbert spied them coming he and his fellowship fled . . . We will summon a court and keep it in haste. You will laugh to hear all that went on there, which is too long to write at this time . . .

Item, I received a letter from you yesterday for which I thank you heartily and pray that I may be as you wrote . . . I have had your worsted ordered, but you may not have it until Hallowmas, but then I am promised that you will have as fine as may be made. Richard Calle will bring it up to you . . .

John III wrote to his father in the following week with more information on events at Cotton. His connection with the Duke of Norfolk's household remained useful.

John Paston III to John Paston                    Early October 1465
Cotton, Suffolk

. . . On Sunday next before Michaelmas Day, as my mother came from London by Cotton, she sent to Hellesdon for me to come to her there, and I have been in this place ever since. And as soon as Michaelmas day was past I began to distrain upon the tenants and gathered some silver – as much, I think, as will pay our costs, even though I keep here a right good company . . . When Debenham heard how I began to gather silver he raised many men within a day and a half, to the number of 300 men, as I was credibly told by one of my Lord of Norfolk's yeomen of the Chamber who owes me good will. This yeoman, as soon as he had seen their fellowship, rode straight to my Lord and informed him of it, and informed my Lord how I had gathered another great fellowship, the numbers of which he reported as one hundred and fifty more than we were. And he said to my Lord and my Lady and their Council that unless my Lord took a hand in the matter there was likely to be great harm done to both our parties, which would be a great disworship to my Lord, considering how he has taken both of us as his men and we are well known as such.

Upon which information . . . my Lord sent for me and Sir Gilbert Debenham to come to him at Framlingham; . . . and he desired of us both that we should gather no further fellowship and those that we had gathered we should send home again, and that the court should not meet until my Lord or such as he should assign had spoken both to you and to Yelverton and Jenney . . .

And then I answered my Lord, and said that at that time I had my master within the manor of Cotton, which was my mother, and until I spoke with her I could give no answer; so my Lord sent Richard Fulmerston, the bearer of this, to my mother this day for an answer, which answer he should bring to my Lord at London . . . And the answer that my mother and I gave him was that at the instance of my Lord and Lady we would adjourn the court and receive no more of the profits of the manor than we had already until we had word again from my Lord and you . . . But before making this answer we had received nearly as much silver as was due according to the books that Richard Calle sent; and as for the possession of the place, we told him that we would keep it, and Sir Gilbert agreed, so long as Yelverton and Jenney would do the same. It was time for him to say so, for my Lord told him that he would otherwise make him fast by the feet [chain him] to ensure that he would make no insurrection until the time that my Lord returned from London . . .

The Duke's visit to London was to receive formal livery of his lands from the King, since he had recently reached the age of twenty-one. This was an occasion of high ceremony for a man of Norfolk's status and John III, like all other members of the Duke's Household and retinue, was ordered to accompany him to London. Thus, like his father, he was away when the final crisis occurred at Hellesdon. The Duke of Suffolk had arrived in Norfolk with a large retinue, including knights and squires from his Suffolk estates. He had the support of the Mayor of Norwich and there were now no royal judges present to whom Margaret could appeal. There is no detailed account of what happened and it is unclear where Margaret and Sir John were, but there seems to have been no resistance when, on 14 October, the Duke's men entered Hellesdon Manor and, over the next few days, destroyed the manor-house and lodge and carried off their contents.

---

Margaret Paston to John Paston                          17 October 1465
Norwich

. . . The Duke came to Norwich on Tuesday at 10 o'clock with some 500 men. And he sent for the Mayor and Aldermen with the Sheriffs, desiring them in the King's name that they should make enquiry of the constables of every ward in the City as to what men had gone to help or succour your men at any time during these gatherings and, if they could find any, that they should take and arrest and correct them, and certify to him the names by 8 o'clock on Wednesday. Which the Mayor did and will do anything that he may for him and his men . . .

I am told that the old Lady [the Dowager Duchess] and the Duke are fiercely set against us on the information of Harleston, the bailiff of Costessey . . . and such other false shrews which would have this matter carried through for their own pleasure . . . And as for Sir John Heveningham, Sir John Wingfield and other worshipful men, they are but made their doggebolds [lackeys], which I suppose will cause their disworship hereafter. I spoke with Sir John Heveningham and informed him of the truth of the matter and of all our demeaning at Drayton, and he said he would that all things were well, and that he would inform my Lord what I told him, but that Harleston had all the influence with the Duke here, and at this time he was advised by him and Dr. Aleyn.

The lodge and the remnant of your place was beaten down on Tuesday and Wednesday and the Duke rode on Wednesday to Drayton and so forth to Costessey while the lodge at Hellesdon was being beaten down. And this night at midnight Thomas Slyforth . . . and others had a cart and fetched away featherbeds and all our stuff that was left at the parson's and Thomas Waters' house to be kept . . . I pray you send me word how I shall act – whether you wish that I abide at Caister or come to you at London . . .

A fortnight later Margaret reported more fully on the destruction at Hellesdon and continued to hope that, by mediation or the intervention of other lords, some redress might be obtained. But, although the Pastons were to seek redress for the loss of Drayton and Hellesdon for many years, the manors were, in fact, to be lost to them for ever.

Margaret Paston to John Paston                                    27 October 1465
[Norwich]

. . . Please you to know that I was at Hellesdon on Thursday last and saw the place there, and, in good faith, nobody would believe how foul and horrible it appears unless they saw it. There come many people daily to wonder at it, both from Norwich and many other places, and they speak of it with shame. The Duke would have been a £1000 better off it it had not happened, and you have the more good will of the people because it was so foully done. They made your tenants of Hellesdon and Drayton, with others, break down the walls of both the place and the lodge – God knows full much against their wills, but they dare not refuse for fear. I have spoken with your tenants of Hellesdon and Drayton and comforted them as well as I can. The Duke's men ransacked the church and bore away all the goods that were left there, both of ours and of the tenants, and even stood upon the high altar and ransacked the images and took away those that they could find, and put the parson out of the church till they had done, and ransacked every man's house in the town five or six times . . . As for lead, brass, pewter, iron, doors, gates and other stuff of the house, men from Costessey and Cawston have it, and what they might not carry away they have hewn asunder in the most spiteful manner . . .

At the reverence of God, if any worshipful and profitable settlement may be made in your matters, do not forsake it, to avoid our trouble and great costs and charges that we may have and that may grow hereafter . . .

# The Art of Dying

A priest sprinkles holy water over the grave as a man is buried. A fifteenth-century view.

The devil attempts to intervene; a scene from Ars Moriendi, a tract about preparing for death.

The obsession with death that some historians have seen in the fifteenth century does not appear in the Paston Letters but all must have been conscious of its imminence. We do not know how many of the children of Agnes and Margaret Paston died in the most dangerous year of life – the first – but of those who reached adulthood only two seem to have reached the age of sixty and five died in their twenties or thirties. Consequently, the importance of the passage to the after-life was supreme. For some this would have consisted of the immediate joys of Heaven, for others of the eternal torments of Hell, but for most, it would have involved 'the purifying pains' of Purgatory. A will which paid obligations to God and Man should be followed by a 'good' death, a suitable funeral and a Christian burial. The funeral, then, was both a mourning and celebration for the life of the deceased and the first stage in easing his soul through Purgatory.

For both purposes, the ceremonies and the money spent on them were expected to befit the status of the deceased. A few testators specifically ask for 'no worldly pomp' at their funerals, but most require burial in accordance with their status. Some are very specific but most, like Margaret Paston, simple state the place of burial and the amount to be spent on alms, torch-bearers, masses and so on, leaving it to the heirs and executors to arrange the details of the funeral itself. The normal place of burial was within the parish-church for a gentleman or woman, and in the churchyard for others; but many gentlemen, like the Pastons, chose to be interred in a monastery or friary.

John Paston's funeral was obviously costly and conducted with due ceremony, but it does not compare with the extraordinary splendour of the funerals of the great lords. The body of Thomas Howard, 2nd Duke of Norfolk, for instance, was accompanied on its journey from Framlingham for burial at Thetford Priory in 1524 by some 900 lords and gentlemen, Garter King at Arms and three other heralds, and 3 coach-loads of friars. The funeral service was taken by a bishop and three abbots, and 400 'messes' were served at the dinner that followed; some 1,900 people were given black liveries. The whole cost was about £1,300, about half the Duke's annual income. It was hoped that the soul of the deceased would be forever remembered in the prayers of those who attended and by the poor who benefited from the alms.

The last months of John Paston's life are not well documented. He certainly spent some time in Norfolk but was mainly engaged in his continued litigation and lobbying in London. A new threat to his property came with the allegation that he was a serf belonging to the Duchy of Lancaster; its steward, Lord Scales, attempted to seize his goods in Norwich. So it was with none of his problems settled that he died at London on 21 or 22 of May 1466. His body was brought back to Norfolk to be buried in Bromholm Priory with great magnificence. A roll of his funeral expenses seems to have been drawn up by James Gloys and other Paston servants under Margaret's supervision.

---

Expenses of John Paston's Funeral                                May 1466

Expenses paid by James Gloys at Norwich when the corpse was there and before.

First, the four orders of friars – £8. Item, alms – 2s.7d. Item, to the 23 sisters of Norman's [Hospital, Norwich], with the Warden, each of them 4d. and the Warden 8d. – 8s. Item, in offering on Pentecost Tuesday for my master – 1d. For the hearse – 40s. For 24 yards of broad white cloth for gowns – 27s.8d. For dyeing of the same – 4s . . . To 38 priests at the dirge at Norwich when the corpse lay there – 12s.8d. To 39 children with surplices within the church and without – 4s.4d. To 26 clerks with 4 keepers of the torches, each of them 2d., – 3s.4d. To the clerks of St. Peter's and St. Stephen's [Norwich] for the ringers at the arrival of the corpse – 2s. To the 4 orders of friars that rode out to meet the corpse – [blank]. To the Prioress of Carrow – 6s.8d . . . To a woman that came from London with the corpse to Norwich – 6s.8d.

Payments by Calle and Gloys at Bromholm

First to the Prior, by my master's bequest – 40s. To 9 monks, each of them 6s. – £3. To another monk of the same place – 20d . . . To 2 men that filled the grave – 8d . . . To the priest that came with the corpse from London – 3s.4d . . . To the Vicar of Upton – 2s . . . To 14 ringers – 7s. To 24 servitors at 4d. – 8s. To 70 servitors at 3d. – 17s.6d. Paid to Daubeney for servitors – 7s. For fish the day after the interment – 6s.10d. For 6 barrels of beer – 12s. For a runlet [cask] of red wine of 15 gallons etc. 12s. 11d . . . to 12 poor men bearing torches from London to Norfolk for 6 days, taking 4d. a day and for 3 days going home, taking 6d. a day. Given to Martin Savage and Denschers waiting upon my master at London for 7 days before he was carried thence 2s.10d. For bread bought – 24s. For 7 barrels of beer – 17s.6d. For a barrel of the best quality – 3s.4d. For 4 barrels of ale – 13s.4d. For bread and ale for 12 men that bore torches – 13d. To a dole [alms given to the poor] at Bromholm – £5.13s.4d . . . To the glazier for taking out 2 panes of the church windows to let out the reek of the torches at the dirge and for soldering the same again – 20d.                                                                        →

Victuals bought by Richard Calle

For 27 geese – 17s . . . 70 capons – 17s.7d . . . 41 pigs – 13s. 10d. 49 calves – 4.13s.4d. 34 lambs – 27s.2d. 10 neat [cattle] – 4.16s.1d . . . 1300 eggs – 6s.6d. 20 gallons milk – 20d. 8 gallons cream – 2s.8d . . . 38 gallons of ale . . .

Given to churches and in alms by [James] Gresham on the way to Bromholm – 5 marks. To the clerk of St. Peter's Hungate and his fellowship when the corpse was in the church there – 12d. To Daubeney for beasts and other stuff for the interment – £20. To him in gold to change into small money for the dole – £40 . . . To the keeper of the inn where my husband died, for his reward – 20s. To Paston Church – 10s. To Bacton Church – 6s.8d . . . To the Parson of St. Peters 6s.8d. For wine for the singers when the corpse was at Norwich – 20s. To Skolehouse in part of his bill for torches and wax made at Bromholm to burn upon the grave – 4 marks . . . To Daubeney to keep the year-day at Bromholm the first year after his death – £8.2s.4d. Given at Caister to 25 householders, every household 2d. To the Master of the College the same time – 6s.8d. To Master Clement Felmingham the same time – 6s.8d. To 8 priests at Caister the same time – 2s.8d . . . For a light kept on the grave – 10s. Given at Christmas next after the yearday to each of the 4 orders of friars 10s. – 40s. To the Vicar of Dalling for bringing home a pardon from Rome to pray for all our friends' souls – 8s.4d . . .

John's will has not survived and did not receive probate until 1473, but he seems to have become sufficiently reconciled with his eldest son to make him an executor together with his widow, Margaret, and, possibly, his brother, William. Sir John, now twenty-four years old, became head of the family, although the landed estate that he controlled personally was quite small. Margaret, of course, kept her own Mauteby inheritance, and certainly had an interest in some of her husband's estates; Agnes still held Paston, Oxnead and other lands and continued to press for a proper share of the Paston inheritance to be given to her younger sons: of these Clement probably died soon after his brother but William, a successful lawyer, was to be closely involved with his mother in disputes with his nephews for many years. Margaret had to bring up her own younger children but continued to maintain the integrity of the East Anglian estates, with the support of John III.

For most of this time Sir John was away in London, Calais or elsewhere, enjoying himself in the military, cultural and amatory pursuits of a young courtier. But he was heavily dependent on the income from the Fastolf estates to maintain his position. He therefore worked hard at obtaining patronage, as well as in the law-courts, to secure or regain his property. The Pastons had some success in ensuring that the inquisition post-mortem taken on John's death gave their version of the Fastolf bequest rather than that of their opponents, but they were unable to make inroads on the Duke of Suffolk's position at Hellesdon and Drayton. On the other hand, they successfully countered the allegations of servile status made against John, which had caused much property to be temporarily seized on behalf of the King and had resulted in John's imprisonment. They produced a mass of documentation before the King's Council to prove their ancient and free descent, and it is here that their alleged French ancestor, Wolstan, apparently makes his first appearance.

---

King Edward IV to the Bailiffs of Yarmouth
Windsor

17 July 1466

. . . Letting you know that our trusty and well-beloved knight, Sir John Paston, our well-beloved William Paston and Clement Paston, with others, have been honourably cleared before us and our Council of the great accusation that was made on our behalf against John Paston, deceased, and them, jointly and severally. So we hold them and each of them sufficiently cleared in the matter and take and repute them as gentlemen descended lineally of worshipful blood since the Conquest until now. And we have also commanded that full restitution be made of the manor of Caister and of all other lands and tenements, with goods and chattels, that the said John Paston, deceased, had of the gift and purchase of Sir John Fastolf, knight, unto our said knight, Sir John Paston . . . Wherefore, in as much as our said knight intends to make his home at Caister, we desire and pray you that for our sake you will be friendly and neighbourly to him in his right . . .

# Monks and Monasteries

*The remains of Bromholm Abbey on the Norfolk coast, where John Paston was buried.*

The main function of the monks was to pray. Eating, sleeping, manual labour, writing, study, teaching and, of course, the administration of their property were all fitted into a round-the-clock ritual of prayer. This was true even in the fifteenth century, when the rules of many orders had relaxed and were frequently criticized for laxity and worldliness. Although the great age of endowment had long passed, the monasteries and nunneries remained an essential part of the religious, as well as the social, landscape and they continued to be supported by the gifts and legacies of the laity.

Three monasteries in particular figure large in the lives of the Pastons: Bromholm, the local house where Clement, John Paston I and generations of their ancestors were buried; St Benet's Hulme, near Ludham, where Sir John Fastolf was buried; and Norwich Cathedral Priory, the burial place of Judge William Paston. Bromholm was a fairly small community, notable for its possession of a piece of 'the True Cross', which made it a place of pilgrimage; St Benet's was so large, old and distinguished that its abbot was summoned as a peer to parliament; and the Cathedral Priory was a great house, with 50 or more monks and landed possessions that 'were the equal of most lords'. Including nunneries but excluding friaries and hospitals, there were between 40 and 50 monasteries in Norfolk, and a thousand or so in the whole of England. These ranged in size from great foundations, such as Westminster and Bury St Edmunds, to small houses of two or three monks.

Whatever their Rule laid down, most monasteries were inevitably involved in worldly affairs as owners of property. The Prior of Norwich is seen as a peacemaker in the Paston Letters but his relations with the citizens of Norwich were far from peaceful. In 1443 there had been a full-scale assault on the Cathedral precinct, with the citizens crying 'let us burn the priory and kill the prior and monks'. Although Norwich was heavily punished for this outrage, conflicts over jurisdiction and privileges continued. Nevertheless, in Norwich, as elsewhere, most of the monks were local men. They employed many local people as servants, and lawyers, like William Paston and John Heydon, as stewards and counsellors; and they fulfilled a significant social role in providing guest-houses for travellers and sometimes schools for local children.

*Choir duty for the seven regular services of the day took up much of the monks' time. Cistercian monks sit in the choir-stalls, while above, a row of skulls look down as reminders of mortality.*

By October Margaret was resident at Caister – through duty rather than choice – and continued to give good advice.

---

Margaret Paston to Sir John Paston                  29 October 1466
Caister

I greet you well and send you God's blessing and mine, desiring you to send me word how you speed in your matters, for I think it right long since I heard tidings from you. And in all ways I advise you to beware that you keep securely your writings that are of value, so that they do not come into the hands of those that may harm you hereafter. Your father, whom God assail, in his troublous time set more store on his writings and evidence than he did by any of his movable goods. Remember that if they were taken from you, you could never get others such as there are for your part . . .

Item, as for your father's will, I would that you should take right good counsel therein, as I am informed that it may be proved even if no-one takes charge [as executor] for a year. You may have a letter of administration to such as you will and administer the goods and yet not take charge. I advise you that you in no way take charge of it until you know more than you yet do . . . As for me, I shall not be too hasty to take it upon me, I assure you.

And at the reverence of God, speed your matters this term so that we may be in rest hereafter, and do not let up, whatever the labour at this time. Remember the great cost and expense that we have had until now and believe verily that this may not endure for long. You know what you left when you were last at home and know truly that there is nothing more in this country to cover more expenses . . .

Written at Caister, the morrow after St. Simon and Jude, where I would not be at this time save for your sake, if I might choose.

---

# The Farming Year

Four out of five English people in the fifteenth century depended on the land. Ploughing, sowing, sheep-shearing, and the hay and corn harvests, made up the shape of their year. After the twelve-day Christmas holiday, which ended at Epiphany on 6 January, work began in earnest; Candlemas on 2 February marked the start of tillage and the end of the period of free grazing on last year's stubble; ploughing, sowing and harrowing went on until Easter; sheep were sheared in early June before Midsummer, St John's Day on 24 June, after which the hay was ready for mowing; Lammas, on 1 August, marked the beginning of the harvest period, the heaviest working-time of the year, whose end was celebrated with sports and fairs. Michaelmas, on 29 September, marked the end of one farming year and the beginning of another.

The rhythms of the agricultural year, punctuated by the great religious feasts, influenced many other aspects of life. The normal accounting year, for instance, ran from Michaelmas to Michaelmas; and the law-terms and much administrative activity were similarly organized around the agricultural seasons, especially in the closedown during the harvest period. Thus, even people who were not directly involved in agriculture were affected by it and conscious of it.

Although the Pastons leased out nearly all their land when they could and drew their profit from rents, like other gentlemen of their status, they were much involved in agriculture. Their letters contain many references to the shortage of money before the harvested grain was sold by their tenants to pay their rents. It is clear that the Pastons took a substantial proportion of their rents in the form of a share of the barley crop of their tenants, which they then sold, either as grain or after malting. The wool-crop of their sheep also provided a considerable income. The letters of John Paston I from London show an intense personal concern with the minutiae of estate administration, though it was Margaret, and later her second son, who directly supervised the work of the leading servants, such as Richard Calle, in making leases, collecting rents and selling the produce.

The Paston estates, particularly Mautby and Caister, included some of the most fertile land in England, where intensive agriculture produced very heavy crops of barley. But the 1460s were a time of low prices for agricultural goods, with good harvests and a static population keeping demand low. The Pastons and Calle had to search around for buyers of their malt, though the good sea-transport from Yarmouth made their position easier than in some areas. When prices were low, so were the profits of their tenants and rents were difficult to collect; Calle had to resort to seizing on the tenants' crops and animals. But there was a limit to the usefulness of such actions, for tenants were not easy to find unless rents were kept very low. At one time Margaret reported to her son that a farmer at Mautby owed her £70 in back-rent which she did not know when she would receive, and therefore she was forced 'to take Mautby into my own hands and to set up husbandry there', (that is, to work the land herself with the help of her servants). 'How it will profit me God knows', she wrote. The complaints of farmers and landlords often need to be treated with a certain scepticism, but it is true that agricultural profitability in the fifteenth century was too low to make it desirable for a lord to cultivate his own lands, as had been common before the Black Death. Nevertheless, the Paston letters show that the gentry considered their estates valuable enough to go to great length in protecting their rights to them.

*A fifteenth-century stained-glass roundel from Brandiston Hall, Norfolk, representing the month of July; the peasant is reaping.*

By January 1467 Margaret had returned to her house in Norwich for the winter and John III had taken up residence at Caister. He reported on measures taken to defend the property and to gather rents against the continued opposition of the Yelvertons and others.

---

John Paston III to Sir John Paston                              27 January 1467
Caister

Sir, may it like you to know that this day my mother sent me your letters, whereby I understand that, blessed be God, all stands in a good way. Also I understand by the letter sent to my mother and me that you would wish your livelode to be gathered as hastily as we can. Sir, as to that, if others do their duty no worse in gathering from other manors than we have done at Caister, I trust to God that you will not long be unpaid. For this day we had in the last coomb [a 4-bushel measure] of barley that any man owed in Caister town, notwithstanding that Hugh Austen and his men have croaked many threatening words while it was being gathered. Hugh Austen's man had twenty coombs carted ready to take to Yarmouth and when I heard of it I let slip a pack of whelps that gave the cart and the barley such a turn that it was forced to take cover in your bakehouse cistern at Caister Hall: it was wet within an hour of returning home and is almost ready to make good malt. Ho Ho! William Yelverton has been at Guton and has set in a new bailiff there and has distrained the tenants and has given them until Candlemas to pay such money as he asks of them. He has also been at Saxthorpe and has distrained the farmer there and taken from him surety to pay him. And this day the said Yelverton and eight men with him, all with jacks and trussing doublets, were ready to ride; and one of the same fellowship told a man that saw them all ready, that they were to ride to take a certain distress in certain manors that were of Sir John Fastolf – I suppose verily that they are going to Guton and Saxthorpe . . . As for the livelode that my Lord claims, I shall do my duty, while we keep our lodging, to take as much profit from it as I may . . .

---

# Norwich

*Bird's-eye view of Norwich, seen from the west, from a woodcut of 1558. The River Yare is in the foreground.*

Although the Pastons held at least half a dozen substantial manor-houses at various times, John Paston and his wife spent much of the year in their houses at Norwich, as did many other East Anglian ladies and gentlemen. Norwich was both the headquarters of the administration of the county of Norfolk and the centre of the diocese which covered both Norfolk and Suffolk. It was in effect a regional capital, the natural focus for one of the richest and most densely populated parts of England.

In the fifteenth century, the population of Norwich was much smaller than it had been before the Black Death, but its prosperity remained high, based on its role as a regional market connected by road and water with a rich hinterland and with foreign markets in the Netherlands. It was a substantial manufacturing city, too, notable for its leather, glass and building industries, and above all for the manufacture of worsted cloth. There was an elaborate structure of craft-guilds but, as in most sizeable towns, political power was controlled by a relatively small group of merchants. These men had

invested heavily in order to achieve self-government by the royal charter of 1404, which gave the City county status. Although the following fifty years were marked by violent divisions among the citizenry and conflicts with the Priory, they also saw a great expansion of civic activity, marked by the building of the Guildhall, the Common Staithe and the New Mills, which were all built with common funds produced by the market and by tolls on the movement of goods. Individual merchants also contributed to the appearance of the City: in 1456 the ex-mayor, Ralph Segryme, left no less than £200 to the repair of the city walls and £10 to cleanse the river. They also financed the rebuilding of many city churches, particularly St Peter Mancroft and of the four great friaries. Norwich's civic and craft pride were fed by regular pageants and plays, with occasional sumptuous shows for royal and ducal visits. Norwich was, as its present authorities claim, 'a fine city', and it is understandable that Agnes and Margaret Paston preferred it, particularly in widowhood and in winter, to their own houses at Paston and Mautby.

The reference to 'My Lord' in the above letter seems to be to the Duke of Norfolk rather than to the old enemy, the Duke of Suffolk. It is an ominous hint of the new troubles that lay ahead. But the first surviving letter from Sir John since his father's death concerned a more peaceful matter which was to become a theme of the correspondence for the next ten years – his brother's marriage.

---

Sir John Paston to John Paston III              March 1467
[London]

Right worshipful and verily well beloved brother, I heartily commend myself to you, thanking you for your labour and diligence that you have in keeping of my place at Caister so securely, both with your heart and mind, to your great labour and trouble . . .

As for my Lady Boleyn's disposition toward you, I cannot in any way find her agreeable that you should have her daughter . . . insomuch that I had so little comfort by all the means that I could make, that I disdained to discuss it with her in person. Nevertheless, I understand that she says 'If he and she can agree I will not prevent it, but I will never advise her thereto in any way'. And upon Tuesday last she rode home to Norfolk. Wherefore you should find the means to speak with her yourself, for without that, in my opinion, it will not happen . . . And bear yourself as lowly to the mother as you like but to the maiden not too lowly, as if you be not too glad to succeed nor too sorry to fail . . .

---

Sir John had long overcome any diffidence he had felt in his early months at the King's Court and was now a well-known and active figure in Court circles, although he does not seem to have held any formal Household post. He shone especially as a jouster, a skill which would have brought him considerable reputation among the King's intimates, of whom the Woodvilles, in particular, were notable figures at tournaments.

---

Sir John Paston to John Paston III              April 1467
London

. . . My hand was hurt at a tourney at Eltham on Wednesday last. I would that you had been there to see it, for it was the goodliest sight provided by so few men that was seen in England this forty years. There was upon the one side within: the King, my Lord Scales, myself and [Thomas] St. Leger; and without: my Lord Chamberlain [Hastings], Sir John Woodville, Sir Thomas Montgomery and John Aparre etc . . .

---

# Tournaments and Jousting

*A tournament in honour of Henry VI's Queen from the* Pageants *of Richard Beauchamp, Earl of Warwick, 1493. The knights confront each other, separated by a barrier, with pages and supernumeraries in attendance.*

In his challenge to the Bastard of Burgundy in 1465, Anthony, Lord Scales, friend and fellow-courtier of Sir John Paston, spelled out the reasons for wanting to fight him in the lists: 'the augmentation of knighthood . . . the glorious school and study of arms, to maintain and follow valour, to avoid slothfulness and to please my fair lady.' It was for this variety of courtly, military and recreational reasons that jousting and tournaments were a feature of the court of Edward IV, as they had not been under the supremely unchivalric Henry VI. The tournament that followed from Scales's challenge in June 1467, for which Sir John's Eltham tournament may have served as a practice match, was notable for the lavishness of its display rather than for the fierceness of its fighting. The tournament had long been 'a form of artistic expression in its own right'; as one historian writes, and months of work by armourers, costumiers, 'stage directors' and craftsmen prepared for the four days of combat at Smithfield. Even this display was overshadowed by the great series of tournaments arranged by Charles of Burgundy to honour his marriage at Bruges in the following year, where a series of romantic dramas were played out by the participants in various 'disguisings' and in surroundings of the most elaborate construction.

Tournaments were not just for display, however. In 1449, for example, a veteran soldier of the French Wars, Thomas Keyll, requested the King's licence to visit France, Scotland, Brittany and elsewhere to challenge and 'have a do' against all-comers. Such feats of knight-errantry remained quite usual in the fifteenth century, stimulated certainly by tales of Arthurian romance, but also concerned, like a modern professional boxer, with winning renown and cash by the exploitation of hard-earned skills. In spite of precautions, the tournament was a dangerous pastime and was still regarded as a training-ground for the soldier. In the three sorts of combat – the mélée, the individual joust on horse-back and the fight on foot – men displayed and practised skills which were still needed in battle.

Sir John's brother was more concerned with the practical problems of defending the Fastolf lands. He reported on the crucial evidence to be given by a friar about the death-bed statement of Friar Brackley, Fastolf's confessor. Although there was much sympathy between the brothers, John clearly found Sir John's courtly pre-occupations irritating, considering the circumstances, and we have the first of many pleas that Sir John should return to play his rightful part in Norfolk affairs.

---

John Paston III to Sir John Paston  
[? Caister]  

April 1467

Sir, please you to know that my mother and I communed this day with Friar Mowght to understand what he shall say in the court when he comes up to London, and he will speak in this way: he says that at the time that he had shriven [given absolution to] Master Brackley and houseled him [given him the Eucharist] he let him know that he was informed by divers persons that the said Master Brackley ought to have a heavy conscience for such things as he had done and said and caused my father, whom God assoil, to do and say in proving of Sir John Fastolf's will. To whom the said Master Brackley answered again . . . that by the destination of his soul, the will that my father put into court was as truly Sir John Fastolf's will as it was true that he would die . . . On the Monday he revived again and was well amended until the Wednesday and on the Wednesday he sickened again and supposed that he would die at once. And in his sickness he called Friar Mowght . . . saying to him '. . . I desire that you will report after my death that I took it upon my soul at my dying that the will that John Paston put in to be proved was Sir John Fastolf's will'. And the said Brackley died the same Wednesday.

. . . And whereas it pleases you to wish that I had been at Eltham at the tourney, because of the spectacle that was there, by my troth, I had rather see you once in Caister Hall than to see as many king's tourneys as might be between Eltham and London.

And, Sir, whereas it pleases you to desire to have knowledge how I have done with my Lady Boleyn, by my faith, I have neither spoken nor done in that matter, nor will do until you come home, even if you come not this seven years. Notwithstanding, the Lady Boleyn was in Norwich in the week after Easter from the Saturday until the Wednesday, together with Heydon's wife [Anne, daughter of Lady Boleyn and wife of Henry Heydon] and Mistress Alice both, and I was at Caister and knew not of it. Her men said that she had no other errand in the town but to amuse herself, but, so God help me, I suppose that she thought I would have been in Norwich so that I could have seen her daughter.

I beseech you with all my heart to hasten home, though you tarry but a day, for I promise you that your folk think that you have forgotten them . . .

By July 1467 John III and Edmund appear to have joined their eldest brother in London, leaving Margaret to perform her accustomed role as keeper of the Norfolk estates. Rumbles of the new threat to Caister were getting louder.

---

Margaret Paston to Sir John Paston                    11 July 1467
Norwich

. . . Also this day was brought me word from Caister that Rising of Fritton had heard in divers places in Suffolk that Fastolf of Cowhawe gathers all the strength he may and intends to assault Caister and to enter there if he may, insomuch that it is said that he has five score men ready and daily sends spies to know what men guard the place. By whose power or favour or support he will do this I know not, but you know well that I have been afraid there before this time, when I had other comfort than I had now: I cannot guide nor rule soldiers well and they set not by [do not respect] a woman as they should by a man. Therefore I would that you should send home your brothers or else Daubeney to take control and to bring in such men as are necessary for the safeguard of the place . . . And I have been about my livelode to set a rule therein, as I have written to you, which is not yet all performed after my desire, and I would not go to Caister till I had done. I do not want to spend more days near thereabouts, if I can avoid it; so make sure that you send someone home to keep the place and when I have finished what I have begun I shall arrange to go there if it will do any good – otherwise I had rather not be there . . .

    . . . I marvel greatly that you send me no word how you do, for your enemies begin to grow right bold and that puts your friends in fear and doubt. Therefore arrange that they may have some comfort, so that they be not discouraged, for if we lose our friends, it will be hard in this troublous world to get them again . . .

---

Early in 1468 Sir John, perhaps with the assistance of Archbishop Neville and the Earls of Warwick and Oxford, his closest patrons at this time, finally persuaded Sir John Fastolf's feoffees [trustees], led by Bishop Waynflete and including Judge Yelverton, to release to him Fastolf's lands at Caister and elsewhere in East Norfolk and Suffolk. The release was part of an attempted settlement of the disputed will. It clearly included provision for replacing the proposed grand collegiate foundation at Caister with further endowment for the college founded by Waynflete at Oxford. William Worcester, who had made his peace with the Pastons since John's death – although he was still actively engaged in promoting what he saw as his old master's real intention – thought Cambridge would be a more suitable location for Fastolf's endowments.

---

William Worcester to Margaret Paston [?1468]

Right worshipful mistress . . . I communed lately with your entirely well beloved son, Sir John Paston, about whether the foundation of my Master Fastolf's college might be at Cambridge, in case it might not be at Caister nor at St. Benet's [Abbey], because that university lies near to the country of Norfolk and Suffolk. For, albeit that my Lord of Winchester is disposed to found a college in Oxford where my said master should be prayed for, yet with much less cost he might make some other memorial also in Cambridge perhaps with two clerks or three or four scholars, endowed at least with the value of good benefices and rich parsonages of which the advowsons [rights to appoint the parson] might be purchased much more cheaply than lordships or manors may. I found your son well disposed to move and persuade my said Lord . . .

Would to Jesus, mistress, that my good master that was formerly your husband could in Master Fastolf's lifetime have found it in his heart to have trusted and loved me as my Master Fastolf did, and that he would not have given credence to the malicious and contrived tales that Friar Brackley, William Barker and others untruly imagined of me, saving your reverence. . . . And I am right glad that Caister is and shall be at your commandment, and yours, especially. A rich jewel it is at need for all the country in time of war, and Master Fastolf would have rather he had never built it than that it should be in the control of any lord who would oppress the country . . .

And, mistress, I pray you recommend me to my best mistress, your mother, Agnes, for she favoured me and did me great charity, to be the better disposed to her son, Master John; and, by my soul, this made me more ready to save the livelode from trouble or claims. I appeal to all the world I never put any part of Master Fastolf's livelode in trouble, nor entitled any creature to any place; and you may speak with her of this when you are alone.

In the middle of June 1468 Margaret, sister of King Edward IV, crossed to Flanders to marry Charles, Duke of Burgundy. It was the culmination of years of negotiations and was intended to consolidate the alliance between the two rulers that was clearly directed against France. Sir John lost, as a consequence, a bet he had made a year earlier with a London merchant that the marriage would not take place within two years. He was, however, among those courtiers whom the King ordered to attend upon Margaret 'for the honour of us and our said sister' and he took with him in his retinue his brother, John. John III's letter to his mother describes one of the great ceremonial occasions of fifteenth-century Europe.

John Paston III to Margaret Paston                          8 July 1468
Bruges

Right reverent and worshipful mother . . . As for tidings here I can send you none except of the festivities. My Lady Margaret was married on Sunday last past at a town that is called Damme, 3 miles out of Bruges, at 5 o'clock in the morning; and she was brought the same day to Bruges for her dinner, and there she was received as worshipfully as all the world could devise, with a procession of lords and ladies, the best arrayed of any people that I ever saw or heard of. Many pageants were played to welcome her on her way into Bruges, the best that ever I saw. And the same Sunday my Lord the Bastard [Anthony, half-brother to the Duke] took upon him to fight with 24 knights and gentlemen within eight days at jousts of peace; and when they had been fought with those 24 and himself should tourney with another 25 the next day after. And those that have jousted with him up to this day have been as richly arrayed, and himself also, as cloth of gold and silver and goldsmith's work might make them; for they of the Duke's court, both gentlemen and gentlewomen, have no want of such gear and gold and pearls and precious stones . . .

And as for the Duke's court, as of lords, ladies and gentlewomen, knights, squires and gentlemen, I heard never of one like it, save King Arthur's court. And, by my troth, I have no ability nor memory to write to you half the worshipful things that are here; but what is lacking, as it comes to mind I shall tell you when I come home which, I trust to God, shall not be long. For we depart from Bruges homeward on Tuesday next, and all the folk that came with my Lady of Burgundy out of England, except such as will be abiding with her, which I think will be but few. We depart the sooner because the Duke has word that the French King is intending to make war upon him very soon, and that he is within 4 or 5 days journey of Bruges. The Duke rides on Tuesday next coming to meet with him: God give him good speed with all his men, for, by my troth, they are the goodliest fellowship that ever I came among, and the best behaved and most like gentlemen . . .

# The Marriage of Margaret of York

*Margaret of York, Duchess of Burgundy, is seen at prayer in this religious treatise written for her in 1475 at Ghent by the theologian David Aubert.*

John Paston's breathless description of the wedding reception given to the young Princess of York by her husband, Charles of Burgundy, illustrates the awe with which the English visitors – themselves acquainted with the splendid court of Edward IV – viewed the wealth and ingenuity of the most cultured and ceremonious court north of the Alps. The display of the Burgundian Court had a political purpose, of course; Charles intended to show to the subjects of his new brother-in-law the power that he would bring to the alliance and he also had to match the large dowry that Edward had provided. Such ceremonies were more than political devices, however; they were part of an aristocratic way of life which reached its apogee in Burgundy.

Another English observer, who left a more detailed description of Margaret's reception, describes a variety of civic performances, some so obscure that 'I fear me to write of them' at the entries into Sluys and Bruges, where pageants on the theme of marriage, Adam and Eve and the feast of Cana were interrupted by 'a storm of the rain'. But it was the Duke's courtly displays, rather than the municipal celebrations, that made the most impression: the men dressed as animals; the nine days of jousting and feasting which followed the marriage, with the tables covered by gold tissue and lit by elaborate chandeliers; and the Duke himself, riding to the jousts with clothes and horses encrusted with splendid jewels. The surviving reactions of English observers suggest that

Charles had indeed created the effect he wanted. His alliance with Edward was sealed by the help he gave during Edward's exile in 1470–1, and in the 1470s the influence of the Burgundian Court and culture increased. Although attitudes to Burgundy became less friendly after the invasion fiasco of 1475 and although Charles is said to have been none too contented with his wife, Margaret remained a powerful pro-English and later pro-Yorkist force in the Burgundian territories – even after the death of her husband in 1477.

*The marriage of Margaret of York to Charles the Bold is signified by the initials C and M on this silver coronet set with pearls and precious stones, worn by Margaret at her wedding in June 1468.*

The two young men returned to England soon afterwards, Sir John to London and his brother back to Norfolk, where he took up residence at Caister. Exposure to the cultural glories of the Burgundian Court no doubt strengthened Sir John's wider interests. Like others of his court circle and, indeed, like Sir John Fastolf, he had a considerable interest in literature – particularly in works of chivalry. It was in 1468 that he ordered the writing of his 'Great Book' which still survives in the British Library. Its scribe, William Ebesham, was not only writing books for him but also recording the testimony of witnesses in the Fastolf litigation. Inevitably he was finding it difficult to get paid.

---

William Ebesham to Sir John Paston                    Autumn 1468
[?London]

My most worshipful and most special master . . . beseeching you
most tenderly to see me somewhat rewarded for my labour in the Great Book
which I am writing for your said good mastership . . . God knows,
I lie in sanctuary at great costs and among those who ask much unreasonably
of me. I moved this matter lately to Sir Thomas Lewis [a priest] and he . . .
told me to write what I have had in money at sundry times from him.
. . . And specially I beseech you to send me as alms one of your old
gowns, which, I know well, will equal in value much of the costs I have listed.
And I shall be yours while I live and at your command. I have great need of it,
God knows, whom I beseech preserve you from all adversity – which I am
somewhat acquainted with.
    Your true man, W, Ebesham.
Here following appear individually divers and sundry manner of writings
which I, William Ebesham, have written for my good and worshipful master,
Sir John Paston, and what moneys I have received and what is unpaid.
    First, I did write for his mastership a little book of physic, for which I had
from Sir Thomas Lewis at Westminster – 20d.
    Item, I had for the writing of half the privy seal from Pamping – 8d.
    Item, for the writing of the whole privy seal from Thomas – 2s.
    Item, I wrote 8 of the witnesses in parchment, at 14d. a piece, for which I
was paid by Sir Thomas – 10s . . .
    Item, as for the Great Book. First, as for the writing of the Coronation and
other treatises of Knighthood in that quire, which contains some 13 leaves
and more at 2d. a leaf – 2s.2d. Item, for the treatise of War in 4 books, which
contains 60 leaves at 2d. a leaf – 10s.; Item, for the Epistle of Othea which
contains 43 leaves – 7s.2d.; Item, for the Challenges and the Acts of Arms
which is 28 less – 4s.8d.; Item, for De Regimine Principum which contains 45
leaves at 1d. a leaf, which is right well worth – 3s.9d. Item, for rubrishing
[inserting headings in colour] of all the book – 3s.4d. . . .

# Books and Bookmen

*In this miniature of 1477, Earl Rivers presents his manuscript to Edward IV, the Queen and the Prince of Wales.*

Courtier and lady's man though he may have been, Sir John Paston was also a man of culture and some learning. An inventory of his English books, drawn up towards the end of his life, includes a variety of the works of Chaucer and John Lydgate, romances, translations of works of ethics and religion, as well as practical treatises on heraldry, tournaments and law. Letters to Sir John from the scrivener, William Ebesham, illustrate the ways in which such libraries were built up. Ebesham wrote business and legal documents to order but his clients also commissioned him to copy particular works on separate quires which, when finished, could either be purchased as units or, like Sir John's *Great Book*, be bound together in a miscellaneous collection. Some scriveners, like John Shirley, mass-produced popular works, such as the poems of Chaucer or the chronicles, to sell 'off the peg' in quires, but most

professionally written books were 'bespoke'.

The growth of literacy in English during the fifteenth century had produced a rapidly increasing demand for books, including translations from Latin and French. The most sumptuous manuscripts were specially commissioned by wealthy patrons as possessions of beauty to go with their tapestries and plate, but the vast majority of books were bought to be read. Books of devotion and guides to heraldry, etiquette, the law and languages were popular just as technical manuals are today, while romances, poetry and history were read for pleasure by the upper and middle classes. Sir John Fastolf was a considerable collector of books and both his stepson, Stephen Scrope, and his servant, William Worcester, wrote or translated for him.

Among Sir John Paston's books is 'a book in print of the *Play of the [Game of] Chess*', one of the first works to come from the printing-press of William Caxton. During the next fifty years Caxton and his imitators were to produce hundreds of titles in printed form, revolutionizing the book trade. The age of the manuscript was drawing to a close. In 1476 Hugh Fenne (whose will mentions various books written 'of my own hand') had left a substantial sum for the repair of books

at Oxford and Cambridge. Nearly fifty years later, when his surviving executor, Edmund Jenney, came to make his will in 1522, he admitted that he had not fully carried out Fenne's bequest. He now left the remaining money for other charitable purposes because times had changed: 'there is so many printed books that there shall not need so great reparation'.

*Dedication page from* The Game and Play of Chess, *translated and printed by Caxton in 1475.*

*Overleaf: Pages from the* Great Book *started in 1468 by the scribe William Ebesham for Sir John Paston.*

The actes of the full honorable & knyghtly armes
don betwene the right noble lordes Sir Antony
Wodevile lorde Scales & of Newselles brothir to
the moost high & excellent Princesse the Queene
of Englonde & of Fraunce and lady of Irlonde Cha-
lenger And Sir Antony the Bastarde of Bourgone
Erle of Roche and lorde of Benee & Beueresse afore
the moost open & victorious Prince Edwarde the iiij.
the kyng of Englond & of Fraunce and lorde of Irlond
the xi. & xij. dayes of Juyne in the vij. yeere of his
vertue defender The Erle of Worcestre their grete
Conestable of Englond in Smythfelde

The fortune of themprise of the saide full noble
& valerouse knyght Sir Antony Wodevile

The Wennesday nexte aftir the solempne & deuoute feste of the
resurrexion of oure blessid Sauyoure & redemptour Jhu Criste For
soone of my besynesse at the departyng from the highmasse I drewe me to
the queene of Inglond and of Fraunce and lady of Irlond my sondayne
lady which I am right humble subiet And as I spake to her ladiship on
knee the bonet from myne hede as me aught I wote not by what ad
venture nor hou it happenyd all the ladies of her companye azovd
aboute me And they of theire beneuolence tied aboute my right thigh
a color of goolde garnysshed with perre And was made with oon letter
And whan I held it it was nere my hert then my knee And to that co
lor was tied a noble floure of soubenaunce enameled and in manor
of an empryse And than oon of them saide to me full dommely that I
shulde take not it a worth as at that tyme And than they withdrowe
them all echone in theire places And I abasshed of this aventure rose
me vp and went to thanke them all of theire right grete honoure that
they did that tyme And as I toke vp my bonet that I had lete fall nygh

to mee. I founde in hit a bille writyn in frenshe parchemyn follid & closed with
a litill thred of goolde & sealled. than thought I well that therein was the
contenue that by them was yoven me. than I thanked right humbly
the quene that of hir good grace hath suffred such honor to be doon to mee
in so high a presence. And also the ladies all of these honor doon to me
that doon I went foorth with the kyng my soveraigne lorde to shewe vnto
his highnesse myne aventure and the emprise that was me chargyd. And
humbly presented vnto his higness the said bille so closed, mekely besechyng
his good grace that it pleasid him to geve me that honoure & grace to agree
& consent to the will of the ladies in that partie And that he wolde geve
me conge to accomplisshe the contenue in the saide bill to be doon. The
kyng vnclosed the saide bille And comaunded the same openly to be redd
in his high presence in which was conteynyng certeyne chapitres that
so redd. the kyng of his aboundaunt grace licenced me to accomplisshe
the contenue of the same.


## The prolog of the saide lorde Scales after the
## redyng of the saide bill before the kyng &
## of the chapitres conteyned in the same
## for doyn armes on horsbak and on foote.


In the worship honorance and helpe of oure blessed Savioure
and triste of the glorious virgyne his modir And Seint Beorse the
vicar and patron and cry of Englisshemen. In augmentacion of
knyghthode & Recommendacion of nobley. Also for the glorious sprede and
study of Armes And for the vaillance thereof to my power to maynteyne
& folowe. And for to voide slowthfulnes of tyme loste. And to obey & please
my faire lady. I Antony Wodevile knyght lorde of Scales & of Nucelles
Englissheman. xxiiij day of Aprill. yere of oure lorde m cccc lxv. Have
resceyved by the ladies the gyft of a riche coler of golde. And in that han-
gyng a noble comendue the which. of theire grace have takyn And
set it vpon my right thigh the which comendue by godes pleasir
conge and licence of the kyng my soveraigne I have takyn the charge for

But more serious – and more expensive – matters were occupying the Pastons' attention by the autumn of 1468. Yelverton and Howes had by now released their rights as Fastolf's trustees for Caister to the Duke of Norfolk who was now attempting to impose his authority there. The Nevilles were still powerful enough to prevent any serious attempt by the Duke to seize the Castle at this time, but the situation demanded constant lobbying. Sir John was residing in Archbishop Neville's household when the following letter was written to him. It is unsigned, but it is clearly from a friend and social equal of the Pastons and illustrates how their problems were affected by the politics of central government. The half-humorous suggestion for dealing with Thomas Howes proved unnecessary, since he died before the end of the year.

---

Anonymous to Sir John Paston                                              28 October 1468

. . . You may tell my Lord of York that there is openly in every man's mouth in this country the language that my Lord of York and my Lord of Warwick had to my Lord of Norfolk in the King's Chamber, and that my Lord of York said that he would come and dwell at Caister himself rather than the land should go in this way. You would marvel how the Lords have people's hearts and how these words put them in comfort. My Lord of Norfolk answered that he would speak with my Lady, his wife, and entreat her. And your adversaries say that my Lord [of York] will never be chancellor till this matter be dealt with, for their [the Duke and Yelverton] bargains are made conditional to stand or not to stand according to whether my Lord is Chancellor or not . . . Pray my Lord [Archbishop] to remember to get a good sheriff for this year, for there is much to be done through the sheriff . . .

If Thomas Howes were approached by Master Tresham and put in hope of the moon shining in the water and I know not what, that he was likely either to be pope or else to be deprived of all ecclesiastical benefice for simony, lechery, perjury and double changeable [two-faced] peevishness and for administering without authority . . . it would make him depart, for Yelverton and he are half at variance now. And entreat my Lord's servants to speak in your matters to all such persons as there is need to. And I shall be hastily with you . . . There are witnesses, it is said, some of them men of £100 a year and many others, laboured to swear against you, some of whom never knew of the matter nor ever heard Sir John Fastolf speak. You know what sort of jury there is in this country in matters that are favoured by those who are against you. It is hard that when a matter rests upon a jury in this country, some of the same jury that found you a bond man will witness against you.

Bbut self-help was also necessary – Caister had to be well defended.

Sir John Paston to John Paston III                    9 November 1468
[London]

Right well beloved brother, I recommend me to you, letting you know that I
have engaged four trustworthy and true men to help you and Daubeney to
keep the place at Caister. They will do all manner of things that they might be
asked to do in safeguarding or strengthening the said place; moreover they
are proved men and cunning in war and in feats of arms: they can shoot both
guns and crossbows well and mend and string them; and they can devise
bulwarks or anything else that should give greater strength to the place; and
they will, when needful, keep watch and ward. They are sad and sensible
men, saving one of them, who is bald and called William Penny, who is as
good a man as can be found on earth except that he is, as I understand, a little
inclined to be cup-shotten [drunk], though he is no brawler but full of
courtesy, much like James Halman. The other three are named Peryn Sale,
John Chapman and Robert Jackson. As yet they have no harness [equipment]
but when it comes it will be sent on to you, and in the meanwhile I pray you
and Daubeney to provide them with some. They also need a couple of beds,
which I pray you, with the help of my mother, to provide for them until I
come home to you. You will find them gentlemanly, comfortable fellows and
they will be prepared to abide by their agreement. I send you these men
because if you think that any assault is likely, men of the country thereabout
would be afraid for fear of loss of their goods. So, if any such thing is
imminent, I would like you to take but few men of the country, and only
trusty men, for otherwise they might discourage all the rest.

And as for any writing from the King, he has promised none shall come;
and if one is sent without his knowledge, your answer should be what the
King has said, and thus delay them until I have word, and I shall soon
provide a remedy.

I understand that you have been lately with the Duke of Norfolk but what
you have done I know not. We hear that he will be here again this day
. . . I shall send you tidings of other things in haste, by the grace of God. I
fear that Daubeney has not all the stores to keep the household long: let him
speedily send me word and I shall relieve him to the best of my power, and
ere long I hope to be with you.

Roger Ree is sheriff of Norfolk and he will be good enough. The escheator
I am not yet informed of . . .

Remember to treat the men I have named as courteously as you can. . . .
As for my Lord Fitzwalter's obligation I do not yet know if any such is
in my award; and as for the Bishop of Norwich's obligation, I never saw it,
that I remember; wherefore I would my mother look it up . . .

# Professional Soldiers and their Weapons

*An assortment of weapons used by foot-soldiers. Polearms were used for hooking heavily armoured horsemen from the saddle; maces and daggers for hacking and bludgeoning.*

The reference to William Penny and his fellows gives us a rare glimpse of soldiers of the lower ranks. They were clearly professionals temporarily out of a job.
Since England had no standing army, like those being developed on the Continent, skilled soldiers made themselves available for private hire and it is probable that these men formed the steady core of many of the armies of the Wars of the Roses. Foreign campaigns were more profitable for the soldier because of the greater chance of booty but, even in England, wages were superior to those of most skilled craftsmen.

The development of new weapons and techniques had produced greater versatility among such men. The difference between archers and men-at-arms had probably narrowed as most of the former were now protected with at least a helmet and a 'jack' or 'brigander' [protective coat] and had hand-weapons as well as bows, while the latter normally fought on foot. Men-at-arms

were paid 1s. a day – twice the rate of an archer, because of their more expensive equipment. But men could and did switch easily from one role to another.
The development of German and Swiss pikemen as a crucial force on the battlefield, and the greater reliability of handguns, were adding new skills to the professional's armoury – skills that demanded a longer and more intensive drilling.

The professionalism of some Burgundian troops is illustrated by the nature of their equipment at the second Battle of St Albans. They had guns which shot lead pellets, arrows with iron heads which could be used to throw wild fire, as well as defensive tackle which included a primitive form of barbed wire. It is true that the London chronicler of the battle 'could not understand that all this ordinance did any good or harm', but the devices do indicate the increasing ingenuity applied to military matters on the Continent.

Throughout the winter, the Duke's men continued to harry the Pastons' tenants. Sir John remained at Court and his mother and brother maintained as best they could the family's interests in East Anglia.

Margaret Paston to Sir John Paston          12 March 1469
[Norwich]

I greet you well and send you God's blessing and mine, desiring you to recommend me to my brother, William [Paston] and to discuss with him and your counsel such matters as I write to you, so that there may be some writing obtained from the King that my Lord of Norfolk and his council cease from the waste that they have done in your lordships, especially in Hainford; for they have felled all the woods and this week they will carry it away and let the waters run out and take away all the fish. And Sir William Yelverton and his son, William, and John Grey and Burgeys, his men, have been at Guton and taken distraints and, unless the tenants will pay them, they will not allow any plough to till the land. They bid them let their land lie untilled unless they pay them. If the tenants have no remedy within seven days, so that they may peaceably harrow their lands without assault or distress by Yelverton or his men or any other in their names, their tilth in the fields will be lost for all the year and they will be undone. And even if you keep it peacefully hereafter you will lose the rents for this year, for they may not pay you unless they can work their lands; they no sooner move a plough out of their gates than a band is ready to seize it.

    And they ride with spears and lances like men of war, so that the tenants are afraid to remain in their own houses. Therefore provide a swift remedy or else you will lose the tenants' hearts and you will be greatly hurt, for it is great pity to hear the sorrowful and piteous complaints of the poor tenants that come to me for comfort and succour, sometimes six or seven together. Therefore, for God's love, see that they be helped, and ask my brother, William, to give you good counsel in this matter . . .

    Labour hastily a remedy for what I have described, or else Sir John Fastolf's livelode, even though you enter it peaceably, will not be worth a groat to you this year, unless you ruin your tenants . . . Remember to labour some remedy for your father's will while my Lord of Canterbury lives, for he is an old man and he is now friendly to you and if he happened to die you do not know who will come after him – if he were to be a poor man he will be the more difficult to deal with, as your father was rumoured to be so rich . . . Therefore, provide hastily and wisely for this while he lives and do not make delays as you did while my Lord of York was Chancellor, for if you had laboured in his time as you have done since, you would have been through with your matters. Beware of that and do not let sloth cause again such fault . . .

During the winter of 1468-9, Sir John Paston became betrothed to Anne Haute, a Kentish lady, who was a kinswoman of the Queen and of Anthony Woodville, Lord Scales, who possessed large estates in West Norfolk, as well as being influential at Court. The relationship brought him a new patron, but seems to have been beset with unknown difficulties from early on. The following letter also hints at the storm which was about to break over the Paston household.

Margaret Paston to Sir John Paston            3 April 1469
[Norwich]

. . . I have no certain knowledge of your betrothal but if you are betrothed I pray God send you joy and worship together, and so I trust you will have, if she is as is reported of her. And in the sight of God you are as greatly bound to her as if you were married, and therefore I charge you upon my blessing that you be as true to her in all ways as if she were married unto you and so you will have the more grace and speed better in all other things. Also, I would that you should not be too hasty to marry until you are more sure of your livelode, for you must remember what expense you will have, and if you cannot maintain it, it will be great shame to you . . .

Your enemies are as bold here as they were before so I cannot but think that they have some encouragement. I sent to Caister, as you wrote to me, that they should be wary in keeping of the place. Hasten to speed your matters as speedily as you can, so that you may have a smaller company at Caister, for the expenses and costs are great if you have no need of them . . .

Also I would that you should provide for your sister to be with my Lady of Oxford or my Lady of Bedford or in some other worshipful place as you think best, and I will help towards her expenses, for we are each of us weary of the other. I shall tell you more when I speak with you. I pray you to do your duty herein if you wish my comfort and welfare and your worship, for divers causes which you shall understand hereafter.

I spoke with the Lord Scales at Norwich and thanked him for the good lordship that he had showed to you and desired his Lordship to be your continual good lord; and he swore by his troth that he would do what he could for you. And he told me that Yelverton, the Judge, had spoken to him upon your matters, but he did not tell me what he said; but I think that if you asked him to tell you, he would. You are beholden to my Lord for his good report of you in this country, for he reports better of you than I think you deserve. I felt that he has been made large proffers on the part of your adversaries to be against you.

Send me word as hastily as you may after the beginning of this term how you have sped in all your matters, for I shall think it right long till I hear some good tidings . . .

# Queen Elizabeth and the Woodvilles

*Contemporary portraits in stained glass of Edward IV and Elizabeth Woodville, from Canterbury Cathedral.*

The secret courtship and marriage of King Edward IV to the young widow, Elizabeth Grey, was one of the more romantic royal episodes of the Middle Ages, but it was deplored by some of his more powerful subjects. Contemporaries accused him of acting 'by blind affection and not by the rule of reason'. Kings were expected to marry for dynastic and political motives and, though Elizabeth did her duty by providing the kingdom with an heir, she contributed neither money nor important connections. On the contrary, she brought with her a large, rather impecunious family – father and mother, five brothers, six sisters and two sons by her first marriage, as well as a mass of more distant Woodville kinsmen. The Woodvilles clearly had a strong sense of kinship and after Sir John Paston's betrothal to Anne Haute, the Queen's cousin, he was accepted into the network. 'Because of marriage agreed with one of my nearest kinswomen,' wrote the Queen's brother, Lord Scales, in 1469 '. . . nature must compel me the rather to show my good will, assistance and favour to the said Sir John.'

The closer relatives had to be helped by the King to live according to their new royal status. Many were helped by arranged marriages, including the 'diabolical marriage' of the Queen's twenty-year-old younger brother, Sir John, to the sixty-five-year-old, three-times widowed Dowager Duchess of Norfolk. Their total of honours, offices and lands earned them the enmity of the Earl of Warwick (who executed the Queen's father and brother in 1469), and later of both the Duke of Gloucester and Lord Hastings. Anthony Lord Scales, who succeeded his father as Earl Rivers in 1469, had acquired large estates in West Norfolk by marriage, but his main connection with the Pastons was through the Court, where his chivalric lifestyle was shared by Sir John. Anthony was the champion jouster of his time, the patron and translator of William Caxton, and a man of austere piety, who was said to wear a hair-shirt beneath his courtly robes. He was charged by the King with the responsibility of educating and supervising his oldest son. On Edward's death, he was seized by the Duke of Gloucester and executed on 25 June 1483 at Pontefract. The Queen, however, survived until 1492, having seen her oldest daughter crowned Queen of England.

During May the domestic storm broke with the revelation that Margery, John and Margaret's older daughter, had entered into a clandestine marriage with their most active and senior servant, Richard Calle. Calle came from a merchant family in Framlingham, which was respectable but hardly suitable to ally with the major gentry family that the Pastons had now become. Pressure from the Duke of Norfolk was increasing as the national political scene became more tense and the King's position weaker.

Family and property problems intertwine in the Paston correspondence of the next six months, as they do in the following letter from John III to his elder brother.

---

John Paston III to Sir John Paston                    May 1469
Caister

Sir, please it to understand that I understand by your letter which you sent me by Jude that you have heard of R.C.'s labour that he makes with the assent of our ungracious sister. But, whereas they write that they have my goodwill therein, they falsely lie . . . Lovell asked me once a question whether I understood how it was between R.C. and my sister. I believe that this was by Calle's suggestion, for when I asked him whether Calle desired him to ask me that question he would have avoided answering by hums and by hays, but I would not be answered so; wherefore he at last told me that his eldest son desired him to inquire whether R.C. was sure of her or not, for he said that he knew of a good marriage for her; but I think he lied, for he is wholly with R.C. in that matter. Wherefore, so that he nor they should take no comfort from me, I answered him that if my father, whom God assoil, were alive, and had consented thereto and my mother and you also, he should never have my goodwill to make my sister sell candles and mustard at Framlingham . . .

Whoever sends you word that I have spent any of your money since you left, they must give you another reckoning, save in meat and drink, for I eat like a horse to eat you out of doors. But that is not needed, for you do not come within them: wherefore, so God help me, the fellowship here thinks you have forgotten us . . .

Also I understand for certain, word being sent me from my Lord's house, that this Pentecost my Lord's council is at Framlingham and they purpose this week and next to hold courts here at Caister and at all other manors that were Sir John F.'s and purchased from Yelverton and Thomas Howes, whom God assoil. It is too late to ask you for advice on how I should act, so if I do well I ask no thanks and if I do ill I pray you lay the fault on too litle wit. But I purpose to use the first rule of hawking, to hold fast if I may. But, so God help me, if they pulled down the house on our heads, though I trust to God to stop them, I would not blame them, for by God that redeemed me, the best earl in England would not deal so with my Lord and Lady as you do.

In June 1469 the King came to Norfolk on pilgrimage to Walsingham. He brought with him a large retinue, including his brother, the Duke of Gloucester, and various members of the Woodville family. The Duke of Norfolk joined him with an entourage of some 200 men, but they did not include the younger John who, after years of service to the Duke, had not this year received the gift of the Duke's livery. His attempts at 'labouring' on his brother's behalf were weakened by the developing estrangement between the King and his brother, Clarence, and the Nevilles, which prevented the King acting vigorously against the Duke of Norfolk, even had he felt so inclined.

John Paston III to Sir John Paston                                     June 1469
Norwich

To begin, God thank you for my hats. The King has been in this country and worshipfully received into Norwich . . . And as for your matters here, I have done as much as I could in labouring of them, to my Lord Rivers, Lord Scales, Sir John Woodville, Thomas Wingfield and others about the King . . . Thomas Wingfield swore to me that when [William] Brandon moved the King to show my Lord [of Norfolk] favour in his matters against you, the King replied to him: 'Brandon, you can beguile the Duke of Norfolk and bring him above the thumb [twist him around your finger] as you wish, but I let you know that you shall not do so with me, for I understand your false dealing well enough.' And he said to him also that if my Lord of Norfolk did not leave that matter, Brandon should repent it, every vein in his heart, for he told him that he knew well enough that he [Brandon] ruled my Lord of Norfolk as he wished . . .

Contrary to these matters and all the comfort that I had . . . my Uncle William says that the King told him by his own mouth, when he had ridden past the lodge in Hellesdon Warren, that he supposed that it might as well have fallen down of itself as have been pulled down, for if it had been pulled down, he said, we could have put in our petitions about it when he and the judges sat on the oyer and terminer at Norwich. My uncle says that he answered the King that you trusted to his good grace to arrange a settlement with both the Dukes; and he says that the King answered that he would neither treat nor speak for you, but would let the law proceed; and so, he says, they parted . . . Wherefore labour your matters effectually, for, by my troth, it is necessary as, for all their pleasant words, I cannot understand what good their labour in this country has done. So be not over-hasty until you are sure of your land, but labour diligently at the law, for, by my troth, until that makes progress you will get but little help.

I had at dinner at my mother's place, she being out, the Lord Scales, Sir John Woodville, Sir John Howard [fifteen others named] and others, and made them good cheer, so that they were content . . .

# Pilgrimages

*Pilgrims enjoy the hospitality of the lady of the manor on their journey home.*

The best-known pilgrims of medieval England are Chaucer's 'nine and twenty in a company of sundry folk', who met at the Tabard in Southwark on their way to Canterbury. Though few can have been so diverse as that particular company, there is plenty of evidence that pilgrims to the more distant shrines did travel in groups, partly for protection. John Paston III probably had company on his journey to Canterbury, and he certainly would have done on the sea-journey to Santiago in Spain, to which transport was often on special pilgrim ships. Margery Kempe of Lynn, one of the great fifteenth-century pilgrims, travelled in large groups to Rome and to Jerusalem – not always to her companions' satisfaction, for she frequently wept and quoted the Gospels and was told firmly to 'sit still and make merry as we do, both at meat and at supper'.

Such pilgrimages needed planning. But, in Margery Kempe's account, at least, the expense and danger was compensated for by the intensity of religious experience at places where Christ and his Disciples had walked or where their supposed relics survived. There were also indulgences to be obtained, shortening substantially the time to be spent in Purgatory by the penitent. St Peter's in Rome offered indulgences of up to 9,000 years to its visitors. Such concessions could be obtained vicariously, too, and wills not infrequently asked for a priest to be sent to Rome for the benefit of the testator's soul.

But, for most people, the great pilgrimages were impossible to undertake. They would have gone to one of hundreds of shrines in England, where saints' relics or images of the Blessed Virgin offered the chance of intercession for a soul or a miracle cure for disease or injury. Margaret Paston had pilgrimages made to Walsingham and to St Leonard's, Norwich, when her husband was ill. Fashions in pilgrimages were changing, however; by the fifteenth century Bromholm and its piece of the 'True Cross' seems to have attracted far fewer pilgrims than in earlier centuries, and Canterbury, though remaining very popular, yielded first place to the shrine of the Blessed Virgin at Walsingham in Norfolk. This was visited barefoot by the Duke of Norfolk in 1457 and by nearly all the fifteenth-century Kings. It grew very rich on the proceeds.

*These tin-lead pilgrim badges, or souvenirs, both from Walsingham, were kept as proof of pilgrimage.*

In late July King Edward was captured by Clarence and Warwick, and some of his closest followers killed, including Lord Rivers and Sir John Woodville. The country virtually dissolved into anarchy, and the preoccupations of both the King and the Nevilles encouraged the Duke of Norfolk to lay regular siege to Caister on 21 August. It was stoutly defended by a small garrison led by John Paston III. The siege dominates the Paston correspondence of the period but a number of letters also chart the progress of the relationship between Margery and Richard Calle.

---

Richard Calle to Margery Paston                                         1469

My own lady and mistress and before God very true wife, I with full sorrowful heart recommend me to you, as one that cannot be merry nor shall be, till it be otherwise with us than it is now. For this life that we lead now is no pleasure to God nor to the world, considering the great bond of matrimony that is made between us and also the great love that has been and, as I trust, is yet between us, and on my part never greater. Wherefore I beseech Almighty God to comfort us as soon as it pleases Him, for we that ought by right to be most together are most asunder. It seems a thousand years ago since I spoke with you and I had rather be with you than possess all the goods in the world. Alas, alas! good lady, those that keep us asunder remember full little what they do: four times in the year are they cursed who prevent matrimony . . .

   Also like you to know that I had sent you a letter from London by my lad, and he told me he could not speak with you, as there was so careful watch kept upon both him and you . . . Alas! What do they mean? I suppose that they think we are not contracted together, and if they do I marvel, for they are not well advised, remembering how plainly I spoke to my mistress at the beginning and, I suppose, you, too, if you did as you ought rightly to have done. If you did the contrary, as I have been informed, you did not speak according to conscience nor to the pleasure of God, unless you did it for fear and to please those who were at that time about you; and if you did it for this reason it was a reasonable cause, considering the great and importunate pressure upon you and that many an untrue tale about me was made to you, which, God knows, I was never guilty of . . .

   I marvel much that they should take this matter so hard as I understand they do, considering that it is in such a case as cannot be remedied, and my deserts are such that there should be no obstacle against it. The worship to them is not in your marriage but in their own marriage, which I beseech God send them one that may be to their worship and pleasure to God and to their heart's ease . . . I pray you let no creature see this letter. As soon as you have read it let it be burned . . .

# Courtship and Marriage

All three aspects of the fifteenth-century marriage – as a religious sacrament, a social institution and, of course, as a personal relationship – are highlighted in the Paston correspondence. The Church saw marriage as a second-best to chastity – a good and necessary institution ordained by God for the procreation of children, the avoidance of lechery and the comfort of man and woman. As Chaucer put it in the *Parson's Tale*, 'it cleanses fornication, replenishes Holy Church with good lineage and makes all one the hearts as well as the bodies of those that be wedded'. Many problems inevitably arose from this sacramental view of marriage as a life-long, indissoluble partnership. What impediments might prevent a valid marriage or might dissolve it? What was necessary to make a valid marriage? What were the duties of husband and wife to one another and what remedy was there if they were not fulfilled? Answers to such problems produced a very elaborate part of the Canon Law which was administered in the Church Courts in England. The historian, F.W. Maitland, described the rules as 'a maze of flighty fancies and misapplied logic' and it is true that parts of the law were excessively ingenious and arbitrary, though they were administered fairly humanely by the courts. Marriage was forbidden, for instance, between those related within the '4th degree', that is between those sharing a common great-great-grandparent. This would have placed an impossible restriction upon kings and nobles, who usually married within a very restricted circle of their own rank. But they sidestepped this by obtaining dispensations, at a price, from the Papacy. More frequent grounds for litigation included alleged lack of free consent (which could not finally be given by a girl until she was twelve years and a boy until he was fourteen) or pre-contract with another. This mainly arose from the rule that *verba de presenti* (words in the present tense spoken with intent, such as 'I take you for my wife') constituted a full and irrevocable marriage, even without the presence of priest or witnesses. It was around this point that the dispute about the marriage of Margery Paston and Richard Calle turned. This case shows that such a marriage had to be accepted even when it was against the will of powerful relatives, and Margaret, though angry, warned her son not to interfere.

Even clandestine marriages usually took place before witnesses, since otherwise their validity rested entirely upon the firmness and honesty of the two parties – and

*A marriage became binding when vows were made in the presence of a bishop and other witness.*

few can have had Margery's strength of character to resist family pressures and to stick to her words. When Sir William Plumpton married secretly at Knaresborough about 1450, the marriage was solemnised in the Church before the curate and several witnesses, who were able to remember years later that the groom wore a green checked garment and the bride wore red. They also recalled Plumpton's words, which were in a form not much different from the later marriage service: 'here I take thee, Jhennet, to my wedded wife, to hold and to have at bed and at board, for fairer or lather [uglier], for better for worse, in sickness and in health, to death us depart, and thereto I plight thee my troth.'

Such ceremonies were usually accompanied by large numbers of family and friends and, like baptism and burial, involved a public display that was appropriate to the status of the participants. The Paston weddings, with the exception of Margery's, were no doubt fully public, with the formal exchange of contracts at the church-door preceding the blessing by the priest and a mass. Marriage linked families as well as individuals: the spouse's parents became 'father and mother', siblings 'brother and sister', and a new set of kinship links were made.

Marriage among most sections of the population involved property. An heiress or widow could bring her land to her husband for his lifetime; where the wife had no land to bring, her relatives would provide a dowry of money and goods which would then become the property of the groom or his parents. In return they would be expected to settle on the couple a 'jointure' – lands which remained with the wife for her lifetime. In any case the wife would be entitled on her husband's death to a third of his estates for life. Thus, negotiations over a marriage, such as that between John Paston III and Margery Brews, often centred upon the exact balance of dowry and jointure and hard bargaining was probably the rule. Many marriage settlements survive and these, together with some notorious cases of the 'sale' of heirs or heiresses, provide a one-sided view of the attitudes of medieval spouses and their parents, which the Paston correspondence does something to modify. The property drive could be considerably more powerful than the sex drive in forming marriages among the upper classes. But the worst cases of child marriage and manipulation were due to the fact that when most noblemen or gentlemen died leaving a minor heir, he or she became the ward of the king or a lord, and the marriage was frequently sold

to the highest bidder. The young Anne Mowbray, heiress to the enormous estates of the Duchy of Norfolk, was married at the age of five years to the four-year-old Richard, Duke of York, in order to secure the estate for the King's second son.

The enquiries as to the wealth of potential spouses, the courting at second-hand, which Sir John did several times for his brother, and the pressures put upon daughters, sisters and wards to marry in the interests of the family, may all seem strange and cold to a modern reader. But, besides these practices, are the religious view of marriage which placed much emphasis upon mutual affection and deplored mercenary motives (however much the clergy might share these where their kin were concerned); and an aristocratic culture in which sexual and romantic love was one of the main features. 'Love' was frequently on the lips of the ladies and gentlemen of fifteenth-century England and there is no reason to believe that it was not frequently in their hearts. The young heir or heiress had little chance of choosing a partner. The older man and the widow did have. Like Edward IV and like the dowagers who married their former husband's handsome young servants, they could let their heart lead their head.

*In this scene from one of the Devonshire Tapestries, woven in Flanders between 1435 and 1450, a young man woos a noblewoman. A rather bored-looking chaperone oversees the courtship, which could not have reached this stage without the knowledge of parents and guardians and their approval of his standing in society.*

$E$arly in September the last act of the drama took place when Margery was examined before the Bishop of Norwich in the hope that her alleged marriage could be annulled: as Richard Calle had realised in the last letter, all depended upon Margery's affirming that the vital words had been said in the correct form – *verba de presenti* – by which each party used the words 'I take you as my husband/wife'.

---

Margaret Paston to Sir John Paston                              September 1469
Norwich

. . . On Thursday last my mother and I were with my Lord of Norwich, and desired him to do no more in the matter touching your sister until you and my brother and others that were executors to your father's will might be here together, for they had the rule of her as much as I. And he said plainly that he had been required so often to examine her that he might not nor would not delay it any longer, and charged me on pain of cursing [excommunication] that she should not be deferred but should appear before him the next day. And I said plainly that I would neither bring her nor send her, and then he said that he would send for her himself, and ordered that she should be at liberty to come when he sent for her . . . My mother and I informed him that we could never understand from what she said that either was bound to the other by the words she had said to him, but that both were at liberty to choose. Then he said that he would speak to her as well as he could before he examined her . . .

On Friday the Bishop sent for her . . . and spoke to her right plainly and put her in remembrance of how she was born, what kin and friends she had and that she should have more if she were ruled and guided by them; and if she did not, what rebuke and shame and loss it should be to her . . . And he said that he had heard say that she loved such a one that her friends were not pleased that she should have, and therefore he would have her right well advised how she did. And he said that he wished to know the words that she had said to him, whether they made a marriage or not. And she repeated what she had said and said boldly that if those words made it not sure, that she would make it surer before she left there, for she said that she thought in her conscience that she was bound, whatsoever the words were. These lewd words grieve me and her grandmother as much as all the rest. And then the Bishop and the Chancellor both said that neither I nor any friend of hers would receive her.

And then Calle was examined apart by himself, to see if her words and his were in accord, and the time and place where it was done. And then the Bishop said that he supposed that there might be found other things against him that might prevent it, and therefore he would not be too hasty to give sentence thereupon, and said he would hold it over until the Wednesday →

or Thursday after Michaelmas, and so it is delayed . . .

I was with my mother at her place when she was examined, and when I heard say what her demeanour had been I charged my servants that she should not be received into my house, as I had given her warning . . . I sent to one or two more that they should not receive her if she came. And she was brought again to my place but Sir James [Gloys] told those that brought her that I had charged them all that she should not be received; and so my Lord of Norwich has set her at Roger Best's to be there till the aforesaid day, God knows much against his will and his wife's, if they dared do otherwise . . .

I pray and require you not to take it too painfully, for I know it goes close to your heart, and so it does to mine and to others; but remember, as I do, that we have lost in her just a brethel [a worthless person] and set it the less to heart, for if she had been good, this would not have happened, in whatever place she had been; and if he [Calle] were dead at this hour, she would never be in my heart as she has been. As for the divorce that you write to me of, I understand what you meant, but I charge you upon my blessing that you do not nor cause anyone else to do anything that should offend God and your conscience, for if you do, God will take vengeance upon it and you would put yourself and others in great danger. For know well, she will sorely repent her lewdness hereafter, and I pray God that she might do so . . .

The Pastons eventually had to accept that they could not break off the marriage. Calle was too valuable a man to lose, and at least for a time he continued to be employed by the family. Margaret was reconciled enough before her death to leave a bequest to her daughter's children in her will.

The affair had been a distraction from the serious business of the struggle for Caister. During August and September the siege was pressed home by the Duke, in spite of the intercession of the Duke of Clarence.

Margaret Paston to Sir John Paston       12 September 1469
[Norwich]

I greet you well, letting you know that your brother and his fellowship stand in great jeopardy at Caister, and are lacking in victuals. Daubeney and Berney are dead and others badly hurt, and gunpowder and arrows are lacking. The place is badly broken down by the guns of the other party, so that, unless they have hasty help, they are likely to lose both their lives and the place, which will be the greatest rebuke to you that ever came to any gentleman, for every man in this country marvels greatly that you suffer them to be for so long in great jeopardy without help or other remedy.       →

The Duke has been more fervently set thereupon and more cruel since Writtle, my Lord of Clarence's man, was there than he was before, and he has sent for all his tenants from every place, and for others, to be there at Caister on Thursday next, so that there is likely to be the greatest multitude of people that ever yet came there. And they purpose to make a great assault, for they have sent for guns to Lynn and other places beside the sea, so that, with their great multitude of guns, with other shot and ordnance no man will dare to show himself. They will hold them so busy with their great number of people that it will not lie in our power to hold it against them without help from God or hasty succour from you.

Therefore, as you will have my blessing, I charge and require you that you see that your brother is hastily helped. And if you can have no treaty, desire writing from my Lord of Clarence, if he be in London, or else my Lord Archbishop of York, to ask the Duke of Norfolk to grant them that are in the place their lives and goods . . . And if you think, as I can suppose, that the Duke of Norfolk will not agree to this . . . then let the said messenger bring other letters from the said Lord of Clarence or else my Lord Archbishop to my Lord of Oxford, to rescue them forthwith, even if it means that my Lord of Oxford should have the place for his lifetime as a reward for his labour. I had rather you lost the livelode than their lives . . .

Do your duty now, and let me send you no more messengers about these matters . . .

$S$ir John replied at once, defending himself from his mother's criticism – a note of exasperation is clearly evident. He was actively 'labouring' potential allies in London, but his failure to achieve any positive action, his continued lack of realism about the prospects of the defenders of Caister and his constant appeals for money must have been equally exasperating to his mother and brother. Political events had, in any case, moved against the Pastons, for the Nevilles had lost control of the King and neither they, Clarence, the King nor anyone else was strong enough to bring the Duke to heel.

Sir John Paston to Margaret Paston                    15 September 1469
London

Mother, on Saturday last Daubeney and Berney were alive and merry, and I suppose that there has come no man out of the place since who could have informed you of their deaths. And, as for the fierceness of the Duke and his people since Writtle departed, I am sure that it was agreed before he left that a truce and abstinence from war should endure until Monday next, and    →

then I think that a truce will be made for another week, by which time I hope that a good conclusion will be found.

And whereas you write to me that I should sue for letters from my Lords of Clarence and York, they are not here, and if they wrote to him, as they have done twice, I know it would not avail; and as for labouring those letters and the rescue [by force] together, they are two separate things, for to prepare the rescue the cost will have to be met . . . so it is hard for me to take that course while I may do it otherwise. But they shall be rescued, if all the lands and friends that I have in England may do it and if God be friendly, and that shall be done as quickly as possible. And the greatest earthly weakness is money and some friends and neighbours to help. Wherefore I beseech you to send me comfort with what money you can find the means to get or borrow upon sufficient surety or by mortgage or even sale of livelode, and send me word in all haste as to what forces your friends and mine could get upon a short notice.

But, mother, I feel by your writing that you think of me that I would not do my duty unless you wrote to me some heavy tidings; but if I had to be woken up by a letter at this time I would be indeed too sluggish a fellow. But, mother, I assure you that I have heard ten times worse tidings since the siege began than any letter that you wrote me, and sometimes I have heard right good tidings as well. But this I can assure you, that they that are within have no worse rest than I have, nor fear more danger. But whether I had good tidings or ill, I take God to witness that I have done my duty as I would have done to me in like case, and shall do so until there be an end of the matter.

I have sent to the King at York and to the Lords [of the Council] and hope to have an answer from them by Wednesday at the latest, and I shall be ruled by that answer, and shall then send you word, for until that time I can make no plan . . . By my troth, I would rather lose the manor of Caister than the life of the simplest man therein, if that may save him. Wherefore, I beseech you to send me word what money and men that you think that I am likely to get in the country, for hasty assembly of money and men will be necessary to get and rescue Caister and the salvation of most men's lives, if we take that way.

Also this day I purpose to send to York to the King for something which may by likelihood be the salvation of all. You must remember that the rescue of it is the last resort, and that it is not easy to achieve. And you send me word that I should not come home unless I come home strong; but if I had another strong place in Norfolk to come to, even though I brought few men with me, I should, with God's grace, have rescued it by this time . . . But, mother, I beseech you, send me some money, for, by my troth, I have but 10s. and I do not know where to get more, and I have been 10 times in a similar case this last 10 weeks. I sent to Richard Calle for money, but he sends me none . . .

Sir John tried to encourage the garrison to continue to fight but after another week, low on food and munitions and with no hope of succour, John III surrendered the castle on fairly honourable terms. The second phase of the struggle for Caister had ended in defeat.

Margaret began the following letter on 22 September in reply to Sir John's of the 15th. It shows a certain asperity at the tone of her son's letter but, by the time it was finished, she knew of the surrender of Caister and she had good reason for lamenting the failure to take her advice. She implies that Sir John's own behaviour had brought down the wrath of God.

---

Margaret Paston to Sir John Paston                    22/30 September 1469
[Norwich]

I greet you well and send you God's blessing and mine, letting you know that it appears, from the letter you sent me by Robin, that you think that I am writing to you fables and imaginings, but I do not do so. I have written as I have been informed, and will continue to do so. It was reported to me that both Daubeney and Berney were dead, but for certain Daubeney is dead, God assoil his soul. I am right sorry for this and wish that God had pleased that it might have been otherwise.

Remember that you have had 2 great losses within this twelvemonth, in him and in Sir Thomas [Howes]. God . . . would that you should know Him and serve Him better than you have done before this time, and then He will send you the more grace to do well in all other things. And, for God's love, remember this well and take it patiently and thank God for his visitation; and if anything has been amiss before this, either in pride or in lavish spending or in any other thing that has offended God, amend it and pray to Him for His grace and help . . .

Item, as for money, I could get but £10 upon pledges, and that is spent on your affairs here, for paying your men that were in Caister and other things . . . And, as for my own livelode, I have received so little payment from it that I fear that I shall be fain to borrow for myself, or else to break up the household or both.

And as for the yielding of Caister, I suppose that Writtle has told you of the agreements by which it was surrendered. I would that this had been done before this time and then there would not have been so much harm done as there has been in various ways. For many of our well-wishers are put to loss for our sake . . .

I would wish that you send your brother and some other whom you trust orders to see your livelode set in order and to gather thereof what you may in haste, and also from the parts of Sir John Fastolf's livelode, which may be gathered peacefully . . .

---

# Sieges and Artillery

*'Mons Meg', built in 1449 at the request of Philip, Duke of Burgundy. It is now at Edinburgh Castle.*

The siege of Caister resembled in miniature many of those undertaken by the King's forces during the fifteenth century, with much of the theory and practice still based on Roman treatises. The techniques of the attackers included the mining of walls, trenches and shields for protection, siege-engines and moveable towers. In response, the defenders strengthened and heightened the walls, added 'crenellation' to them, dug moats and ditches all around, and devised flanking towers and barbicans at the gateways.

The development of artillery affected siege-warfare much more than it did the battlefield. Henry V's reduction of Normandy in 1417–21 and its recapture by the French in 1450–1 had owed much to the threat and use of artillery. By the 1460s some very big guns were available, such as the famous Mons Meg at Edinburgh. Improved casting methods had made accidents less frequent – although James II of Scotland was 'slain with a gun which broke in the firing' before Roxburgh in 1460. The larger guns even had their own names as well as their own ammunition: 'London' and 'Dijon', for example were among those that battered Bamburgh Castle into submission to Edward IV in June 1464.

Apart from the throwing out of defensive bulwarks – at which some of John Paston's troops were said to be skilled – and some changes in the design of fortresses, the main defensive response was to stuff the town or castle with artillery of its own. We know from an inventory of their losses, drawn up in 1470, that John had at least twenty 'serpentines', 'fowlers', 'pot-guns' and 'organ-guns' at Caister to resist the Duke of Norfolk. The Duke himself had artillery shipped round from Lynn and, although Caister was battered by his guns, the bombardment was not decisive. Caister was eventually surrendered by agreement – the normal end to most sieges in the fifteenth century. Even with the use of artillery, well-fortified and supplied towns or castles were difficult to capture, as the siege of Harlech from 1462 to 1468 illustrates. Assaults usually cost the lives of many attackers but, by the laws of war, slaughter and sacking were the fate of the defenders if the place was taken. There was, therefore, pressure on both sides for an agreed surrender once the defenders' position had deteriorated beyond a certain point. An early surrender might allow a garrison to depart with all its equipment, but, considering the political situation and the expense to which he had put the Duke, John Paston received reasonable terms at the surrender of Caister.

*Overleaf: Besiegers take cover behind shields and moveable towers, crossbows are armed, and an artilleryman positions the large gun. The defenders of the castle respond with arrows from their longbows.*

John Paston III did not engage in any recriminations when he wrote to his brother to report on the surrender.

---

John Paston III to Sir John Paston                    Late September 1469

Right worshipful sir, I recommend me to you. And as for the surrender of
Caister, John Chapman can tell you as well as myself how we were forced to
it. As for John Chapman and his fellows, I have provided that each of them
be paid 40s. and, together with the money that they had from you and
Daubeney, that is enough for the time that they have done you service. I
pray you give them thanks, for, by my troth, they have as well deserved it as
any men that ever lived; but, as for money, you need not give them any
unless you wish, for they are pleased with their wages. Writtle promised to
send you the details of the agreement. We were sore lacking in victuals,
gunpowder and men's hearts, and lack of certainty of rescue drove us to
make the treaty . . .

---

In the wake of the fall of Caister, the few surviving letters of the next six months are much
concerned with financial matters, but there are also references to a growing coldness
between the younger Pastons and their Uncle William, whom they suspected of influencing
their grandmother to settle her estates upon him. The political situation remained
confused, an apparent reconciliation between the King and the Nevilles and Clarence
failing to disguise continued enmity; the Duke of Norfolk's position remaining powerful.

Sir John remained characteristically resilient in the face of failures but the early part of
1470 brought one positive development. On 13 February 1470 Bishop Waynflete was
granted the authority to administer Sir John Fastolf's goods. Sir John and Yelverton had
agreed to accept the arbitration of the Bishop in the disputes between them, and Paston
hoped for a renewal of friendship with the Yelvertons and the isolation of the old enemy,
John Heydon. He continued to have time for marriage matters and for court-gossip.

Sir John Paston to John Paston III                    [Late February] 1470
London

. . . Item, as for Mistress Katherine Dudley, I have many times recommended you to her and she is nothing displeased with it. She does not mind how many gentlemen love her: she is full of love. I have spoken on your behalf, as I told her, without your knowledge. She answers me that she will have no-one these two years, and I believe her, for I think she has a life that she is well content with . . .

I am still offered to have Mistress Anne Haute and I shall have help enough, as some say . . .

Item, I am half intending to come home within the next month or about Mid-Lent, or before Easter, if you agree and if you think that my mother would help me with the costs – 10 marks or thereabouts. I pray you to feel out how she is disposed and send me word.

Item, I cannot tell you what will befall in the world, for the King is verily disposed to go into Lincolnshire and men do not know what will result from that nor thereafter: they say that my Lord of Norfolk will bring ten thousand men.

Item, there has arrived here a little Turk, who is a good-looking fellow of the age of 40 years; and he is shorter than Manuel by a handful and shorter than my little Tom by the shoulders, and smaller above the breast. He has, as he said to the King himself, 3 or 4 sons, children still, each one of them as tall and as handsome as the King himself. And he has good legs, and it is reported that his penis is as long as his leg.

Item, I pray you show or read to my mother such things as you think are right for her to know of, after your discretion; and let her know of the articles of the agreement between Sir William Yelverton and me . . .

I pray you always keep an eye on Caister to know the rule there, and send me word, and tell me whether my wise Lord and Lady [of Norfolk] are as besotted upon it as they were, and whether my Lord resorts there as often as he did or not, and of the disposition of the country.

J ohn III's response to this letter shows that he remained a loyal friend to his brother, but his mother's attitude was more critical and she was certainly unwilling to pay to see her eldest son again. John III felt that his mother and her chaplain, James Gloys, exaggerated their poverty. As the senior representative of the family in Norfolk, however, he felt a greater responsibility than his brother for the fate of their dependants and their reputation in the shire. He was still looking for a wife, but his Biblical justification for marriage is not very accurately remembered.

John Paston III to Sir John Paston                              1 March 1470
Norwich

. . . I have communed with my mother for your coming home, but I cannot find that she will part with any silver for your costs, for she and her curate allege more poverty than there ever was . . . Item, I pray that you will make acquittance [acknowledge that Daubeney was clear of debt to the Pastons] to the parson of Mautby and John Seyve as executors of John Daubeney, for they will not take administration of his goods until they are acquitted by you and my mother. You may well do so, God help me, for I know well that you owe him money and not he you, if he were truthful when he died, and I know well that we never found him untrue when he lived. But his friends and others of the country find great fault in me that there is nothing done for him, saying that he could do no more for us than lose his life in your service and now he is half-forgotten among us. Wherefore I pray you let this be sped . . .

   I pray you, get us a wife somewhere, for *melius est nubere in Domino quam urere* [It is better to marry in the Lord than to burn] . . .

   Item, as for our affrays here, John Pamping can tell you; but they have sworn that if they get me, you will lose a brother . . . I assure you that while our Duke is thus cherished with the King neither you nor I shall have a man unbeaten or unslain in this country, nor ourselves, neither . . . The Duke and Duchess and their council are angry that you make no approach to them yourself.

# Parsons and Chaplains

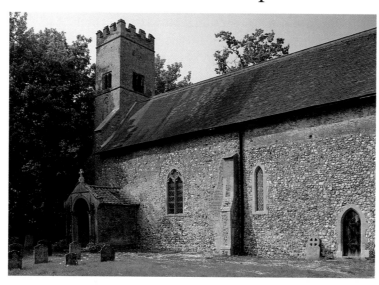

*The 'little and reasonably pleasant' Church of St Michael, Oxnead, Norfolk.*

Parsons and chaplains make frequent apearances in the Paston Letters but rarely in a spiritual role. No doubt James Gloys, for instance, said mass daily in the Paston household but it is donning his 'jack and sallet', quarrelling with John Paston III or acting as Margaret's secretary that we normally see him. Similarly, it is as an aged and sickly farmer, deprived of his horses by the Duke of Suffolk's men, that we encounter the parson of Hellesdon in the correspondence. Nevertheless, most parish priests performed their religious duties reasonably assiduously, either in person or by deputy, saying mass and the canonical hours, celebrating the main feast-days, giving some instruction and visiting the sick.

There were over 9,000 parishes in England, each with its rector or vicar, and some of the better-endowed had a number of subordinate chaplains and clerks as well. Most of these men were from the lower classes and of elementary education, though standards were rising in the fifteenth century. Each rector or vicar was 'presented' to his living by a patron, who might be the King, a bishop or abbot, or a layman. Comparatively few benefices provided a high income and, except for a sprinkling of gentlemen and university-trained 'high-flyers', the parson's standard of living was close to that of the better-off peasant or middling townsman. A description of Oxnead Rectory, when it was vacant in 1479, mentions its 'little and reasonably pleasant church', its 'well repaired parsonage', two orchards, a dovehouse and 22 acres of land. These resources, together with the tithes, brought in about £10 per annum, from which the parson had to give alms and keep part of the Church in good repair. Oxnead had the advantage of proximity to Aylsham and Norwich, and 'it is but an easy cure to keep for there are not 20 persons to be yearly houseled [given the sacraments]'. There was, therefore, plenty of time for other, more lucrative activities.

Many priests, either by choice or lack of patronage, did not have a benefice but held other less secure jobs. Some, like Gloys, accepted appointments as domestic chaplains with a variety of administrative, clerical and teaching, as well as religious, duties. Fastolf granted his domestic chaplain, Thomas Howes, the rectory of Castlecombe in Wiltshire – Howes drew the revenue but had to pay a curate to perform the duties. It was an economical way of rewarding servants and Fastolf would have liked to have done the same for William Worcester, but William had not taken Holy Orders. There were many like him who had taken the first steps into the ranks of the clergy, but had then drawn back from full commitment, perhaps because the rewards were not rich enough. Like Worcester, the poet and Privy Seal clerk, Thomas Hoccleve, settled for marriage as second best:

> *I gazed long first and waited fast*
> *After some benefice, and when none came,*
> *By process I me wedded at the last.*

In two letters sent during June, John III had mainly bad news to tell his brother. They and two of their servants had been indicted for the death of two of the besiegers of Caister and would probably have to face appeals [private prosecutions] from the two widows; John, however, hoped to use his remaining connections with the Duke's council to arrive at a settlement. Their Uncle William was clearly attempting to influence their grandmother, Agnes, to make over her estates to him, in spite of the fact that she had made a binding settlement by a 'final concord' many years previously. On the other hand, John had by now scraped together enough money to make a pilgrimage to Canterbury, perhaps to secure God's pardon, if not the Duke's, for any deaths he had been responsible for at Caister.

---

John Paston III to Sir John Paston                    25 June 1470
Norwich

As I sent you word by a letter that John Wyndham brought to London, J. Pamping is indicted of felony with Edmund Broom as principals, and you as accessory, for shooting of a gun in August last which killed two men; and I think that my Lord of Norfolk's council will have one or both of the widows bring an appeal upon the same indictment this term. Wherefore I pray you see well to this matter, so that when it is certified into the King's Bench, Broom and Pamping may have warning so that they may look after themselves if there is issued a capias [a writ ordering the seizure of the defendant] against them . . .

Also, you must in every way be prepared, for my grandmother and my Lady Anne [Beaufort, wife of William] and my Uncle William will be at London within the next 8 or 10 days, and I know well that this is for nothing else but to make my Uncle William sure of her lands. She made a fine [settlement] of them in my grandfather's days before Goodred, the Justice, and my mother tells me that you have a copy of it: I would advise you to have it ready, whatever happen . . .

This day seven-night at the latest I trust to God to be forth to Canterbury, and on Saturday come seven-night I trust to be in London; wherefore I pray you to leave word at your place in Fleet Street where I shall find you, for I purpose not to be seen in London till I have spoken with you . . .

---

Margaret Paston was clearly becoming increasingly irritated by the lack of activity of her eldest son and by her continued responsibility, particularly when John III was away, for his financial affairs.

Margaret Paston to Sir John Paston                    15 July 1470
[Norwich]

I greet you well and send you God's blessing and mine, letting you know that your farmers have brought me a great bill for repairs, which I send you, together with 60s. in money. I would have had the rest of the money from them but they said that it was in your agreement that these repairs should be done and allowed for in this payment, and so I could get no more money from them. And they say that the parson [Thomas Howes] was aware of the repairs. If you were thus agreed and will have the repairs examined you may send word, but I wish you would settle your affairs as hastily as you may, and come home and take heed to your own [property], and mine as well, otherwise than you have done before this, both for my profit and yours. Or else I shall arrange otherwise for myself in haste, in a way that, I trust, shall be more to my ease and profit and no ease nor profit to you in time to come. I have yet little help nor comfort from any of you, God give me grace to have more hereafter. I would that you should consider whether it would not be more profitable to serve me than to serve such masters as you have served before this . . . I pray God we may be in quiet and rest with our own property from henceforth. My power is not as great as I would wish it for your own sake and for others, and if it were, we should not for long be in danger. God bring us out of it, who have you in His keeping.

  Written without ease of heart the Monday next after Relic Sunday.

  By your mother.

On 14 July 1470 Sir John came to an agreement about the Fastolf lands with Bishop Waynflete. He agreed to release much of the estate to the Bishop in order to perform the will of Sir John Fastolf; in return, the Bishop recognised Sir John's rights in most of the Norfolk lands and promised to try to recover Caister, Hellesdon and Drayton, although half the value of the last two manors would go to the estate. It was the best that could be done, although it left the Pastons with an estate sadly diminished from the vast inheritance John Paston had claimed in 1459 – particularly since the main manors remained in practice with the Dukes of Norfolk and Suffolk.

The political situation, however, was changing in favour of the Pastons. The flight of Clarence and Warwick to France in April 1470 was followed in September by their return as loyal subjects of Henry VI. King Edward fled to the Netherlands. Warwick and his brother, Archbishop Neville, who was appointed Chancellor, dominated the new regime and the Pastons could certainly hope for favour from them and from their brother-in-law, the Earl of Oxford, who became all-powerful in East Anglia. Glittering prospects were opened up and the two brothers hurried to London.

---

John Paston III to Margaret Paston          12 October 1470
London

. . . Please you to know that, blessed be God, my brother and I are in good health, and I trust that we shall do right well in all our matters speedily. For my Lady of Norfolk has promised to be ruled by my Lord of Oxford in all such matters as concern my brother and me, and, as for my Lord of Oxford, he is better lord to me in many ways, by my troth, than I can wish him. For he sent about my affairs alone to my Lady of Norfolk by John Bernard and without my knowledge or any prayer from me, for when he sent to her I was at London and he at Colchester, which shows that he remembers me. The Duke and Duchess sue as humbly to him as ever I did to them . . .

As for the offices that you wrote to my brother and me for, they are not for poor men, but I trust we shall have other offices suitable for us, for my master, the Earl of Oxford, bids me ask and I shall have. I believe my brother, Sir John, shall have the constableship of Norwich Castle with £20 fee – all the lords are agreed to it.

For tidings, the Earl of Worcester is likely to die this day or tomorrow at the latest . . . The Queen that was and the Duchess of Bedford [the Queen's mother] are in sanctuary at Westminster; the Bishop of Ely, with other bishops are in St. Martins [sanctuary]. I pray God send you all your desires . . .

# The Widow's Might

However powerful her position in the fifteenth-century household, the legal status of the married woman was decidedly inferior to that of any free man. Although she was responsible for her own criminal actions, she could not enter into contracts on her own behalf; her husband was responsible for all her debts; her personal goods were her husband's property and, if she inherited any property or land, its use belonged to him; and she could make a will only with his permission.

Once widowed, however, she was in a much stronger position. Her private rights in law became the same as a man's and she had absolute rights in her own property, including the large share of her husband's goods left to her; she also had a minimum of a third of her husband's estates for life. Her position in the marriage-market suddenly became extremely strong and second – and sometimes third and fourth – marriages were common. Although widows of noblemen might have to pay the King for a licence to marry, they were much more able to follow their own desires in choosing a second husband. Sir John Heveningham may have complained bitterly to Margaret Paston about his mother's intention to marry John Wyndham in 1459, but only peaceful persuasion could be used to prevent the match. Noble widows frequently married younger men of lower rank. The outstanding example is Queen Katherine's marriage to Owen Tudor, but there are many others: the widows of each of the first two Dukes of Norfolk, for instance, married gentleman-servants of their first husband, and the widow of Lord Roos had to pay the King £1,000 in 1424 for marrying 'dishonourably' a Suffolk squire.

Many widows, such as Agnes and Margaret Paston and their friend, Elizabeth Clere, did not remarry, however – even though Elizabeth was desired by the Queen 'to have a husband'. Each preferred the independence of long years of widowhood. Agnes and Elizabeth formed part of a group of wealthy widows, also including Lady Morley and Lady Felbrigge, who lived in Norwich in the 1450s and who must have exerted a formidable influence on Norfolk society in that period. Even more formidable was Alice, Duchess of Suffolk, who remained a powerful political force for twenty-five years after her husband's murder in 1450.

By retaining so much of the family land in their hands for so long, dowagers could change the course of local and even national politics. The 3rd and 4th Dukes of Norfolk, for example, were much weakened by the fifty years during which a large part of the Mowbray estates lay in the hands of Duchess Catherine. And if Agnes had died earlier, John Paston and his sons would have been in a much better position to fight their legal battles. On the other hand, Margaret's early death might have led to the dissipation of the estates by her oldest son; a long widowhood here may well have been the saving of the Pastons' 'livelode'.

*The finely carved features of Alice de la Pole, Duchess of Suffolk, from her alabaster funeral effigy.*

John III soon returned to Norfolk where a formal visit from the Earl of Oxford was expected. Sir John stayed in London to complete the negotiations which led to the Duke of Norfolk's surrender of Caister in December, but he had advice for his brother on how best to present their case to the Earl. The Earl's visit may have coincided with the election of knights of the shire to the parliament that had been called to meet on 26 November. The election returns for this parliament do not survive and it is possible that Sir John and Richard Roos were the successful candidates, although the letter does not specifically mention the election. Heydon, though now an old man, was still seen as the main enemy.

---

Sir John Paston to John Paston III                    15 November 1470
London

Brother, I commend me to you, praying you that you act thus, if other folk will agree to the same – that Mr. Roos, old [John] Knyvett, you, and the most worshipful that will act for our sake, such as Arblaster, John Jenney, Wodehouse and all other gentlemen that will be in Norwich on that day, shall come all together as one body, so that my Lord of Oxford may understand that some strength rests therein, and if it be well handled, I believe Heydon's party will be but weak in comparison . . .

Item, be very wary of [John] Clopton, for he has advised my Lord to be altogether advised by Heydon, in so much as he has reported that all things and matters of my Lord's and in all the country should be guided by Heydon. If Clopton, or Higham or Lewis John be busy, press into my Lord before them . . . praying them not to cause my Lord to owe his favour for the pleasure of some folks there present . . . Also, if you and Mr. R[oos] could find the means to cause the Mayor to tell my Lord in his ear, though he should bind my Lord to secrecy, that the love of the country and city rest on our side, and that other folks are not beloved, nor never were, this would do no harm . . .

Brother, I pray you recommend me to my Lord of Oxford. And whereas I told my Lord that I would wait on him in Norfolk, I would give £100 to have done so, but, in good faith, those matters that I told my Lord I thought might prevent me were not finished till yesterday, and that is the reason. And also since Hallowmas every other day I might not hold my head up, nor yet may, in so much that since the said day in Westminster Hall and other places I have gone with a staff, like a ghost, as men said, more as if I rose out of the earth than out of a fair lady's bed; and I am still in the same case, though I am in hope to amend . . .

A few days later Margaret wrote to her sons that there was likely to be a challenge to the return of knights of the shire made by the sheriff, but otherwise all was well – 'all the country thinks that you should now overcome all your troubles', she wrote. Caister was, indeed, regained, and the future looked rosy, but the 'world' was soon to change again.

In March 1471 King Edward landed in Northumberland and marched on London, soon to be joined by his brother, Clarence. It was left to the Nevilles and Oxford to gather forces to resist him. Among these forces were both the older Paston brothers who, with their servants, fought at the Battle of Barnet on 14 April. Sir John reported to his mother four days later.

---

Sir John Paston to Margaret Paston          18 April 1471
London

Mother, I recommend me to you, letting you know that, blessed be God, my brother, John, is alive and fares well and is in no peril of death. Nevertheless, he is hurt with an arrow in his right arm beneath the elbow: I have sent him a surgeon who has dressed it and he tells me that he trusts that he shall be all whole in right short time. It is true that John Mylsent is dead, God have mercy on his soul! And William Mylsent is alive and it is likely that his other servants have all escaped. Item, as for me, I am in good case, blessed be God, and in no jeopardy of my life, I think, for I am at my liberty if need be.

Item, my Lord Archbishop is in the Tower. Nevertheless I trust to God he will do well enough: he has a promise of safety both for himself and me. Nevertheless, we have since been troubled, but now I understand that he has a pardon, and so we hope well.

There were killed upon the field, half a mile from Barnet on Easter Day, the Earl of Warwick, the Marquess Montagu, Sir William Tyrrell, Sir Lewis John and divers other esquires from our country, such as Godmerston and Bothe. And on King Edward's party, the Lord Cromwell, Lord Say, and Sir Humphrey Bourchier of our country, who is much lamented here, with other people of both parties to the number of more than a thousand.

As for other tidings, it is understood here that the Queen Margaret is verily landed with her son in the West Country, and I believe that tomorrow or else the next day the King Edward will depart from here towards her to drive her out again . . .

God has showed Himself marvellously like Him that made all things and can undo again when He pleases; and I can think that in all likelihood He will show Himself as marvellous again, and that in short time . . .

Item, it is so that my brother is unprovided with money. I have helped him to my power and more. Wherefore, as it pleases you, remember him, for, being in the same case, I cannot even provide for myself . . .

# Battles of the Wars of the Roses

*The Battle of Barnet, 1471, which was fought in heavy armour, gave Edward IV victory over Warwick.*

A dozen pitched battles or 'fields' were fought on English soil between 1455 and 1487, besides a number of lesser skirmishes. Very little detail is known about some of these, particularly those fought far from London, and even those which are fully described by contemporaries are difficult to interpret in terms of tactics and the reasons for success or failure. These seem fairly straightforward, however, for the first battle of the wars, which was fought at St Albans on 22 May 1455, when the King's forces, largely consisting of his own Household and the retinues of a few lords, were intercepted by a larger army led by the Duke of York and the Nevilles. The royal army was surprised from behind by Warwick's breaking through the streets; it was insufficiently organized to change face quickly and was devastated by volleys of arrows, one of which wounded the King. Abbot Whethamstede of St Albans, who was present, ascribes the victory to the fact that the King's forces were from the East of England and thus softer and less warlike than York and Warwick's men who were Northerners 'for whom wheat and barley [the expected spoils] are

like gold and ebony'. Other battles of the wars do not seem to support the idea of an inherent superiority of Northern soldiers, although their reputation as plunderers remained high.

There are no details of the fighting at Blore Heath on 23 September, when the Earl of Salisbury, on his way to join his allies in Shropshire, was intercepted in Cheshire by hastily gathered troops on whom he inflicted a bloody defeat. The encounter between the armies of the King and the Yorkists at Ludford on 12 October produced no fighting at all, as the Yorkist forces disintegrated at the sight of the 'King's banners openly displayed'. But when Salisbury, Warwick and March returned from Calais in the summer of the following year, having regrouped their forces, a decisive battle was inevitable. It took place near Northampton on 10 July 1460, when a strong loyalist defensive position was broken through the treachery of the commander of the vanguard, Lord Grey of Ruthin. The whole encounter was over in half an hour: Henry VI was captured and Warwick gave orders to slay, rather than capture, the nobility.

From this encounter on, the forces in the major battles can accurately be described as 'Lancastrian' or 'Yorkist', for the dynastic issue had been brought openly to the fore by York's claim to the throne. His attempt to suppress the Queen's army at Wakefield on 30 December 1460 was a disaster, however; York appears to have been tricked by the opposing commander, the Duke of Somerset, and both he and the Earl of Salisbury lost their lives as a consequence. A month later, on 2 February, his son, the Earl of March, defeated a Lancastrian force, mainly consisting of Welshmen, at the obscure Battle of Mortimer's Cross. In the event, this proved more decisive than the Lancastrian victory over the Earl of Warwick and an army from the south-eastern counties at the Second Battle of St Albans on 17 February. There are two lengthy contemporary accounts of this battle, although they do not always confirm each other. The Queen's army included a motley collection of Northerners and Scots, who had struck fear into the inhabitants of the towns on their route south. The southern chronicler asserts, however, that most of these men fled early in the battle, and that the field was won by the household men and retainers of the Duke of Somerset, the Earl of Northumberland and other lords of the Queen. Warwick, leading the Yorkist army, appears to have changed his position at a critical time, unaware of the proximity of the Lancastrian army, and the substantial artillery that the Yorkists possessed was unable to be brought to bear before the Queen's army was upon them. It was a long and bloody battle, ending with Warwick's flight and the recapture of King Henry by his wife's army.

Compared with St Albans, the decisive Battle of Towton on 29 March 1461 is poorly documented. The two armies were probably the largest of the entire civil wars; besides the retinues of the Nevilles, King Edward had the Duke of Norfolk and other nobles, and large contingents from the counties and towns of Southern England, who were convinced of the threat to their lives and property if the northern lords were not crushed. The battle was fought in a blinding snow storm; it lasted many hours and ended in the rout and slaughter of the Lancastrians. The death-roll was very high. Other battles of the 1460s – Hexham and Hedgeley Moor in 1464, where the Lancastrian forces in the North were finally defeated, and Edgecote in 1469, where the northern rebels allied to Warwick and Clarence defeated Edward's forces under the Earls of Devon and Pembroke – were not major encounters, though politically important.

The two battles by which Edward IV regained his throne in 1471 are more fully documented. The Battle of Barnet on 14 April, Easter Sunday, 1471 was apparently the first pitched battle in which the Paston brothers fought. Though several accounts survive, there is little precision on detail. The 'fog of war' descended quite literally on the battlefield and even the participants can have had little knowledge of what was going on more than a few yards away. Early manoeuvring apparently took place at night, which allowed Edward IV's army to approach closer than his opponent, the Earl of Warwick, realized. Consequently, Warwick's field artillery fired over the heads of the King's men and, in order to keep his position secret, Edward forbade any return of fire. At dawn, Edward attacked in a heavy mist. Neither commander realized that the right wings of the armies had both outflanked their respective opponents. The Earl of Oxford, commanding Warwick's right, and probably accompanied by John Paston III, surrounded and broke the enemy's left wing. As Oxford and his men returned from the pursuit, the badge they wore – Oxford's 'star with streams' – was mistaken by Warwick's men for the Yorkist 'sun with streams' badge. Warwick opened fire on his own side, causing Oxford's men to cry 'Treason' and flee. Meanwhile, Edward's right flank had disposed of Warwick's left and was now free to join in the attack on the centre which broke. It had been a dour and bloody fight with casualties high on both sides.

The Battle of Tewkesbury on 4 May 1471, where Edward finally disposed of the Lancastrian opposition, is described in several accounts. The Lancastrians seem to have held a strong defensive position but their vanguard was harried by superior gunfire into leaving their prepared positions in order to attack King Edward's main 'battle'. They were then attacked on the flank, which broke. Edward followed this success by a frontal attack on the main force of his enemy – already disorganized by fleeing troops from the vanguard – and rapidly destroyed all resistance.

The Battle of Bosworth in 1485, which brought the Tudor dynasty to the throne, seems to have been a more fluid encounter. The crisis arrived with Richard III's attack on Henry Tudor's main position and was resolved by the decisive intervention of the Stanleys on Henry's side. At the Battle of Stoke on 16 June 1487, where John Paston III was knighted, the large, ill-equipped Irish contingent of the Yorkist rebels finally broke under the advance of Henry VII's vanguard and exposed Lincoln and his German troops to destruction.

Three weeks later, the Pastons still hoped that Queen Margaret's forces would avenge their defeat. On 4 May, however, the Battle of Tewkesbury dashed all their hopes. By July the Duke of Norfolk had re-entered Caister and the Pastons were back to the situation that had prevailed before the 'Re-adeption', but now without possible Neville or De Vere patronage. Sir John, perhaps through his Court connections, soon had a royal warrant for a pardon, but his brother had more difficulty and was eventually indebted to the good offices of the courtier and Suffolk knight, Thomas Wingfield. Both brothers had to wait another six months before their pardons were formally sealed and during that time their position remained delicate.

---

John Paston III to Margaret Paston      17 July 1471
[London]

. . . Please you to understand that this Wednesday Sir Thomas Wingfield sent for me and let me know that the King had signed my bill of pardon which the said Sir Thomas delivered to me; and so by Friday at the latest I trust to have my pardon sealed by the Chancellor, and soon after, if I can equip myself, I trust to see you, if it happen that any of the King's Household come to Norwich . . .

 Also, if Sir Thomas Wingfield comes to Norwich, may he have as good cheer as it pleases you to make to that man that I am most beholden to for his great kindness and good will; for he fully takes my part against my greatest enemies, the Brandons and his brother, William. For at my first coming to Sir Thomas Wingfield both William Wingfield and William Brandon the younger were with him and had great words to my face, and especially William Wingfield. And wheresoever he may meet me on even ground, he says, he will do much, but if we meet evenly, no force [no worry], so long as I have your blessing.

 I pray you, let there be but few words said of this pardon, unless it be to Lady Calthorpe . . .

---

# The Earls of Oxford

*Castle Hedingham,
Essex, home of the
Earls of Oxford,
as it looked at the time
of John, the 13th Earl.*

The De Veres were one of the few noble families of the fifteenth century who were directly descended in the male line from a companion of William the Conqueror. The family had held its great castle at Hedingham in North-East Essex since the eleventh century and had been Earls of Oxford since 1142. Their involvement in Norfolk affairs and their association with the Pastons, however, derived from their acquisition by marriage of extensive estates in West Norfolk around East Winch near Lynn. The Pastons formed a series of links with the Earls; William II, in particular, became a trusted councillor of the widow of the 12th Earl who had been executed in 1462, together with his oldest son, for treason against Edward IV. His second son, John, was permitted to inherit as 13th Earl and married the sister of

the Earl of Warwick. In 1470 he rebelled with his Neville relations against Edward IV and, even after the Battle of Tewkesbury, he remained loyal to the Lancastrian cause. After an attempted invasion in 1474, he was captured and imprisoned near Calais, but in 1485 he escaped to join Henry of Richmond in Brittany and was one of Henry's chief captains at the Battle of Bosworth. After 1485 he became one of the great men of the realm, being rewarded with offices such as Lord Great Chamberlain and Lord Admiral. He was also the leading figure in East Anglia and John Paston III and his family, who were closely associated with him, benefited greatly from his patronage. He built extensively at Hedingham Castle and lived in much magnificence, with large numbers of retainers, until his death in 1513.

### THE EARLS OF OXFORD

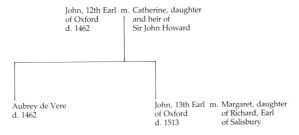

John, 12th Earl m. Catherine, daughter
of Oxford      and heir of
d. 1462        Sir John Howard

Aubrey de Vere    John, 13th Earl m. Margaret, daughter
d. 1462           of Oxford         of Richard, Earl
                  d. 1513           of Salisbury

*The family tree of the Earls of Oxford.*

207

John III must shortly after have returned to Norfolk, for it was to him and his mother that Sir John addressed a fairly optimistic letter in mid-September. He seems to have been staying in the household of Bishop Waynflete. Pestilence was raging in the towns and he was concerned for the safety of his family. John III was apparently now courting the widow of Sir Humphrey Bourchier, killed on the opposite side at Barnet. She later married the son and heir of Sir John Howard, a more suitable match for an heiress.

---

Sir John Paston to John Paston III          15 September 1471
Bishop's Waltham, Hants.

. . . I intend to be in London the first day of term: send me word whether you will be there or not . . .

Item, I would know whether you have spoken with my Lady of Norfolk or not and of her disposition and that of the household towards me and you, and whether it be possible to regain Caister and their goodwill; and also I pray you to find out how large is the company at Caister and how well it is looked after and have a spy going in and out, so that you may know the secrets among them.

There is much ado in the North, men say; I pray you to be careful of your behaviour and especially of your language, so that henceforth no man may perceive by your language that you favour any person contrary to the King's pleasure. I understand that the Lord Rivers has a licence from the King to go to Portugal now within this seven-night.

Item, I pray you send me word if any of our friends or well-willers be dead, for I fear that there is great death in Norwich and in other borough towns in Norfolk, for I assure you that it is the most universal death that ever I knew in England. For, by my troth, I hear from pilgrims that pass through the country and from other men that ride or go in any country that no borough town in England is free from that sickness; may God end it when it pleases Him. Wherefore, for God's sake, let my mother take care that my young brothers be in no place where sickness reigns, and that they do not disport with any other young people who resort where any sickness is; and if there be any dead or infected of that sickness in Norwich, for God's sake let her send them to some friend of hers in the country, and you do the same, by my advice; let my mother rather remove her whole household into the country . . .

I pray you send me word how you do with my Lady Elizabeth Bourchier. You have spoiled it a little, but I do not know how; send me word whether you are in better hope or worse . . .

Soon after, John III joined his brother in London and the first surviving letter from their brother, Edmund, was sent to him there. Edmund had been educated at Staple Inn and was looking for a job – but he was more concerned about clothes.

Edmund Paston to John Paston III                    18 November 1471
Norwich

. . . I send you now by the bringer of this some money, which I pray you bestow as I write to you . . . to Christopher Hanyngton 5s.; to the Principal of Staple Inn 5s. in part payment. Also I pray you to buy me 3 yards of purple camlet [a fine cloth], price 4s. a yard; a bonnet of deep murrey [blood-red] , price 2s.4d.; a hose-cloth of yellow kersey [a coarse, ribbed cloth] at, I think, 2s. an ell [cloth-measure of 45 in.]; a girdle of plunket [grey-blue] ribbon, price 6d.; 4 laces of silk, 2 of one colour and 2 of another, price 8d.; 3 dozen points [tying laces] with red and yellow, price 6d.; 3 pairs of pattens [footwear]. I pray you let William Mylsent purchase them. I was wont to pay but 2½d. for a pair but I pray you do not let them be left out, even if I have to pay more. They must be low pattens: let them be long enough and broad about the heel . . .

   Also, sir, I send Parker his money by the bringer hereof and I have desired him to lend me a gown of puce, and I have sent him a tippet of velvet to border it round about: and I pray you be at the choosing thereof . . .

   Also, sir, my mother greets you well and sends you God's blessing and hers, and prays you that you will buy her a runlet [cask] of malmsey . . . And if you send it home, she bids you have it wound in a canvas, to stop it being broached by the carriers, which she says she has known happen before . . .

   All the Court recommends them to you. I pray you that if you can get me any profitable service, try to do so . . . I would have a right easy service until I am out of debt . . .

Margaret remained concerned about the family's financial position and what she saw as her eldest son's failure to carry out his responsibilities. She was particularly worried about money which she had borrowed from Elizabeth Clere on Sir John's behalf and which he showed little sign of being able or willing to repay.

---

Margaret Paston the John Paston III        29 November 1471
[Norwich]

. . . I have a letter from your brother, by which I understand that he cannot nor may make provision for the 100 marks. This, with other things that he tells me he is in danger of, causes me to be right heavy. For, remembering what we have had before this and how lightly it has been spent and to little profit to any of us, and that we are now in such a case that none of us may well help another, unless we were to do what would be of great disworship for us to do – either to sell wood or land or such stuff as is necessary for us to have in our houses – so, may I answer to God, I do not know what to do for the said money and the other things that I am charged to do, while saving my worship. It is a death to me to think upon it . . .

He [Sir John] writes to me also that he has spent this term £40. It is a large sum, and I think that with discretion much of it might have been spared. Your father, God bless his soul, had as great matters to do as I believe he has had this term, and did not spend half that money on them in so little a time, and did right well. At the reverence of God, advise him still to be careful of his expenses and behaviour, so that it be not a shame to us all. It is a shame and a thing that is much spoken of in this country that your father's gravestone is not made. For God's love let it be remembered and provided for in haste. There has been much more spent in waste than would have been necessary to make that. I think, by your brother's attitude, that he is weary to write to me, and therefore I will not encumber him with writing to him. You may tell him what I write to you . . .

As for my runlet of wine, I would send you the money for it, but I dare not put it in jeopardy, there are so many thieves about. John Loveday's man was robbed down to his shirt as he came homeward. I suppose that if you ask Townshend or Playter or some other good countryman of ours to lend it to you for me till they come home, they will do so for me and I will content [recompense] them again . . .

Item, James Gresham has been passing sick and still is. Jude tells me that your brother is advised to sue him. For God's sake let no unkindness be showed to him, for that would soon make an end of him. Remember how kind and true-hearted he has been to us to the best of his power . . .

# Death with Honour

*The magnificent funerary effigy of Richard Beauchamp, Earl of Warwick.*

The splendid funeral service of the Duke of Norfolk in 1524 was concluded by a reading of the exploits of his life, possibly composed by the Duke himself for the tomb which he had had designed some years earlier. Such a practice was not uncommon. The tomb where the deceased was to await the Resurrection was a matter of great importance to him and his family. 'It is a shame', Margaret wrote to her son, 'and a thing that is much spoken of in this country that your father's gravestone is not made'. She herself described in her will the tomb which she wished to be laid over her. Elizabeth Tendring, who died in 1466, wished to have the arms of her family and her husband's inscribed on her tomb at Holbrook, Suffolk, but she also left £20 for figures of herself and her husband 'in the dress which we wore in life' to be set in brass on the marble slab. Similar requests are made by a number of gentlemen. William Hanningfield of Benacre, Suffolk, for instance, asked in 1426 for a brass representing himself, his three wives and twelve children to be made for his tomb – an early example of the representation of a whole family that was to become more common in the following century.

Many such 'brasses', and the tombs from which they have frequently been ripped, survive as some of the best known memorials of the Late Middle Ages. But the Pastons', except for one unidentifiable slab in Paston Church, have all gone. Margaret's tomb at Mautby and many others in parish churches have fallen victim to the ravages of time and, often, to the renovating or metal-hunting instincts of eighteenth- and nineteenth-century parsons and parishioners.

*Alabaster effigies of Sir Ralph Fitzherbert, who died in 1483, and his wife Elizabeth Marshall. Sir Ralph displays the Yorkist 'sunbursts' around his collar.*

211

John III returned home for Christmas, but Sir John stayed on in London, spending part of the Christmas holiday with his Aunt Elizabeth and her second husband, Sir George Browne of Betchworth, Surrey. Sir John ignored his financial problems when he sent a fairly cheerful New Year's letter to his mother. His pardon had finally been formally sealed, and prospects seemed brighter. He even had hopes of regaining Caister, although his main concern at this time was to get back the personal property which he had left at Caister and which had been seized by Norfolk's servants. He suggested that Lady Brandon, the wife of the Duke's chief councillor, might be persuaded to help.

---

Sir John Paston to Margaret Paston　　　　　　　　8 January 1472
The Moor [Herts]

. . . Please you to know that I have my pardon, as the bearer can inform you, for comfort whereof I have been the merrier this Christmas. I was for part of the time with Sir George Browne and my Lady, my aunt, his wife, and before Twelfth Night I came here to my Lord Archbishop [of York], where I have had as great cheer and been as welcome as I could wish; and if I had been sure that Caister would be regained I would have come home this day . . .

I beseech you to remind my brother to do his duty that I may have again my stuff, my books and vestments and my bedding, whatsoever he do, even though I should have to give 20 ecus by his advice to my Lady Brandon or some other good fellow . . .

As for any tidings there are none here, save that the King kept a royal Christmas. Now they say that he will hastily go to the North, but some say that he will go to Wales, others to the West Country. As for Queen Margaret, I understand that she is removed from Windsor to Wallingford, near to Ewelme, my Lady of Suffolk's place in Oxfordshire . . .

I beseech God send you good health and greater joy in this one year than you have had this seven years . . .

---

For reasons that are unkown, Sir John was by now concerned to break his relationship with Anne Haute. The consequent negotiations and process in the ecclesiastical courts were to occupy him for the rest of his life and made another marriage impossible. The following letter also refers to the sale of Sporle woods, which was to figure large in the correspondence for several years and to cause more ill-feeling between Sir John and his mother. He continued to provide Court gossip, here referring to the quarrel between the King's two brothers over the division of the inheritance of their wives, the daughters of the late Earl of Warwick.

---

Sir John Paston to John Paston III                    17 February 1472
[London]

Brother, I commend me to you and pray you to look out my Temple of Glass [a poem by John Lydgate] and send it me by the bearer hereof.

Item, as for tidings, I have spoken with Mistress Anne Haute at some length and I promised her that the next time I had leisure I would come again and see her . . .

Yesterday the King, the Queen and my Lords of Clarence and Gloucester went to the pardon at Sheen; men say that they were not all in charity with one another. What will befall, men cannot say. The King entreats my Lord of Clarence for my Lord of Gloucester; and, it is said, he answers that he [Gloucester] may have my Lady, his sister-in-law, but they will part with no livelode, as he says; so what will fall I cannot say . . . This day I purpose to see my Lady of Norfolk again, may it be in a good hour!

Buyers have offered me money for Sporle Wood. God send me a good sale when I begin: that poor wood is sore menaced and threatened.

I do not yet know whether I shall come home before Easter or not. I shall send you word . . .

The family's financial position continued to drive Margaret almost to despair and her report on happenings in East Anglia suggests that Sir John's optimism about Caister was misplaced. On the other hand, there was a chance for a good marriage for her younger daughter, Anne, although it was to be four years before this took place.

---

Margaret Paston to Sir John Paston            5 June 1472
[Norwich]

. . . It is told to me that Harry Heydon [son of John] has bought from the said Lord both Saxthorpe and Titchwell and has taken possession therein. We beat the bushes and have the loss and disworship, and other men have the birds. My Lord has false and simple counsel that advise him thereto, and, as I am told, Guton is likely soon to go the same way. As for Hellesdon and Drayton, I suppose that it is likely to stay as it is now. What shall befall the rest, God knows – I suppose as bad or worse. We bear the loss among us. It ought to be remembered and they that are at fault should bear it in their conscience. And, may I thrive, it was told me but lately that I am likely to have but little good from Mautby if the Duke of Norfolk continues to have possession of Caister: and if we lose that we lose the fairest flower of our garland . . .

As for your sister, Anne, Master Godfrey [Joye] and his wife and William Grey of Merton are agreed with me and your brother, John, if you will agree thereto and be her good brother. She shall have to her jointure his mother's livelode after the deaths of her and her husband, and I am to pay £10 a year to maintain her and her husband till £100 be paid. And if his grandsire's livelode fall to him hereafter, he has promised to improve her jointure. Master Godfrey has promised him for his part 40s. a year and so they are but 4 nobles [26s.8d.] short of 20 marks a year, which they hope that you will make up for your part. William Grey told me that he would speak with you when he came to London this term . . .

---

For most of 1472 John III and Edmund stayed with their mother in Norfolk, but they found the company of their mother and her chaplain, James Gloys, increasingly irritating – a feeling perhaps reciprocated. Gloys had been in the family's service for a quarter of a century but the three oldest Paston sons seem by this time to have regarded his influence over their mother as pernicious. Unfortunately we do not have direct evidence of Gloys's viewpoint, though he wrote some of Margaret's letters and perhaps infused them with some of his own feelings. Edmund reported that Gloys had been responsible for the dismissal of a valued servant. The incident throws a vivid light on life at Mautby.

---

Edmund Paston to John Paston III                              May [?1472]
Mautby

. . . Please you to know that my mother has caused me to put Gregory out of my service and I write to tell you the reason. He happened to have a knavish lust – in plain terms, to have a tart – and had her in the Konyne Close. He happened to be seen by two of my mother's ploughmen, who were as keen as him on the business and asked him for a share. As good companionship demanded, he did not deny them, so that the ploughmen had her all night in their stable. Gregory was quite rid of her and swears he had nothing to do with her in our mother's place. But my mother thinks he began the matter so there is no remedy but for him to go. And as you asked to have him when you were last here, if he should ever leave me, I am sending you what my mother says was the cause of his dismissal. But I am sure that the real cause is that he cannot please all parties. That gentleman [James Gloys] is his worst lord; he has said he will get rid of whoever he pleases . . . and now he has been the causer of Gregory's leaving . . . If we three [brothers] do not get rid of him may God make us never thrive and I think that is his intention. Wherefore I require you, if you will please to have him, that you will be the better master to him for my sake, for I am as sorry to part from him as any man alive from his servant, and, by my troth, as far as I know he is as true as any one alive.

---

John Paston III shared his brother's animosity to the chaplain.

John Paston III to Sir John Paston                    8 July 1472
[Norwich]

. . . Item, the proud, peevish and evil-disposed priest to us all, Sir James, says
that you commanded him to deliver the book of the Seven Sages to my
brother, Walter, and he has it . . .

Item, my mother would that you should in all haste get her acquittance
[acknowledgment she had none] from the Bishop of Winchester for Sir John
Fastolf's goods: she prayed you to make it sure by the advice of your counsel
and she will pay for the costs . . .

Item, she would that you should get yourself another house to put in your
stuff that came from Caister. She thinks one of the Friars' houses would do.
She purposes to go into the country and sojourn there once again. Many
quarrels are picked to get my brother, Edmund, and me out of her house: we
go not to bed lightly unchidden, all that we do is ill-done and all that Sir James
and Pecock do is well-done. Sir James and I are at odds. We fell out before my
mother, with 'Thou proud priest' and 'Thou proud squire', my mother taking
his side, so I have almost burned my boats as far as my mother's house is
concerned; yet summer will be over before I get me any master.

My mother proposes to make a new estate [settlement] of all her lands, and
upon that estate to make her will of the said lands: partly to give to my
younger brothers for term of their lives and after to remain to you; part to my
sister, Anne's, marriage till £100 be paid; part to make her aisle at Mautby;
and part for a priest to sing for her and my father and their ancestors. And as
a result of this anger between Sir James and me she has promised that my
part will be nought: what your part will be I cannot say. God speed the
plough! In faith you must provide for my brother, Edmund, to go over with
you [to Calais], or he is done: he will bring 20 nobles in his purse. My mother
will neither give nor lend either of you a penny henceforward. Provide a
means to have Caister again before you go over: my Lord and Lady (who for
certain is great with child) are weary of it, and all their household also.

If you wish me to do anything more in this country, send me word and I
shall do as well as I can, with God's grace, who preserve you . . .

I pray you, burn this bill, for danger of losing it.

The reference to Sir John's 'going over' relates to the new firm connection he had made with Lord Hastings. Hastings was described by Sir Thomas More as 'an honourable man, a good knight and a gentle, of great authority with his prince', though his womanising in the King's company brought enmity of the Queen and the Woodvilles. He served Edward as Chamberlain of the Household throughout his reign and his loyalty was rewarded with great estates in the Midlands and, from 1471, the command of Calais. The end of the Anne Haute marriage negotiations had presumably lost the Pastons the goodwill of the Woodvilles but Hastings, their rival, was potentially an even more powerful patron. The new relationship, and the recovery from the disasters of 1471, allowed Sir John to hope for election as knight of the shire for Norfolk to the parliament that was to meet in October 1472. His brother clearly acted as his local agent, and in September had to report failure. The letter gives an illuminating insight into attitudes to parliamentary elections in the fifteenth century. John attempted to find Sir John a borough seat and he eventually obtained one, perhaps in Cornwall, through the patronage of Lord Hastings.

---

John Paston III to Sir John Paston            21 September 1472
Norwich

Right worshipful sir, I recommend me to you, letting you know that your desire for the knights of the shire was impossible to be brought about, for my Lord of Norfolk and my Lord of Suffolk were agreed more than a fortnight ago to have Sir Robert Wingfield and Sir Richard Harcourt, but I did not know it until last Friday. Before I rode to Framlingham I had sent to as many of your friends as I could to be at Norwich this Monday to serve your intent [vote for you], but when I came to Framlingham and knew the agreement that had been made for the 2 knights I sent warning again to as many as I might to stay at home. And yet there came to Norwich this Monday as many as produced total costs of 11s.1½d., paid and reckoned by Pecock and R. Capron, and yet they did but break their fast and departed. And I thanked them in your name, and told them that you wished to have no voice this day, for you supposed that you would not be in England when the parliament would meet. So they came not to the shire-house: for if they had, it was thought by your friends here that your adversaries would have reported that you had made labour to be one of the knights and that you had failed in your purpose.

I have sent to Yarmouth, but they have promised also to Dr. Aleyn and John Russe more than three weeks ago. James Arblaster has written a letter to the Bailiff of Maldon in Essex to have you a burgess there . . .

Sir, I have twice been at Framlingham since your departure, but now, the last time, the council was there and I saw your letter, which was better than well written . . . When they had read it they showed it to my Lady . . . She →

would not speak in that matter, but remitted me again to the council, for she said that if she spoke about it before my Lord and the council were agreed, they would lay the blame on her, which would be reported to her shame: but she promised to be helpful, so long as it was first moved by the council.

Then I went to the council and offered before them your service to my Lord and to make him a gift of £40 for the having again of your place and lands in Caister, not speaking of your stuff or anything else. So they answered me that your offer was more than reasonable, and if the matter was theirs, they said, they knew what conscience would drive them to. They said they would move my Lord to it, and so they did, but then the tempest arose, and he gave them such an answer that none of them would tell me it; but when I asked an answer of them they said that if some Lords or greater men moved my Lord with it, the matter would be yours (but keep this secret) . . .

If you are not chosen burgess [MP] for Maldon you may be in another place, if my Lord Chamberlain wishes: there are a dozen towns in England which choose no burgess which ought to do, and you may be set into one of those towns if you are well befriended. Also, in no way forget to get in all haste some goodly ring, price 20s., or some pretty flower of the same price, to give to Jane Rodon [the Duchess's maid] for she has been the most special labourer in your matter and has promised her good will henceforth, and she can do anything with her mistress . . .

I ask no more goods of you for all the service that I shall do you while the world stands, but a goshawk, if any of my Lord Chamberlain's men or yours go to Calais, or if any are obtainable in London: that is a mewed [caged] hawk, for she may make you sport when you come into England for a dozen years hence: I call upon you hourly, nightly, daily, at dinner and supper for this hawk . . .

Now think of me, good lord, for if I have not a hawk I shall grow fat for lack of labour [exercise] and dead for lack of company, by my troth. No more, but I pray God send you all your desires and me my mewed goshawk in haste – or, rather than nothing – a sore [young] hawk. There is a grocer dwelling right over against the well with two buckets a little away from St. Helen's, who always has hawks to sell . . .

Rather than fail, a proved tercel [male goshawk] will occupy the time till I come to Calais.

John III continued to report on domestic strife in his mother's household, and on her anger at Sir John's mortgaging of East Beckham Manor, which was not to be recovered for thirty years. He continued to press for his hawk.

---

John Paston III to Sir John Paston                    16 October 1472
[Norwich]

. . . I send you herewith the indenture between you and [Roger] Townshend. My mother has heard of that matter through old [William] Wayte, who runs on with open mouth in his worst fashion. My mother weeps and takes on marvellously, for she says that she knows well it will never be got back; wherefore she says that she will arrange for her land so that you shall sell none of it, for she thinks that you would if it came into your hands. As for her will and all such matters as were in hand at your last being here, they think that it will not lie in our power to stop it in any point.

Sir James is ever chopping at me, when my mother is present, with such words as he thinks anger me and also cause my mother to be displeased with me – just as if to say that he would wish me to understand that he thinks nothing of the best of us. And when he has the most unfitting words to me I smile a little and tell him it is good to hear these old tales. Sir James has been made parson of Stokesby by gift of John Berney: I think he bears himself the prouder for it . . .

Item, I pray you send me some tidings how the world goes and whether you have sent any of your folks to Calais . . . and whether you have spoken anything of my going to Calais.

Item, as for a goshawk or tercel. I thought to have had one of yours in my keeping before this time, but 'far from eye, far from heart'. By my troth, I die from want of labour. If it may be by any means possible, for God's sake let one be sent me in all haste; for if it be not had by Hallowmas the season shall have passed. Remember me, and, by my troth, you shall not lose by it . . .

---

# The Sport of Kings and Country

*A group of noblemen hawking. The* Book of St Albans *tells us that Eagles were for Emperors, Peregrine Falcons for Princes and Earls, Merlins for Ladies, Goshawks for Yeomen and Sparrowhawks for Priests.*

John Paston's enthusiasm for falconry was shared by many of his contemporaries. Treatises on hawking and hunting, together with one on heraldry, make up the late-fifteenth-century *Book of St Albans*, a frequently reprinted guide to the arcane lore and terminology used in these pastimes of 'gentlemen and honest persons'. Hawking and hunting were the passions of kings and nobles: the most famous treatise on falconry was written by Emperor Frederick II of Germany and that on hunting by Gaston, Comte de Foix, and the courtly literature abounds with references to them. John was being quite modest in his request for a goshawk, since this creature came well down the hierarchy of birds of prey, which was headed by the Gerfalcon – to be owned only by a king. North Norfolk was ideal for falconry, but there were no forests in East Anglia and the Pastons make no reference to hunting, although they probably took part in hunts at the Duke of Norfolk's great deer-park at Framlingham.

Deer were also hunted with crossbows, a sport in which ladies participated. Archery with the longbow was another sport – Sir John Howard spent 6s. on 'shooting' at Chester in 1463 and lost bets on it as well (most games and sports provided an opportunity to gamble). Fishing and physical exercises, such as running and jumping, wrestling and ball-games, particularly tennis, were practised by all classes, though football – 'nothing but beastly fury and extreme violence,' as Thomas Elyot calls it – seems to have been exclusively a lower-class or schoolboy activity. Probably the most famous all-round sportsman was the young Henry VIII, for whom jousting was the supreme sport.

Many other entertainments were available in towns and in the larger villages: cock-fighting and bear-baiting were popular among all classes, and performing animals and troupes of minstrels, often employed by a nobleman, frequently toured the 'provinces'. But gentlemen's amusements were mainly made by members of their households: even without the professionals employed in the great houses, many members of the family and servants could sing, play the lute or harp and act in 'disguisings'. The great period for indoor pastimes was Christmas. Margaret Paston's advice from Lady Morley as to what games would be suitable at Christmas during the mourning for Sir John Fastolf refers to the 'disguisings, harping, luting, singing, and lewd disports' that were normal, but advises that Margaret should only permit playing at the tables [backgammon] and chess and cards. The two board-games, like dice, had long been popular; playing-cards were a newer amusement that began to replace them as a pastime for the long, badly lit winter evenings.

Sir John, with Edmund in his train, was due to go to serve at Calais, but most of the latter part of the year he lingered on in London. He was concerned that he had offended the Duchess during his visit to Norfolk during the summer.

Sir John Paston to John Paston III                    4 November 1472
London

Worshipful and well-beloved brother, I recommend me to you, letting you know that I sent you a letter and a ring with a diamond, in which letter you might understand what I would like you to do with the same ring . . .

Also, I pray you to feel out my Lady of Norfolk's disposition towards me and whether she took any displeasure at my language or mocked or disdained what I said to her at Yarmouth between the place where I first met with her and her lodging. For my Lady Brandon and Sir William also asked me what words I had to her at that time. They said my Lady said I was not polite to her and that I was supposed to have said that my Lady was worthy to have a lord's son in her belly, for she could cherish it and care for it. In truth, I did have these words, or similar, with her, and meant what I said . . . But I am also supposed to have said that my Lady was of good stature and had long and large sides, so that I was in hope that she would bear a fair child: he was not laced nor braced in to hurt him, but she left room for him to play in. They say that I said that my Lady was large and fat, and that it should have space enough to go out of. And thus, whether my Lady mocks me or they do, I know not. I meant as well, by my troth, to her and to the child she is with, as any that owes her the best will in England. If you can by any means know whether my Lady takes it to displeasure or not, or whether she thinks I mocked her, or if she thinks it but my own lewdness, I pray you send me word, for I do not know whether I may trust this Lady Brandon or not . . .

I sent you word of a hawk: I heard not from you since, I do and shall do what is possible in such a need . . .

Lord Hastings's patronage brought Sir John fully back into favour at Court, in spite of his activities in 1470-1. The King was persuaded to send one of his secretaries, William Slyfeld, to the Duke and Duchess in favour of Paston's claim to Caister.

---

Sir John Paston to Margaret and John Paston III        22 November 1472
[London]

May it please you to know that I have obtained letters from the King to my Lord of Norfolk and to my Lady of Norfolk and to their council: I have not addressed the letter to their council, because we are not certain which members of the council would be present when the letter comes. I think, therefore, that the names must be somewhat by your advice . . . The King has acted specially for me in this case, and has pity on me, and so have the Lords, and so I have right good comfort in this case, that if this fail, I shall have undelayed justice. The King has sent a man of worship and one in favour with him on this message, which has not often been seen . . . I have given him £5 for his costs: God send him good speed in his work . . .

Item, if it be thought useful, I think that, though neither Slyfeld nor you, brother John, may come into my Lady's chamber, my mother, if she were at Norwich, might speak with her, for she is a woman and of worship. I think that my mother would move my Lady well. I think that there must be somebody who has authority to settle it for me or else . . . they might make delay and say that at the King's command they were willing to commune with me, but I was not present. Wherefore, rather than fail, I will, if need be, without any delay, come home, if I hear from you . . .

Item, you may say largely on my behalf about such service that I should do for my Lord and Lady hereafter, which, by my troth, I intend to do. Nevertheless, do not say that I will be his sworn man [sworn to serve him], for I was never yet a lord's sworn man, yet I have done good service and not left any lord when he was in need . . .

Item, brother, I am agreed with my Lord that you shall be at Calais if you wish, and have three paid men under you, of whom my Lord says that William Loveday must be one until he has provided some other place for him . . . My Lord promised that he would write to Elkinhead, the Treasurer of Calais, for you by the next messenger that went . . .

This letter clearly crossed with one from John III who had already been actively lobbying at Framlingham, where the Duchess was awaiting her lying-in.

---

John Paston III to Sir John Paston                          24 November 1472
Framlingham

Right worshipful sir, I recommend me to you, thanking you most heartily for the diligence and cost which you have had in getting of the hawk which you sent me, for I know well that your labour and trouble in the matter were as much as if she had been the best in the world. But, so help me God, as far as the most cunning falconers that I have spoken with can imagine, she will never serve but to lay eggs, for she is not only a mew de haye [hedge-hawk] but also has been so bruised by bad carrying that she is as good as lame in both her legs, as every man's eye may see. Wherefore all such folk as have seen her advise me to cast her into some wood, where I shall have her for eggs. But I will do therein as you wish – whether you wish me to send her to you again or to cast her into Thorpe Wood and put a tercel with her, for I know where one is. But now I dare not put you again to the cost of a hawk, but, for God's sake, if there be any tercel or cheap goshawk that might be got, let the bearer of this have her to bring to me, and I assure you, by my troth, you shall have Dollys and Browne bound to you to pay you at Candlemas the price of a hawk. Now, if you have as many ladies as you used to have, I require you for the sake of her that you love best of them all, to trouble yourself once more for me in this matter and so be finished with my clamour.

Item, as for the ring, it is delivered, but I had as great pains to make her [Jane Rodon] take it as ever I had in such a matter. But I have promised that you will be her knight and she has promised to be more at your commandment than any knight's in England, my Lord [of Norfolk] reserved . . .

I marvel that I never heard word of the letters that my Lord Chamberlain should have sent to my Lord and my Lady for Caister . . .

Item, I think that you do wrong not to agree with my Lady of Suffolk for Hellesdon and Drayton: for money would come to you from it which would pay your debts to Roger Townshend and all others, and set you up for always . . .

Anne, the daughter and eventual heiress of the Duke and Duchess of Norfolk, was born on 10 December 1472 and a large party assembled at Framlingham for the christening. Among those attending was Bishop Waynflete, who was to baptize the baby and stand as godfather. He took the opportunity to talk to the Duchess about Caister. As one of his servants pointed out to the Duchess, the Bishop's honour was engaged in the matter as he had promised Sir John its peaceable possession. John III had recently paid a visit to his brother in London and, when he returned to Framlingham, found himself out of favour.

---

John Paston III to Sir John Paston                    18 December 1472
Framlingham

. . . Sir, as for the matter of Caister, it has been moved to my Lady's grace by the Bishop of Winchester as well as he could imagine it, considering the little leisure he had with her; and he told me that he had a right agreeable answer from her, but what the answer was he would not tell me. Then I asked him what answer I should send you, inasmuch as you made me a solicitor to his Lordship for that matter. Then he made me answer that I should send you word in confidence that her answer was more to your pleasure than to the contrary, and you shall have more full knowledge of this next term, at which time both my Lord and she shall be at London.

The Bishop came to Framlingham on Wednesday night and on Thursday by 10 of the clock before noon my young Lady was christened and named Anne. The Bishop christened it and was also godfather, and within two hours and less after the christening was done he departed towards Waltham . . .

And I tell you plainly that I am not the man I was, for I was never so rough in my master's [the Duke] opinion as I am now, and that he told me himself before Richard Southwell, Tymperley, Sir W. Brandon and twenty more; so that they that lowered now laugh upon me . . .

---

# Birth and Baptism

*A practising midwife is assisted by several ladies at the birth of a noblewoman's child.*

The rituals of birth and baptism within the Paston household probably resembled – to an appropriate degree – those of their social superiors. The Duchess of Norfolk's pregnancies were more public events, however, and Sir John Paston's ill-phrased compliments to her seem to have been regarded as discourteous rather than indelicate. Great ceremony surrounded the later stages of the pregnancy of a queen and, no doubt, of a duchess. Some four to six weeks before the birth the duchess formally 'took to her chamber', after which she was attended only by women. Female midwives, like the Elizabeth Peverel who had offered to come to Margaret in a wheelbarrow, assisted in the labour, no doubt with the help of experienced matrons such as Margaret herself. It was an anxious time for all, since the risk for both baby and mother was high. Hasty baptism was necessary, therefore – usually on or immediately after the day of birth. The priest, godparents and guests were doubtless on stand-by.

In about 1482 Sir William Stonor listed those he had chosen for his son's christening: 'to lead the child my brother Thomas and my brother Rokys; to bear the salt Thomas Lyne; to bear the basin John Doyly; to bear the gifts Edmund Romsey . . . ,' The child of a king or duke would have such ceremonies on a much grander scale: there would be a procession from the mother's chamber bearing the baby, the salt, basin, towels, tapers and perhaps the gifts from the godparents: the baby would be blessed at the font, undressed and immersed in the water (warmed, at least for royal babies) with the help of the godparents; it would then be presented at the altar for confirmation, before being led back to the mother's chamber. A great feast would follow.

Births were occasions for display and for an assertion of status. The choice of godparents could be equally important. It was usual to choose two of the baby's sex and one of the opposite sex. Although grandparents were not uncommon choices, many parents took this opportunity to strengthen or extend ties of kinship and friendship or to create a connection for the child and themselves with a powerful patron. The chief godparent usually gave the child its name, usually his or her own: John Paston II's godfather may have been his mother's uncle, John Berney. But a later letter from Margaret which asks her husband to name the coming child 'in remembrance of your brother [otherwise unknown] Henry' shows that this practice was not universal. Becoming a godparent created a spiritual kinship with the child and its parents which was seen by the Church as close enough to prevent future marriage among the parties. Margaret Paston certainly left money to her own godchildren in her will.

During the forty days after the birth, the mother remained in her chamber: after that she left it, again with ceremony befitting her station, to proceed to the ceremony of churching, which in turn was followed by more feasting. After this she resumed her normal role in the household until the next pregnancy.

There is no evidence that Margaret Paston intervened with the Duchess as her son had suggested, but she was to continue to play an active role in the affairs of the family for the rest of the decade. By January 1473, however, Norwich had ceased to be her main residence and she was living at Mautby when she wrote the following letter, probably to her chaplain and confidant, James Gloys, whom she commissioned to take her younger son, Walter, to Oxford. Why Oxford was preferred to Cambridge for Walter is not known, but Walter was to be a priest and both bishops well-known to the Pastons, Lyhert of Norwich (recently deceased) and Waynflete of Winchester, were Oxford graduates.

---

Margaret Paston to [James Gloys]                       18 January [1473]
Mautby

. . . I pray you heartily, if it be no dis-ease to you, that you will take the labour of bringing Walter to where he should be, and to provide for him that he may be set in good and sad rule. For I would be loth to lose him, for I trust to have more joy of him than I have of those that are older. Though it be more cost to me to send you with him, I hold myself pleased with it, for I know well that you will better provide for him and for such things as are necessary to him according to my intentions than another would do. And as for a horse to carry his gear, I think it would be best to obtain one at Cambridge, unless you can get any carriers to go from there to Oxford more hastily . . . And I would like Walter to be paired where he is going with someone better than Holler's son, though I would not want Walter to look down on him, for he is his countryman and neighbour. And also I pray you to write a letter in my name to Walter according to what you have known my intentions are towards him. So that he do well, learn well and be of good rule and disposition, there will be nothing lacking to him that I may help him with, so long as it is necessary to him. And bid him not to be too hasty in taking [holy] orders that would bind him, till he be 24 years of age or more, even though he is counselled to the contrary, for often 'rape rues'. I will love him better to be a good secular man than to be a lewd priest.

    And I am sorry that my cousin, [John] Berney is sick, and I pray you give him my white wine or any of my waters or any other thing that I have that is in your keeping that may do him any comfort; for I would be right sorry if anything but good should come to him. And, for God's sake, advise him to have his will made, if it be not done, and to do well to my cousin, his wife, or it would be a pity; and I pray you recommend me to her and to my aunt and to all the gentlemen and women there . . .

    And I remember that water of mint or millefleurs [a distillation of flowers] would be good for my cousin, Berney, to drink, to make him brook [digest] his food; and if they send to Dame Elizabeth Calthorpe you will not lack one or the other – she has other waters, too, to make folk brook their food . . .

# Oxford and Cambridge

Most East Anglians, such as William Worcester, saw Cambridge as their natural university. Their return from it to parsonages, schools and manor-houses in their own counties helped to create the strong regional affiliations that for some colleges were to last until modern times. John Paston I and his brothers, and his grandson, William III, certainly spent time there and so, probably, did most of the other male Pastons. John's son, Walter, was an exception in that he was sent by his mother to Oxford probably because, as a future priest, he received patronage from the Bishop of Norwich or Bishop Waynflete.

Cambridge had traditionally been the poor relation of Oxford but during the fifteenth century it was catching up, partly as a result of royal patronage, exemplified by the foundation of King's and Queen's Colleges. It has been estimated that there were some 1,600 students of all sorts at Oxford and perhaps 1,300 at Cambridge. As the population of neither town can have been above 4,000, the universities clearly dominated their hosts in numbers and also exercised considerable jurisdiction over them. The student body was undoubtedly a hazard to the local communities. It always included a good many of those who, as Oxford statutes of 1432 allege 'sleep all day and at night haunt taverns and brothels' and unruly behaviour continued through the fifteenth century. In 1441, for instance, there was a riot at Oxford when a group of southern students attacked some northerners, shouting 'Scots dogs' and fired arrows at them in their hall (the northerners got the best of the fight and went on to beat up a group of Welsh students). Such incidents explain why the authorities insisted increasingly that students live in licensed halls, if they were not members of the few colleges, which had strict discipline: the statutes of King's College, Cambridge, for example, forbade students from hunting, fishing, shooting arrows and throwing stones, owning animals, playing with dice or ball and from dancing and wrestling.

The later fifteenth and early sixteenth centuries saw a great expansion in the numbers of colleges and the size of their membership. Waynflete's foundation of Magdalen College was typical of the new fashion in making substantial provision for undergraduates and for the teaching duties of the fellows. A central function of all colleges remained the commemoration of patrons by prayers and intercessory masses; in this they resembled the many secular colleges like that proposed by Fastolf

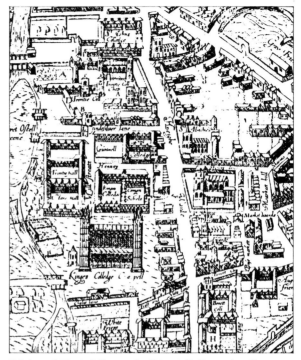

*Trinity and King's Colleges; a detail from a bird's-eye view of Cambridge engraved in 1574. The River Cam is on the left.*

for Caister. But increasingly the endowment of an institution for the better education of the clergy became seen as a pious act in itself. In 1476, for instance, Hugh Fenne, the friend of the Pastons, left, among his numerous religious bequests, £400 'for the increase of learning of good scholars in the Universities of Oxford and Cambridge'. Small sums were to be loaned to the 'poor, virtuous scholars, not vicious nor wasters nor haunters of taverns or alehouses'.

Only a minority of scholars graduated as a Bachelor of Arts after four years of study or as a Master of Arts after a further three years; the many sons of gentlemen who, like the Pastons, were by now spending time at the universities, were there to improve their general education before moving on to life on the land, at court or in the law. The universities welcomed such potentially useful connections and the statutes of Magdalen make specific provision for the sons of noblemen to be educated there at their own expense. The gentry's 'invasion' of Oxford and Cambridge had already begun.

The parliament was adjourned between the end of November 1472 and the beginning of the following February. Sir John spent part of that time in the Calais garrison but John III did not join him there. Sir John was back in London and attending the parliament when John III asked him to help remove a relative from the burdensome job of tax-collector. Sir John persuaded Richard Harcourt, knight of the shire for Norfolk, to remove Blennerhassett's name.

---

John Paston III to Sir John Paston      26 March 1473
[Norwich]

. . . Sir, my cousin, John Blennerhassett is informed that he has certainly been chosen to be one of the collectors of the tax in Norfolk, whereas in very truth he has not a foot of land in the shire. Wherefore, I beseech you that, as hastily as you may after the sight of this letter, it may please you to take the trouble to commune with Sir Richard Harcourt and to let him know that this gentleman has nothing within the shire, and that the two of you may find the means to get him out of that thankless office, for I promise you that it troubles him greatly and my mistress, his wife, and all of us, his friends, here. If it be that you and Sir R. Harcourt may not find the means between you, then may it please you to approach my Lord Chamberlain with this matter, and so Master Hassett prays you to do, and Mistress Jane, his wife, also, for she has no liking for the office . . .

---

Sir John Paston to John Paston III      2 April 1473
London

Well beloved brother, I recommend me to you, letting you know that at the request of Mistress Jane Hassett and you I have laboured the knights of the shire of Norfolk and Suffolk. I understand that there has been labour for such a thing as you wrote me of but now it is safe. Rafe Blaunderhassett is a name to start a hare. I warrant there shall come no such name in our books, nor in our house: it might, perchance, start 20 hares at once . . .

As for tidings, the worst that I heard was that my mother will not do so much for me as she assured me she would . . .

Item, of beyond the sea, it is said that the French King's host has killed the Earl [Count] of Armagnac and all his merry men . . . Furthermore men say that the French King is, with his host, upon the water of the Somme some 60 miles from Calais: I leave them where I found them . . .

After the end of the parliamentary session, Sir John returned to Calais. He was able to send some more diplomatic information, as well as news of a threat from their old master, the Earl of Oxford, who had not made his peace with the King; later that year, he was to land at St Michael's Mount in Cornwall. Sir John also had problems with his retinue.

---

Sir John Paston to John Paston III                     16 April 1473
Canterbury

. . . As for tidings, there was a truce taken at Brussels about the 16th day of March last past between the Duke of Burgundy and the King of France's ambassadors and Master William Atcliffe for the King here; this is a peace by land and water till the first day of April next, between France, England and the Duke's lands. May it hold forever, by God's grace.

Item, the Earl of Oxford was on Saturday at Dieppe and intends to sail to Scotland with about 12 ships. I mistrust that venture . . .

No more, but I have been and am troubled with my over-generous and courteous dealings with my servants, and now with their ingratitude. Platting, your man, told me this day he will bid me farewell tomorrow at Dover notwithstanding that Thurston, your other man, and John Myrell and W. Woode have gone from me; although he promised you and Daubeney, God rest his soul, at Caister, that if you would take him in again to be with me, he would never go from me; and thereupon I have kept him this 3 years to play St. George and Robin Hood and the Sheriff of Nottingham, and now when I would have a good horseman, he is gone into Barnesdale, and I am without a keeper.

Written at Canterbury on the way towards Calais . . .

Item, the most part of the soldiers that went over with Sir Robert Greene have left and have come home, so the highway is full. My carriage was 2 hours longer behind me than I expected and I thought I might have eaten suitable fare for Good Friday [i.e. fasted], all my gowns and finery having been gone, but all was safe . . .

---

$S$ir John spent the rest of 1473 commuting between London and Calais, where Edmund had become part of the garrison. John III stayed in Norfolk, except in July when he went on a pilgrimage to Santiago in Spain. Sir John wrote regularly to his brother with news of the Court and politics and with instructions for the management of his estates. Negotiations continued fruitlessly over the Caister lands and over the dissolution of the relationship with Anne Haute. Sir John finally proved his father's will (though this has not survived) but finances were still a problem and they exacerbated his relations with his mother. The death of James Gloys in October, however, was a relief to the brothers.

---

Sir John Paston to John Paston III                    22 November 1473
London

. . . I received a letter from you written about the 6th of October, in which you let me know of the decease of Sir James and that my mother is intending to be at Norwich, and I am right glad that she will now do somewhat by your advice. Wherefore beware henceforth that no such fellow creeps in between her and you, and if you like to take on a little work, you may live right well and she be pleased. It is as good that you ride with a couple of horse at her cost as that Sir James or Richard Calle should do so.

You send me word also that she in no way will provide the £100 for the redeeming of Sporle. Let it go . . . Nevertheless, if Cokett will pay £120 I would that he have it for 7 years, as long as my mother is agreeable to the same, for she has an interest in it on behalf of my brother, William, who will not be of age this 7 years. Nevertheless, as you know, my old intention was to provide for him in another place better than there . . .

You prayed me also to send you tidings how I sped in my affairs, chiefly with Mistress Anne Haute. I have answer from Rome that there is a well of grace and an ointment sufficient for such a sore, and that I may be dispensed with [i.e. the betrothal annulled]; nevertheless, my proctor [representative] there asks for a thousand ducats, which he thinks necessary. But Master Lacy, another Rome-runner [agent at the Papal Court] here, who knows my proctor there, as he says, as well as Bernard knew his shield, says that he means but a hundred ducats or two hundred at the most . . .

Item, as touching Caister, I trust to God that you will be in it to my use before Christmas be past . . .

---

# Rome and the Papacy

*Left to right: Pope Calixtus III (1455–58), Pope Paul II (1464–71) and Pope Innocent VIII (1484–92). Their papal crests are shown above.*

Rome was a place of pilgrimage and thousands, like Margery Kempe of Lynn and, later, Martin Luther, went there to pray at the shrines of what was, apart from Palestine, the holiest place in Christendom. Margery stayed at one of the hospices for English visitors – until, typically, she was forced to leave by the complaints of the other guests. But it was not just pilgrims who stayed there. The Papal 'Curia' headed both a substantial territorial state and the hierarchy of church-courts throughout Europe; consequently many visitors to Rome were there on diplomatic or legal business. Only the Pope or his senior officials could, for instance, grant dispensations to breach the elaborate rules governing marriage. Henry VII, like many other fifteenth-century noblemen, had to seek a dispensation from Rome in order to marry his kinswoman, Elizabeth of York, in 1486, and Sir John Paston needed Papal approval to extricate himself from his entanglement with Anne

Haute. His worries about the probable expense were undoubtedly justified. In order to negotiate the Papal bureaucracy successfully, you needed to employ a proctor, whose fees could be high – as could those charged by the Popes for any grants they made.

Sir John's father and grandfather had both been involved in litigation at Rome and, for most of the laity, it was practical matters such as this which provided first-hand experience of Rome and the Papacy. With Lollardy over in England and Protestantism still to come, few doubted that the Pope was the divinely ordained head of the Church. The fifteenth-century Papacy was an important legal and financial, as well as a religious, institution.

*Overleaf: Pilgrims visiting the seven churches of Rome to pray at the shrines of the saints. The engraving, by Antonio Lafrevi, was made for the 1575 papal jubilee.*

·S·MARIA· MAGIORE·

GIOVANI LATRANO.

LE SETTE CHIESE DI ROMA
Per esser uenuto lanno del santo Jubileo con:
cesso da Nostro Sig.re Gregorio XIII secondo
lantico consueto e fatto questo disegno, con il
circuito de Roma, doue si uedeno dette chiese
cauate dal naturale, et se non sono poste nel
suo luogo, ogni persona iuditiosa conoscera
depender la causa per non hauer piu spatio
Di queste sette chiese quattro sono le piuile:
giate segnate con li Santi a chi sono de:

Margaret's younger daughter, Anne, seems to have spent several years in other ladies' households. This was a normal enough practice but, in this case, it may have been intended to keep her from following her sister's example with another servant, John Pamping.

---

Sir John Paston to John Paston III               25 November 1473
London

. . . Item, I pray you take good care of my sister, Anne, lest the old love between her and Pamping renew. I pray you send me word how my mother is disposed towards her and what she would part with if a good marriage might be had.

Item, I pray you that you remind her about the tomb of my father at Bromholm and also the chapel at Mautby, and send me word how she is disposed in these matters.

Item, if I have Caister again, ask whether she will dwell there or not; I will find her a priest at my expense and give her the dovehouse and other resources there; and if any horsekeeper of mine lie there I will pay for his board as well as for the priest's . . .

---

Over the Christmas and New Year of 1473-4 Sir John visited his mother, and the tone of the letters between them seems rather more friendly thereafter. He remained optimistic about Caister, but there was little progress on that front, nor on the Anne Haute affair. John III was increasingly active in seeking a marriage for himself and Sir John acted as go-between to more than one potential bride. But the negotiations came to nothing.

---

John Paston III to Sir John Paston              25 July 1474
Norwich

. . . I pray you to remember, before you depart from London, to speak with the wife of Harry Eberton, draper, and to inform her that I am offered a marriage in London which is worth 600 marks and better, and that I prayed you to discuss it, as I might not stay in London myself, but that I insisted that if Mistress Eberton would deal with me, you should not conclude in the other place . . . because I have such an attraction towards Mistress Elizabeth Eberton . . .

Also, that it please you to speak with your apothecary, who was sometime the Earl of Warwick's apothecary, and to learn from him what the widow of Black Friars is worth and what her husband's name was . . .

---

The Eberton match continued to be mentioned for several months, but there were other possibilities. By December John III had set his sights on the probably young and certainly wealthy widow of Sir Thomas Waldegrave – but without much chance of success, in spite of Sir John's dedicated wooing on his brother's behalf .

---

Sir John Paston to John Paston III            11 December 1474
London

. . . I have, as I promised you, done my duty to know my Lady Waldegrave's attitude towards you, which, as God help me, and to be plain with you, I find in no way gives me cause for comfort. She will in no way receive nor keep your ring, even though I told her that she would in no way be bound thereby, but that I knew of old from your heart that you would be glad to give up the dearest thing in the world so that it might be daily in her presence and cause her once a day to remember you; but it would not be. She would not, as she said, put you nor keep you in any comfort thereby. And moreover, she prayed me that I should not labour further therein, for she would hold by such answer as she had given you before . . .

When I understood all this and that the previous night she had asked the woman who went between us to tell me to bring back her muskball [perfumed ball] I asked her if she were displeased with me for it, and she said, no. Then I told her that I had not sent it to you for fear my soul would be in sin . . . But now, I told her, as God help me, I would send it to you and give you advice not to hope over much on her, because she is too hard-hearted a lady for a young man to trust, but I thought that, for all my words, you could not nor would not obey.

On the other hand, she is not displeased and did not forbid me to give you the keeping of her muskball, so do with it as you like. I would that it had gone well: by God, I spoke for you in such a way that I could, in faith, not speak so well again. Wherefore I send you herewith your ring and the unhappy muskball. Make of it hereafter what you can. I am not happy to woo either for myself, nor for another . . .

Preparations were now well under way for a great royal expedition to France in alliance with the Duke of Burgundy. Such an invasion had been talked of for several years but was now clearly planned for the following summer. It was to be the biggest army sent abroad for nearly fifty years and, as it was to be led by the King himself and was intended to recapture some of the glories of the great campaigns of Henry V, a large proportion of the gentlemen of England were eager to go to win both honour and, possibly, spoils. Fitting out for such an expedition was neither cheap nor easy and the letters of the first part of 1475 contain many references to the attempts by the Pastons to acquire men, horses and equipment. Sir John had returned to Calais and did not come back to England for the last session of parliament, which had sat intermittently since 1472 and had granted taxes for the royal expedition. He preferred to visit the Duke of Burgundy's siege of Neuss, in Germany.

---

Sir John Paston to John Paston III                    17 January 1475
Calais

I recommend me to you, praying you heartily that I may know when my Lord and Lady of Norfolk will be at London, and how long they will be there, especially my Lord of Norfolk; for I will decide my action when I know when they are in London. Nevertheless, I should be sorry to go there unless I needs must . . .

For tomorrow I propose to ride into Flanders to provide myself with horse and harness, and perchance I shall see the siege of Neuss before I return, if I have time; wherefore, if I do, it will be, in all likelihood, 14 days before I am here again. And afterwards, according to what I hear from you and others about it, I propose, God willing, to come to London by the next passage. God send me good speed, chiefly for the matter above-written, and secondly to agree with the King and my Lord [Hastings] for such retinue as I should have now in these wars in France. Wherefore I pray you, commune in Norfolk and other places with those in gentlemen's houses and elsewhere who are disposed to take service and whom you think suitable for you and for me, so that we may be the more ready when the need is. Nevertheless, at this time I would be glad to have with me 3 or 4 more likely men than I have now, for I lack such numbers in my retinue. I pray you send me what tidings you hear and how my brother, Edmund, does.

As for tidings here, there are but few, save that the siege of the Duke of Burgundy before Neuss still lasts, and that the Emperor [Frederick III of Germany] has also besieged a castle not far from there occupied by the Duke's men. And also, men say, the French King has come right to the River Somme with 4000 spears [men-at-arms], and some men say that, at the day when the truce ends or before, he will set upon the Duke's country here [around Calais]. When I hear more I shall send you more tidings . . .

# The King's Armies

*Archers with protective helmets and quilted tunics, and horsemen in full armour, engage at the decisive Battle of Tewkesbury in 1470.*

'Since King Arthur's day', wrote the contemporary French observer, Philip de Commines, about the expedition of 1475, 'never king of England invaded France with so great a number of the nobility and such a formidable army.' Although he is critical of the lack of discipline of the inexperienced troops and has some caustic comments on their behaviour after the truce was concluded – 'some were singing, some were asleep and all were drunk' – there is no doubt that it was the best-prepared army to have left English shores since the reign of Henry V. Like Henry V's armies, it was composed largely of the retinues of some 200 captains who had contracted with the Crown to provide a specified number of troops. These companies varied in size from those of the Dukes of Clarence and Gloucester who each brought 120 men-at-arms and 1,000 archers, to many petty esquires and officials who brought, perhaps, three or four archers each. The Royal Household not only provided the financial and administrative control but also the largest contingent of troops: all members of the Household down to the King's physician and cook were expected to bring men. The Treasurer of the Household, who acted as war-treasurer, was also responsible for the large artillery train and the soldiers and craftsmen who serviced it.

There seem to have been at least 11,000 combat troops. Most young gentlemen, such as the Pastons, would have wanted to serve on such an expedition, led by the King in person; there was the hope of glory, the chance of finding the favour of the King or some other patron, and the reasonable possibility of spoils and ransoms. The army also contained a number of servants, 'pioneers', ancillary craftsmen and camp-followers who may have raised the total to well over 20,000. The troops were well victualled, mostly horsed, and strict rules of discipline were drawn up, though not necessarily enforced. During battle, the various contingents would have been marshalled into divisions with specified commanders, and there is no reason to doubt that they would have given a good account of themselves, even though few were experienced in fighting a continental army.

The armies of the Wars of the Roses attracted a less universal response from the gentry and were inevitably far less organized. Usually they were gathered together with little prior planning and depended heavily on the retinues of those lords who were deeply involved on one side or the other. Both Lancastrians and Yorkists, however, exploited the ancient duty of all adult men to fight in defence of the King and sought contingents from towns and counties. Norwich, for instance, sent 120 men with a captain to King Henry's army before the battle of Northampton in 1460, supplying them with some victuals and plenty of beer. County levies were more difficult to organize and John Paston's report of the Norfolk levies 'straggling about by themselves' on the way to London in March 1461 probably represents the behaviour of many groups of archers mustered to join one of the armies but with no effective leadership. In 1461, however, Edward and Warwick were able to raise large numbers of men from the South-East to fight against the dreaded Northerners and it may well be that their presence was decisive at Towton, where the opposing lords almost certainly had many retainers.

*Overleaf: Edward escapes from the Lancastrians to Calais in 1459, with the Earls of Warwick and Salisbury. The garrison there provided loyal professional soldiers for the planned Yorkist counter-attack.*

John Paston contracted to serve with three archers in the King's army; his brother, Edmund, contracted to take the same number to the Duke of Gloucester's retinue; while Sir John was with Lord Hastings's Calais contingent. One or more of the younger brothers also served in the army, as a letter from Margaret, who had reverted to her position as local agent of the family, shows. She was also very concerned about the level of taxation. When he came to the throne Edward had promised to 'live of his own', that is from traditional royal revenues, but the planned war with France needed heavy grants of personal taxes from parliament, which were supplemented by a 'benevolence', supposedly voluntary offerings from his richer subjects. In practice a mixture of threats and more subtle royal pressures virtually made it an extra tax.

---

Margaret Paston to Sir John Paston　　　　　　　　　　　　23 May 1475
Mautby

. . . I marvel that I have heard no tidings from you since you sent me the answer about the £20 for which I have laid pledges to my cousin, Clere – which letter was written the 22nd of February. And as for the money, I can get no repayment day longer than Midsummer or a fortnight after . . . By my troth, I know not what to do [for money]: the King is so hard on us in this country, both poor and rich, that I know not how we shall live unless the world amend. God amend it when it is his will. We can neither sell corn nor cattle at any good price. Malt is here at but 10d. a coomb, wheat 28d. a coomb, oats 10d. a coomb; and there is little to be got here at this time. William Pecock will send you a bill of what he has paid for you for two taxes at this time and how he has provided for the rest of your corn . . .

For God's love, if your brothers go over the sea, advise them as best you can for their safekeeping. For some of them are but young soldiers, and know full little what it means to be a soldier, and to endure as a soldier should do. God save you all, and send me good tidings of you all. And send me word in haste how you are, for I shall think it long until I hear from you . . .

---

After the anti-climax of the expedition which saw no action at all, the younger sons returned home in September, but Sir John stayed on at Calais for a time, though promising Margaret to come home, if need be, 'to be your husband and bailiff'. The King had spoken to the Duke of Norfolk about Caister, and Sir John still had hopes of a speedy settlement. But he continued to rely upon his brother's contacts in the Duke's household, and John did not let him down, though, like his brother, he had ended the campaign with a bout of illness. Sir John had returned to London and was lodging at 'The George by Paul's Wharf' when John reported on his negotiations with the Duke's council.

---

John Paston III to Sir John Paston                    10 October 1475
Norwich

. . . I have talked with Barnard and other of your well-wishers with my Lord of Norfolk, and they advise me that, for the best means of getting Caister again, you should labour to get a letter from the King to Richard Southwell, James Hobart and other of my Lord's council . . . and in the said letter to let them know that the King moved my Lord about the said matter when beyond the sea, and how my Lord answered the King that on his return into England he would consult with his council about the said matter and give the King an answer . . .

My Lady [of Norfolk] swears, and so does Barnard on her behalf, that she would be as happy for you to have it as anybody: but she did not say this to me since I came home, for I have only spoken once with her since I saw you last. She lies in Norwich and shall do until she be delivered [of her child], but I have been sick ever since I came to this side of the sea. I trust to amend soon, for all the sickness that I had at Calais and since I came over also, came only from the cold. But I was never so well armed for the war as I have now armed myself against the cold; wherefore, I advise you to take example from me, if you happen to be sick as you were when I was at Calais, in every way keep yourself warm . . .

My mother sends you God's blessing and hers, and she would fain have you at home with her: and if you are once at home, she tells me, you shall not easily depart till death do depart you . . .

# Medicine and Physicians

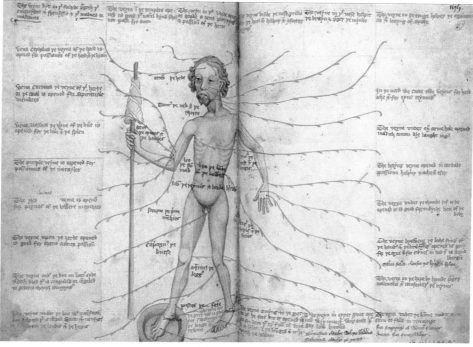

*Blood letting was a popular remedy for many ailments in the fifteenth century.*

Doctors with formal qualifications from a university were few and far-between in fifteenth-century England. And even they were often regarded as ineffective in their treatment and excessive in their charges; as Chaucer wrote ironically of his Physician 'For gold in physic is a cordial, Therefore he loved gold in special'. In 1452, when Margaret Paston's uncle, Philip Berney, was very ill, he went to stay with his sister because she lived near a good physician. But he died later 'with the greatest pain that ever I saw a man' and, by 1464, Margaret was warning her husband, 'For God's sake beware what medicines you take of any physicians of London. I shall never trust them because of your father and my uncle.'

The science of medicine, structured around the theory of 'humours' and with a strong astrological element, had advanced little in England during the Middle Ages. Bleeding was the most popular remedy and was usually applied by surgeons, educated through apprenticeship rather than at universities. If carried out at the right time – when the weather was neither too hot nor too cold and when there was no new moon – bleeding would 'clear the mind, . . . feed the blood . . . get rid of

pestilent diseases and cure pains, fevers etc.'

Many other forms of treatment were employed too. During the insanity of Henry VI, his medical advisers were licensed to bleed him as they thought best, to apply poultices of all sorts and to administer potions, laxatives and electuaries, as well as waters, syrups and confections. It was these confections that were mainly used by the numerous 'leeches', or unqualified physicians, who provided most of the medical treatment in the period, as well as by women such as Lady Calthorpe or Margery Paston. There was often an element of magic and astrology involved in these cures but also some classical learning and practical experience. Remedies in 'leech-books' of the time include some monstrosities, such as the grease from a roasted fat cat stuffed with bear and hedgehog fat and herbs, which was recommended for quinsey, but most recipes specify combinations of herbs or treacle. One recipe for 'swelling on the knee', for example, was a poultice of rue and borage mixed with honey. Perhaps it was something like this that Margery sent to James Hobart; it would have done as much good as most of the physicians' remedies.

A fortnight later John III reported that he had spoken with the Duchess: her account of her husband's conversation with the King suggested that he was still in no mood to give up Caister but the Duchess's attitude was more friendly. John was still a sick man in spite of his precautions against the cold.

John Paston III to Sir John Paston                          23 October 1475
Norwich

. . . I have spoken with my Lady since I wrote to you last; and she told me that the King had no such words about Caister as you told me, but she says that the King asked my Lord at his departure from Calais how he would deal with Caister, and my Lord answered never a word. Sir William Brandon stood by and the King asked him what my Lord [of Norfolk] would do in that matter, saying that he had commanded him before that time to move my Lord in that matter. Sir William Brandon answered the King that he had done so, and the King asked Sir W.B. what my Lord's answer was to him; and Sir W.B. told the King that my Lord's answer was that the King should as soon have his life as that place. And the King asked my Lord whether he said this or not, and my Lord said, yes. And the King said not another word, but turned his back and went away; but my Lady told me that if the King had spoken any word in the world after that to my Lord, my Lord would not have said him nay. And I have given my Lady warning that I shall do my Lord no more service, but before we parted she made me make her a promise that I should let her know before I committed myself to any other man's service. And so I departed and saw her not since, nor intend to do until I have spoken with you.

I pray you bring home some hats with you, or, if you do not come home soon, send me one, and I shall pay you a coomb of oats for it when you come home.

My mother would fain have you at Mautby: she rode there out of Norwich on Saturday last to prepare your lodging ready for your coming.

I have been right sick again since I wrote to you last, and this very day I have been quite sick: it will not shift from my stomach by any means. I am undone. I may not eat half enough when I am most hungry: I am so well fed, but yet it will not be. God send you health, for I have none 3 days together, whatever I do . . .

It is uncertain whether Sir John spent Christmas 1475 in Norfolk, but in January he was certainly at Framlingham, pursuing his case with the Duke. It was from there that he reported to his mother the sudden death of the Duke, who was still a young man – a death which was to have momentous consequences not only for the Pastons but for East Anglia as a whole. It would provide new opportunities to regain Caister, but John's immediate reaction was to ingratiate himself with the late Duke's widow and council by contributing to the elaborate funeral that was being organised.

---

Sir John Paston to Margaret Paston                    17 January 1476
[Framlingham]

Like you to know that, not at the most happy time for me, it so happened that, whereas my Lord of Norfolk was yesterday in good health, this night about midnight he died. It is now the duty of all that loved him to help in whatever may be for his honour and the welfare of his soul. And as it appears that this country is not well provided with cloth of gold for the covering of his body and the hearse, and as every man should help to the best of his power, I promised my Lord's council that I hoped to get one for that day if it has not been broken or put to other use.

   Wherefore may it please you to send me word if you have or can come by the cloth of tissue that I bought for our father's tomb, and I undertake, on my peril, that it will be returned for you unhurt. I think by this to get great thanks and great assistance in time to come. May either Syme or Mother Browne deliver it to me tomorrow by 7 of the clock . . . And within 4 days I hope to see you . . .

---

# Framlingham

*Framlingham Castle, Suffolk, the fortified residence of the Dukes of Norfolk. The Pastons, through their associations with the Mowbrays and the Howards, frequently visited Framlingham. The twelfth-century curtain wall is 44 ft (13 m) high and 8 ft (2.4 m) thick.*

By the fifteenth century, the great castle of Framlingham in North-East Suffolk had been the chief seat of the Earls and Dukes of Norfolk for three hundred years.

The curtain-wall, with its gate-tower and thirteen other towers, reflected its owner's might, enclosing the residential buildings appropriate for a great lord. On the west side was the Great Hall, with chambers for the lord and the domestic apartments; on the east was the large, richly appointed private chapel; while scattered around the rest of the walls, and in the towers and great gate-tower, were the chambers and lodgings for the servants and soldiers. Just outside the postern-gate was the 'prison tower' and within the large outer court, or bailey, surrounded by a ditch and fence, were other lodgings for servants, together with stables and domestic and farm-buildings.

When the lord was in residence, Framlingham Castle was a community of several hundred men and women, apart from the small town which lay outside its walls. It could and did act as the political focus for the whole region – a court in miniature. The Pastons came here to plead for 'good lordship', to seek redress and assistance against their enemies, to pay respects to a newly born heir or a newly adult lord, to advise the Duke and to consult with him and his council on the affairs of the region; no doubt, they hunted, too, in his great deer-park. Framlingham remained the centre of the ducal estates until the Howard dukes built their new palace at Kenninghall in the sixteenth century.

After the fall of the Howards in 1571, the castle was neglected and most of its interior buildings were pulled down in the seventeenth century.

Sir John did make a brief visit to Norwich, although it is uncertain whether he saw his mother since he was very busy in arranging to make good his claims to Caister. After he had gone, John III reported to him that his action in taking formal, though not actual, possession of Caister, which was an essential step in a future legal claim, had offended some of the Duke's council. The Duchess was pregnant and, if a son were born this time, she might be angry enough to resist Paston's occupation. Sir John justified himself in a letter sent by return of post. Interestingly, there was already a rumour that the King designed the young Anne Mowbray for his younger son; clearly this would not take effect, however, if a son were born and she ceased to be the heir.

---

Sir John Paston to John Paston III                   27 January 1476
London

. . . I have received a letter from you written on Tuesday last.

Item, whereas some who are close to my Lady of Norfolk complain that I behaved unkindly to send so hastily to Caister as I did, there is no sensible person that thinks so, for even if my Lord had been as kind to me as he might have been and behaved according to such service as my grandfather, father, yourself and myself have owed and done to past Dukes of Norfolk, and even if I had married his daughter, I must have done as I did.

And, moreover, if I had had any idea of my Lord's death 4 hours before he died it would have been foolish not to have entered in the hour before his death. Indeed, it is those that have always been hostile to me in that matter that invent that rumour against me. But no-one who was his true well-wisher or loved his soul would be sorry that I had it . . . And although it is thought that my Lady will be heavy lady to me for that deed, I think that she is too reasonable to be so, for I did not do it unbeknown to her council . . .

Item, as for my matter here, it was this day before all the lords of the Council, and among them all it was not thought that I dealt unkindly or unfittingly in sending Wheteley there immediately after the decease of the Duke, but they felt that I was unreasonably dealt with. Wherefore, let men think what they will, 'greatest clerks are not always wisest men' . . . .

Item, I pray you recommend me to my mother, and let us all pray God that he send my Lady of Norfolk a son, for upon that rests much. For if the King's son marry my Lord's daughter, the King will want his son to have a fair place in Norfolk, even though he might give me twice the value in other lands, as I am given to understand. I pray you send me word of my Lady's speeding as soon as you can . . .

Item, there is offered me a good marriage for my sister, Anne, in Skipwith of Lincolnshire's son and heir, a man of 5 or 6 hundred marks a year . . .

Before a final settlement of the Caister affair was arrived at, Sir John had to accompany Lord Hastings to Calais, from where he wrote at some length about the defeat of Charles, Duke of Burgundy by the Swiss at the Battle of Grandson: 'men told him they were hard churls [tough men] but he would not believe it'. A year later Charles was killed in battle against the same enemy.

In East Anglia, the Duchess of Norfolk's pregnancy was nearing its end and John III, who was with her household at Norwich, hoped to use his mother's expertise to soothe any offence that his brother had given the Duchess by his actions over Caister in January.

---

John Paston III to Margaret Paston                     [late March] 1476
Norwich

. . . The chief cause that I write to you at this time is because I understand that my Lady would be right glad to have you about her when she gives birth; in so much that she has questioned divers gentlewomen whether they thought that you would wait on her or not, and they answered that they dared say that you would with a right good will, await on her at that time and at all other times that she might command you. And so I think that my Lady will send for you, and if it were your pleasure to be here, I would be right glad that you should be here, for I think that your being here would do great good to my brother's matters that he has to speed here. Wherefore, for God's sake, have your horse and all your gear ready with you, wheresoever you be, out or at home, and as for men, you will not need many, for I shall come for you and wait on you myself and one or two with me. But I shall need to know where to find you, or else I shall perhaps be seeking you at Mautby when you are at Fritton, and my Lady might then chance to be far gone on her journey before you came, if she were as swift as you were once on Good Friday . . .

Also a man of the Prior of Bromholm was here with me yesterday to let me have knowledge of the evil speech which is recently in that country that the tomb is not made. And he also says that the cloth that lies over the grave is all torn and rotten and not worth 2d. and he says he has patched it once or twice. Wherefore the Prior has sent to you at the least to send there a new cloth for Easter.

---

By May Sir John had arrived back in London, and slowly and expensively was securing recognition of his title to Caister, although he still seems to have been tempted to make a sudden entry to obtain possession. Any baby the Duchess had produced, assisted or not by Margaret, did not survive, and the young Anne was to be the heiress to the great Mowbray estates. The King, however, seems to have given up the idea of acquiring Caister for his son, who was to marry Anne two years later. John III, still with the Duchess, continued to counsel caution, but he was concerned with his own marital plans, which now have an air of desperation.

---

John Paston III to Sir John Paston                     6 May 1476
Norwich

. . . To the best of my power you are welcome again into England. And as for the Castle of Sheen [Caister] there are no others in it but Colley and his mate, and a goose might take it; but I certainly would not take that course of action and my mother thinks the same. Take not that way if there be any other.

I understand that Master Fitzwalter has a sister, a maid, to marry. I think that if you entreated him, she might be given into a Christian man's hands. I pray you speak with Master Fitzwalter about it for me, and you may tell him that, since he wishes to have my service, if an agreement be made that she and I would serve him and my mistress, his wife, at our own cost, it would be as good as if I were to await upon him at his cost. For if I had such a reason to keep me at home he could be sure I would not be flitting about. If I had his goodwill, it would not be impossible to bring about.

I think to be at London within 14 days at the latest, and possibly my mistress also, but keep this to yourself . . .

---

Johan III's days of seeking a wife were soon to be over, however. Sometime in the latter part of 1476 he became acquainted with Margery, the daughter of Sir Thomas Brews of Woodbridge in Suffolk. The Brews family was an old and distinguished one, and Margery's mother was the daughter of Gilbert Debenham who, with his son, had earlier been in conflict with the Pastons. Elizabeth Brews, however, seems to have been in favour of the relationship from early on; all her help and John's determination were to be necessary to see the courtship through to a successful end. Although Margery was not an heiress, it was an ambitious match for a 32-year-old younger son with few resources of his own – though his elder brother's continued bachelor status and the entanglement with Anne Haute that prevented its changing obviously gave hope for the future. It is much the best documented of all the Paston courtships but many of the letters are difficult to date with precision. The following is probably one of the earlier in the series.

---

Dame Elizabeth Brews to John Paston III              [? late 1476]

Right worshipful cousin, I recommend me to you etc. I sent my husband a letter of the matter that you know of and he wrote another letter to me again touching the same matter. And he would that you should go to my mistress, your mother, and try if you might get the whole £20 into your hands, and then he would be more ready to marry her to you and give you a £100. And, cousin, the day she is married my father will give her 50 marks. But, if we agree, I shall give you a greater treasure, that is a witty [clever] gentlewoman, and, though I say it, both good and virtuous: for, if I should take money for her, I would not give her for £1000. But, cousin, I trust you so much that I would think she was well deserving you if you were worth much more

. . .

---

By St Valentine's day 1477 the relationship between the couple had developed fast, undoubtedly with the sympathetic help of Margery's mother, although major financial obstacles remained.

Dame Elizabeth Brews to John Paston III                    [circa 10 February] 1477

Cousin, I recommend me to you, thanking you heartily for the great cheer that you made me and all my folk the last time that I was at Norwich. And you promised me that you would not break the matter to Margery until such time as you and I were agreed. But you have made her such an advocate for you that I may never have rest night or day, for her calling and crying upon me to bring the said matter to a conclusion etc.

And, cousin, on Friday is St. Valentine's Day and every bird chooses for himself a mate; and if you like to come on Thursday at night and so arrange that you may stay till Monday, I trust to God that you shall speak to my husband, and I shall pray that we shall bring the matter to a conclusion etc. For, cousin,

'It is but a simple oak

That is cut down at the first stroke'.

For you will be reasonable, I trust to God, who have you ever in his merciful keeping etc . . .

John appears to have made the visit to the Brews's Norfolk house at Topcroft. No financial agreement was arrived at but Margery's heart was certainly won. The following letter was written by one of the Brews's clerks, but, as has been seen previously, this does not detract from the sincerity and spontaneity of the sentiments, although it is likely enough that her mother gave some advice. The verses are crude enough to be her own.

---

Margery Brews to John Paston III                               February 1477
Topcroft

Right reverent and worshipful and my right well beloved valentine, I recommend me unto you, full heartily desiring to hear of your welfare, which I beseech Almighty God long to preserve to his pleasure and to your heart's desire. And, if it please you to hear of my welfare, I am not in good health of body nor heart, nor shall be till I hear from you:

'For there knows no creature what pain I endure,
And I should rather die than dare it discover.'

And my lady, my mother, has laboured the matter to my father full diligently, but she can get no more than you know of, for which, God knows, I am full sorry. But, if you love me, as I trust verily you do, you will not leave me therefore. For, if you had not half the livelode that you have, and I had to work as hard as any woman alive might do, I would not forsake you.

'My heart me bids ever more to love you
Truly over all earthly things
And if they be never so wroth [angry],
I trust it shall be better in time coming'.

No more to you at this time, but the Holy Trinity have you in keeping. And I beseech you that this bill be not seen of any earthly creature save only yourself etc.

And this letter was written at Topcroft with full heavy heart etc.

By your own, Margery Brews.

---

Further letters exchanged between the lovers during the next few months show that the size of Margery's dowry remained the sticking point but after John III visited Topcroft again in March he was fairly optimistic about gaining concessions from Sir Thomas Brews, though, as usual, Margaret's help was needed.

---

John Paston III to Margaret Paston                    8 March 1477
Topcroft

. . . Mother, please you to know that the cause that Dame Elizabeth Brews desires to meet you at Norwich and not at Langley, as I agreed with you at my last being at Mautby, is by my suggestion, for my brother, Thomas Jermyn, who knows nothing of the matter, tells me that the causeway by which you come to Buckenham Ferry is so flooded that no-one can pass it, however well-horsed he is; which is no suitable way for you to pass over, God forbid you should try. But, all things reckoned, it will be less cost to you to be at Norwich for a day or two, and go no further, than to meet at Langley, where everything is dear. And your horse may be sent home again the same Wednesday.

Mother, I beseech you for divers causes that my sister, Anne, may come with you to Norwich. Mother, the matter is in a reasonably good state and I trust with God's mercy and with your good help, that it shall take effect better to my advantage than I told you of at Mautby; for I think there is no kinder woman living than I shall have to my mother-in-law, if the matter takes effect, nor yet a kinder father-in-law than I shall have, even though he is hard to me as yet . . .

Dame Elizabeth Brews will lie at John Cook's. If it might please you, I should be glad that she might dine in your house on Thursday, for you can talk more privately there. And, mother, for God's sake, take care that you make sure you take no cold on the way to Norwich, for it is the most perilous March that ever was seen by any man living . . .

---

On the same day Sir Thomas Brews wrote to Sir John Paston to explain some of the financial problems which obstructed the match. Both families were trying to maximise the contribution made by the other, and John III was also trying to get as much as possible from his mother and elder brother. The impression given by this and other letters, however, is that both sides were increasingly committed to the marriage but that neither wanted to seem to have the worse side of the bargain.

---

Sir Thomas Brews to Sir John Paston                    8 March 1477
Topcroft

. . . And, cousin, the cause of my writing to you at this time is that I understand from my cousin, John, your brother, that you know of the discussions touching a marriage to be concluded, with God's grace, between my cousin, your brother, and my daughter, Margery, which has been much discussed and not yet concluded, nor shall be till I hear from you of your good will and assent to the said matter and also to the obligation that I send you herewith. For, cousin, I should be sorry to see either my cousin, your brother, or my daughter driven to live so mean a life as they would do if the £120 had to be paid from their marriage-money. And, cousin, I have taken myself so near [strained myself] in paying this £120, that, whereas I had laid aside £100 for the marriage of a younger daughter of mine, I have now lent the £100 and £20 on top of that to my cousin, your brother, to be repaid by such easy days as the obligation on which I send you specifies. And, cousin, I would be right loth to bestow so much on one daughter that her other sisters should fare the worse. Wherefore, cousin, if you will that this matter should go forward in the form that my cousin, your brother, has written to you, I pray you give it your right goodwill and some of your money, as I have done of mine more generously than I purpose to do to any two of her sisters, as God knows my intent, whom I beseech to send you your dearest heart's desire . . .

Sir John, however, had had to accompany Lord Hastings to Calais, where he had been sent to strengthen the defences of the town. This was at a time when Western Europe had been thrown into turmoil by the death of Charles, Duke of Burgundy, at the hands of the Swiss on 5 January 1477. Sir John was in Calais on this occasion for two or three months, and among the letters he received were some far less serious than that of Sir Thomas Brews. Several letters from a Kentish gentleman, John Pympe, a kinsman of Anne Haute, survive: the following is a specimen of the more light-hearted, purely social letters which must have been numerous, but of which few were kept.

---

John Pympe to Sir John Paston · 16 May 1477

Honour and joy be to you, my right good master and most assured brother; letting you know that all your well-willers and servants that I know in these parts fare well and would be better if they might hear of your well-being together with some of your French and Burgundian tidings. For we in these parts are in great dread lest the French King, with some assaults, should in any way disturb you from your soft, sweet and sure slumber, but as yet we cannot hear that he disposes himself to do so.

Marry, we have heard say that the fraus of Bruges, with their high caps, have given some of you great claps, and that their feat of arms is such that they smite at the mouth and at the top end of the thigh; but, in faith, we do not worry about you, for we know that you are good enough at defence. But we hear say that they are of such courage that they give you more strokes than you give to them and that they strike sorer than you, also . . . But in one thing we much praise your sadness and discretions, that is in keeping of your truce and peace with the King of France as the King has commanded; and the reason why is that it would be too much for you to have war with all the world at once . . .

Sir, furthermore, I beseech you, if you will do anything for me, that you look one day, for my sake and your pleasure, at all the good horses in Calais, and if there be among them at any price a horse of good performance that is to sell, especially one that trots well from his own courage, without being spurred, and also if he be a mettlesome horse the better, I pray you send me word of his colour, deeds and courage, and also of his price, pretending that you wished to buy him yourself. Also, I would have him large, not among the largest but no small horse . . . I pray you above all things to have this in remembrance, and as hastily as possible . . .

I think that the Frenchmen must have taken up all the good horses in Picardy, and, anyway, they are usually heavy labouring horses, and those I love not, but a horse heavy of flesh and light of courage I love well, for I love no horse that is always lean and slender like a greyhound . . .

$S$ir John no doubt replied to Brews's letter more expeditiously than he did to those of Pympe, who complains in all his letters of having no answer. The letter to Brews does not survive, but in late March he wrote to his mother, giving his views on the marriage negotiations. Margaret had promised to make over the Mauteby manor of Sparham to the young couple, but Sir John, though approving the action, refused to ratify it formally.

Sir John Paston to Margaret Paston                    28 March 1477
Calais

Please you to know that I have received your letter, wherein you remind me of the great hurt that might befall my brother if it happen that this matter between him and Sir Thomas Brews does not take effect – for which I should be as sorry, within reason, as he himself. And you also speak of the wealthy and convenient marriage that it would be if it take effect, and I should be as glad of this as any man and am better content now that he should have her than any other that he was ever previously going to have, considering her person, her youth, and the stock that she comes from, the love on both sides, the tender favour that she has from her father and mother, the kindness of her father and mother in parting with her and the favour and good opinion that they show towards my brother, as well as the worshipful and virtuous disposition of her father and mother, which suggests that, in all likelihood, the maid will be virtuous and good . . . All which considered, together with the necessity of my brother for some support, I am not surprised that you have parted with and given him the manor of Sparham . . .

Item, another inconvenience is that I understand that the manor is given to my brother and his wife and the issue begotten between them. If it happened that they had one or more daughters and his wife died and he married another afterwards and had issue a son, that son would have no land, though his father's heir. I know of inconvenience that still exists between a gentleman and his sister in Kent in a similar case, and I would that you took the advice of your counsel in this point . . .

Item, I think that she is made sure enough of her rights in the land and I think that they should make no obstacles about my not ratifying, for I had never any rights in the land, nor do I wish to have . . .

# Calais

Two of the early series of private correspondence in English – the Cely Letters, written by a family of fifteenth-century wool-merchants, and the Lisle Letters, written by the family of the Lieutenant of Calais in the 1530s – are much concerned with the affairs of Calais. The Pastons' connection was less close, although the town was important for Sir John and his brothers during the 1470s when Lord Hastings was its Lieutenant. Calais had been captured by Edward III in 1347 and, from 1453 until its loss in 1558, it was the last surviving English possession on the Continent. Unlike other conquered French territory, Calais had been settled by Englishmen; it was a mainly English-speaking colony which comprised the town itself and about 120 square miles of the 'Pale' around it, including outlying forts such as Hammes and Guisnes. Its importance was both strategic and economic. As a fifteenth-century observer wrote, it was a 'town royal', commanding the Narrow Seas, one of the major trade-routes of Europe, allowing the free movement of armies across the Straits and acting as a listening-post and spy-centre through its relations with both France and the Netherlands. It was heavily fortified and regarded as almost impregnable, but its exposed position demanded a substantial permanent garrison, which became the main standing army paid for by the English kings during the century. Calais was thus a major factor in the Wars of the Roses and its command, first by the Earl of Warwick and then by Lord Hastings, gave its Lieutenants great power.

But the town's greatest value was economic: all exports of wool from England to Northern Europe had to be shipped to its splendid harbour. This provided not only a massively profitable trade for the 'Merchants of the Staple', who had a monopoly of wool exports, but also, through the heavy customs duties imposed, the single most important source of royal revenue for most of the century. In this way, royal and mercantile interests coincided, ensuring that any threats to its safety were met vigorously.

Calais contained the houses of many rich men as well as warehouses to collect the large quantities of wool shipped every year. It was also, a bridge to the culture and wealth of Flanders, where most of the wool was sold. From the Paston Letters we know that hawks and horses were sold there, and from the Cely Letters that lessons in dancing, singing, and playing the harp and lute were available. There were always a lot of gentlemen in the garrison, some of whom, like Sir John, travelled into the Netherlands, and it is probable that Calais was one of the routes by which the arts and fashions of the courts and towns of the Netherlands and France were brought into England.

*Edward IV lands at Calais in 1475, at the beginning of his invasion of France. The Dukes of Norfolk and Suffolk each contributed 40 men-at-arms and 300 archers to the army.*

Sir John promised to be 'kind' in the matter in a letter to John of 14 April, but when he wrote again, later in the same month, he showed an unusual degree of asperity towards his brother, while explaining why he could not accede to all his requests. After years of acting as matchmaker and courting on his younger brother's behalf, he seems piqued at not being consulted over the Brews match, even though he approved of the potential bride.

Sir John Paston to John Paston III            [April 1477]
Calais

. . . You need not ask me more often than once to do what might be done for your profit and worship . . . for I would do for you, to my power, and take as much pains for your welfare, and remember it when, perhaps, you might not even think of it yourself. I would, by my troth, be as glad that someone gave you a manor worth £20 a year as if he gave it to me myself.

Item, whereas you think that I might with conscience repay it to our family from other lands that I have of that value in fee simple, [he explains in detail why this is impossible] . . .

I need not make these excuses to you, but I know your mind is troubled. I pray you do not rejoice too much in the hope of obtaining something that all your friends may not help you get . . . Establish yourself on good ground and grace will follow. Your matter is widely spoken of but if it prove no better, I would that it had never been spoken of. Also it is rumoured that I am so unkind that I am preventing everything. I do not think any matter happy nor well-handled nor politicly dealt with, when it cannot be finished without an inconvenience; and to any such bargain I shall never be consenting or of counsel. If I were at the beginning of such a matter I should have hoped to make a better conclusion, if they do not deceive you. This matter is gone so far without my counsel, so I pray you make an end of it without my counsel. If it goes well, I should be glad; if it be otherwise, it is a pity. I pray you trouble me no more in this matter . . .

The negotiations appear to have reached a stalemate, but Margaret, possibly spontaneously or possibly at the urging of her son, tried to heal the breach by another direct meeting with Elizabeth Brews.

| | |
|---|---|
| Margaret Paston to Elizabeth Brews | 11 June 1477 |
| Mautby | |

. . . Madam, may it like you to understand that the chief cause of my writing to you at this season is this: I know well that you have not forgotten the great discussions that have been had divers times touching the marriage of my cousin, Margery, your daughter, and my son, John, of which I have been as glad, and recently as sorry, as ever I was for any marriage in my life. And where, or in whom, the fault is in causing the breach, I have no clear knowledge, but, madam, if it be in me or any of mine, I pray you assign a day when my cousin, your husband, and you think you will be at Norwich on the way to Salle [another Brews manor] and I will come there to you. And I think that, before you and I part, we shall know where the fault is and also, with your and my advice and help together, we shall take some course so that it will not break. For, if it did, it would be no honour to either party, and particularly not to those in whom the fault lies, considering that it is so widely spoken of.

And, madam, I pray you that I may have exact knowledge by my son [-in-law] Yelverton, bearer of this, when this meeting shall be, if you think it expedient, and the sooner the better in preventing worse things. For, madam, I know well that if it is not concluded in a right short time, my son intends to do right well by my cousin, Margery, and not so well by himself, and that would be no great pleasure to me nor, I trust, to you, if it so fortuned, which God forbid, Whom I beseech to send you your fondest desires.

Madam, I beseech you that I may be recommended by this bill, to my cousin, your husband, and to my cousin, Margery, to whom I supposed that by this time I should have given another name.

Sir John returned to England in June and the last two surviving letters concerning the marriage are between him and his mother. He remained in financial difficulties and complained of his inability to do more for his brother. Margaret's reply returned to the mood of some of her earlier letters to her eldest son. She was extremely critical of his financial practices in one of the stiffest of her letters.

Margaret Paston to Sir John Paston                    11 August 1477
Mautby

. . . You would have knowledge of how I would behave in Cokett's matter . . . I must leave you in no doubt that I will never pay him from my own purse a penny of what is due to him, even though he sue me for it, for I will not be compelled to pay your debts against my will, and even if I would I cannot . . .

I marvel that you have dealt so foolishly with Sporle, considering that you and your friends had so much to do to recover it previously. You have had no greater expenses than you had when it was last mortgaged, and this causes me to be in great doubt of what your disposition will be hereafter, concerning such livelode as I have been disposed to leave you after my death. For I think truly that you would be disposed hereafter to sell or mortgage the land that you should have from me, your mother, as gladly, and more gladly, as you have that which you had from your father. It grieves me to think upon your behaviour considering the great property you have had in your control since the death of your father, whom God assoil, and how foolishly it has been spent. God give you grace to be of serious and good disposition hereafter to His pleasure and to that of your friends, and to your worship and profit hereafter.

And as for your brother, William, I wish you to provide for his upkeep, for as I told you the last time that you were at home, I will no longer find for him at my cost and charge. His board and school charges are owing since St. Thomas's Day before Christmas, and he has great need of gowns and other gear that are necessary for him to have in haste. I would that you should remember and provide for them, for, as for me, I will not. I think you set but little by my blessing, and, if you did, you would have asked for it when you wrote to me. God be pleased to make you a good man . . .

Unfortunately there is no evidence of how the final obstacles to the marriage of John and Margery were removed, nor exactly when they were finally married, but the marriage took place late in 1477, and in the same year John's sister, Anne, was at last married to William Yelverton.

Sir John Paston was elected by the borough of Yarmouth to the parliament which met on 16 January 1478 – a reflection not only of his influence in the area now that Caister was recovered, but also of his standing at Court, particularly through the connection with the Lord Chamberlain. It must have been widely known that the main purpose of the parliament, which lasted for only a month, was to deal with the Duke of Clarence, who had been a prisoner in the Tower since the previous June. But for East Anglians almost as interesting was the marriage of the young Anne Mowbray to Richard, Duke of York, which took place with magnificent ceremony on 15 January. Sir John had begun legal actions in the court of Chancery against the Duke of Suffolk over Hellesdon and Drayton – apparently stirred by the Duke's cutting down and selling off the timber. John Paston III continued to act as his brother's agent in these matters, but had other things on his mind: Margery was already in the early stages of pregnancy and, in spite of the wintery weather, he had taken her to her parents' home at Woodbridge: when he wrote to his brother, they were at the house of the Pastons' old friend and agent, Thomas Playter, at Soterley in Suffolk, on the way to visit Margaret Paston at Mautby.

---

John Paston III to Sir John Paston             21 January 1478
Soterley

. . . I have communed with divers folk of the Duke of Suffolk now this Christmas and since, who let me know in secret that he is short of money. Wherefore, sir, at the reverence of God, let it not be delayed, but act now, while he is in London, and my Lady, his wife, also: for I assure you that 100 marks will do more now in their need than you shall, perhaps, do with 200 marks in time to come, if this opportunity be not taken. And always find the means that my Lady of Suffolk and Sir Robert Chamberlain may be your guides in the matter, for, as for my Lord, he need not be moved with it until it be as good as ready for the sealing . . .

And, as for tidings here, we have none, but we would fain hear of all your royalty at London, such as the marriage of my Lord of York and other parliament matter . . .

And, sir, as for my housewife, I am fain to carry her to see her father and her friends now this winter, for I think that she will be out of fashion in the summer. And so, in my progress from my father Brews to Mautby, I took in Master Playter on my way, at whose house I wrote this bill the 21st day of January, in the 17th year of King Edward IV . . .

Sir John was still entangled in the interminable negotiations to dissolve his ties with Anne Haute but, being, as one of his friends put it, 'the best chooser of a gentlewoman I know', he had not lacked for mistresses during these years.

He was still promising that he would soon make a tomb over his father's grave 'that there shall be none like it in Norfolk'. It is doubtful whether his mother was too impressed with such promises, particularly as the tomb was to be paid for by the sale of some cloth of gold – probably that which had been removed from his father's tomb for the funeral of the Duke of Norfolk and which had since been used as pledge for a loan. Margaret had now redeemed it for 20 marks and hoped that it would be used as her son had promised. But Sir John remained very occupied during 1478 with Hellesdon and Drayton. The Duke of Suffolk clearly remained adamant against making any concessions and Sir John's servant, John Whetley, wrote scornfully of his behaviour at a recent visit to Hellesdon.

| John Whetley to Sir John Paston | 20 May 1478 |
| Norwich | |

. . . As for Drayton Wood, it is not all down yet, but it is fast drawing towards finishing . . . And as for Hellesdon, my Lord of Suffolk was there on Wednesday in Whitsun Week and dined there and netted a great number of fish from the stew [fish-pond]. But he has left you a pike or two, if you come again, which would be great comfort to all your friends and discomfiture to your enemies. For at his being there that day, there was never a man who played Herod in a Corpus Christi Play better and more in character than he did. You should understand that it was afternoon and the weather hot, and he so feeble for sickness that his legs would not bear him, but two men had great pains to keep him on his feet. And there were you judged. Some said 'slay'; some said 'put him in prison'. And forth came my Lord, and he would meet you with a spear and have no other amends for the trouble that you have put him to but your heart's blood and that he would get with his own hands – for you will not have Hellesdon and Drayton while he lives. And so he comforted your enemies who have dealed and still deal with the wood, the principal of whom is now Nicholas Ovy . . .

And so my Lord has set in there the bailiff of Costessey and all is done in his name. And, as for his servants, they daily threaten to slay my master, your brother, and me for coming on their lord's ground . . .

And as for my mistress, your mother, she has been very sick, so sick that she thought she would die and she has made her will, which you shall hear about more when I come, for there is every man for himself. I do not know all the details as yet, and therefore I write no more to you of this, but I am promised that I shall know before I depart . . .

When Whetley left for London he took the cloth of gold with him. Margaret felt she had to remind her son, as so often before, of his responsibilities, but she was pleased that he was in favour with the King and hoped that rumours of a good marriage were true. This is, unfortunately, the last of Margaret Paston's letters to survive, though she lived for another six years. Appropriately it contains the same mixture of family feeling, practical advice and exhortation that had characterised so many of her letters over the previous thirty years.

Margaret Paston to Sir John Paston                     27 May 1478
Mautby

I greet you well and send you God's blessing and mine, letting you know that I have sent you by Whetley the cloth of gold, charging you that it be sold to no other use than to the making of your father's tomb, as you should send me word in writing. If you sell it for any other purpose, by my troth, I shall never trust you while I live. Remember that it cost me 20 marks to redeem it and if I did not want to see the tomb made I would not part with it. Remember what expense I have had with you of late, which will harm me for two years: when you are in better state I trust you will remember this.

My cousin, [Robert] Clere is spending up to £100 at Bromholm upon the desks in the choir and in other places, and Heydon similarly, and if nothing should be done for your father it would be too great a shame for us all, especially to see him lie as he does.

Also, as I understand, my cousin, Robert Clere, thinks you and Pecock have dealt very unkindly with him . . . I think that this dealing is not as it should be. I would that each of you should help the other and live as kinsmen and friends; for such servants may make trouble between you, which is not courteous, you being such near neighbours and he a man of substance and worship, and so will be taken in this shire. I should be loth that you should lose the goodwill of such as may be able to help you.

Item, whereas you have begun your claim to Hellesdon and Drayton, I pray God send you good speed and furtherance in it. You have as good an opportunity as you could wish, considering that your adversary does not stand in best favour with the King. Also, it is said in this country that you may do as much with the King as any knight that belongs to the Court: if it be so, I pray God let it continue. It is also said that you are to marry right near to the Queen's blood. Who she is we are not certain, but if it be so that your land may be returned and set at rest by reason of your marriage at the reverence of God forsake it not if you can find it in your heart to love her, and if she be such a one as you can have issue by – otherwise, by my troth, I had rather you never married in your life . . .

The youngest of Margaret's sons, William, now about twenty years old, was near the end of his time at Eton. He was already concerned with the inevitable search for a bride, though in the event he was never to marry.

---

William Paston III to Sir John Paston          23 February 1479
Eton

. . . letting you know that I received a letter from you in which letter was 8d., with which I was to buy a pair of slippers. Furthermore, the 13s.4d. which you sent by a gentleman's man called Thomas Newton for my board, was delivered to my hostess and so to my creancer [tutor], Master Thomas Stevenson, and he heartily recommends himself to you.

Also you sent me word in the letter of 12 pounds of figs and 8 pounds of raisins. These have not been delivered as yet, but I doubt not [that they] will be, for Alwedyr told me about them and he said they came on afterwards in another barge [up the Thames from London].

As for the young gentlewoman, I shall certify you how I first fell into acquaintance with her. Her father is dead. There are two sisters, and I was present with my hostess at the wedding of the elder, also being invited by the gentleman himself, called William Swan, whose dwelling is in Eton. It so happened that my hostess reported about me better than I was worth, so that the mother commanded her [the daughter] to make me good cheer and so, in good faith, she did. She does not live where she is now, as her dwelling is in London, but her mother and she came to a place of hers 5 miles from Eton, where the wedding was, because it was near to the gentleman who married her daughter. And on Monday next coming . . . her mother and she will go to the pardon at Sheen and so forth to London, there to abide in a place of hers in Bow Churchyard.

And if it please you to inquire of her, her mother's name is Mistress Alborow. Her daughter's name is Margaret Alborow, and she is probably about 18 or 19 years at the most. And as for the money and plate, it is ready whenever she marries, but as for the livelode, I believe not until after her mother's death – I cannot tell you for certain, but you may find out by inquiring. And as for her beauty, judge that when you see her, if you take the trouble to do so; and especially look at her hands, for, if I am told correctly, she is inclined to be fat.

And, as for my leaving Eton, I lack nothing but versifying, which I trust to have with a little more time . . .

    'Arbore iam videas exemplum. Non die possunt
    Omnia suppleri; sed tamen ille mora.'
[You should take example from a tree. All things may not be fulfilled in a day, but only gradually.]
    And these two verses aforesaid are of my own making . . .

# The Poor Scholars of Eton

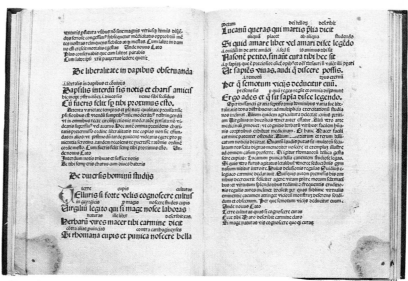

*Pages from the popular school-book,* Cato, *a series of Latin verses on civilized behaviour.*

In the Middle Ages schools were under the supervision of the church although, by the fifteenth century, most of the students would remain as laymen rather than embark on a clerical career. In the 'song schools', boys of up to ten years old would be taught elementary reading and the ability to sing the services of the Church; they might then proceed to 'grammar schools' and next to the 'schools' of the universities. Less is known about the numerous private schools which taught the practical skills of reading and writing in English, some elementary Latin and how to keep accounts. In fifteenth-century Norfolk at least a dozen places are known to have possessed schools, apart from the ancient grammar school in Norwich: these included Aylsham and, probably, North Walsham, so it is likely that the young Pastons spent some time at one of these. Sons of such gentlemen as the 2nd Earl of Suffolk and John Hopton of Blythburgh are known to have attended local schools.

Because a royal licence was necessary for their endowment, more is known about the newly-founded schools, which were often associated with a college or chantry. The greatest of these foundations was Eton College, which had been richly endowed by Henry VI. Although suffering from the fall of its patron, the school had largely recovered its standing and wealth by the time that the young William Paston went there in the late

1470s. Eton was a religious college with a provost, fellows, clerks and choristers for divine service, but the Master and twenty-five poor scholars were an important feature of the foundation. Other students included the fee-paying sons of gentlemen. William was clearly one of these but, although the status brought some privileges, he probably shared much of the austere life and discipline of the scholars, who rose at 5 a.m. and began a working day which lasted, with breaks for meals and divine service, until 5 p.m. Learning and discipline at Eton were enforced through the birch – 'The birch twigs are so sharp, It maketh me have a faint heart', wrote one schoolboy poet. The academic year was punctuated by numerous short holidays around the major feasts of the Church. Latin, which was seen as the foundation of all the liberal arts, was almost the only subject taught – mainly orally, in large classes, although prose and verse composition were essential skills for the older boys (it seems doubtful whether William's couplet would have passed the scrutiny of the Master). His letters do not suggest, however, that the harsh regime harmed his spirits. Indeed, the bequest by the Pastons' neighbour, John Barnard of Guton, of a vestment and jewel to Eton College, 'where I was brought up in my youth in learning', implies that by 1499 it was already possible to look back with pleasure to one's schooldays.

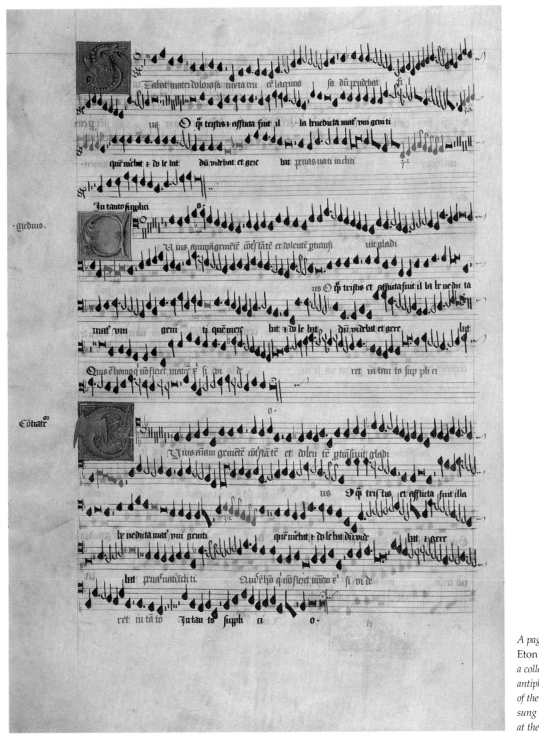

*A page from the Eton Choir Book, a collection of antiphon in praise of the Virgin Mary, sung by the choir at the daily services.*

John Paston III's first child, a boy, was born in the summer of 1478 but must have died in infancy; the eventual heir, William, was born a year or so later. Margaret Paston was still, however, concerned with her own two younger sons. Early in 1479 she was clearly trying to place Walter in an ecclesiastical living, although he was still too young for priest's orders and had not yet graduated. She found herself, perhaps for the first time since her husband's death, receiving rather than administering a rebuke for this attempted breach of Church law – from William Pickenham, chancellor of the diocese. In the summer of 1479, however, Walter was about to graduate and wrote to his brother, then staying at Caister, about his expenses and the possibility of preferment from Bishop Waynflete.

---

Walter Paston to Sir John Paston                      22 May 1479
Oxford

. . . I received a letter from my brother, John, by which I understood that my mother and you wished to know what the costs of my proceeding [graduating] would be. I sent a letter to my brother, John, certifying my costs and the causes for my proceeding, but, as I have sent word to my mother, I purpose now to tarry until Michaelmas, for if I wait until then some of my costs will be paid; for I supposed when I sent my letter to my brother, John, that the Queen's brother [Lionel Woodville, later Bishop of Salisbury] would proceed at Midsummer, but now he is going to tarry until Michaelmas. But, as I sent word to my mother, I want to be Inceptor [to be examined for his degree] before Midsummer, and therefore I besought her to send me some money, for it will be some cost to me, but not much.

Also, sir, I beseech you to send me word what answer you have had from the Bishop of Winchester about the matter which you spoke to him for on my behalf when I was with you in London. I thought I would have word before this time. I would that it should come, for our help from the Bishop of Norwich begins to be slack in payment. And if you do not know what the term 'Inceptor' means, Master Edmund, who was my governor at Oxford and brings this letter can tell you, or any other graduate.

Also, I pray you send me word what is done with the horse that I left at Tottenham, and whether the man whom I had it of is paid or not . . .

---

The summer of 1479 saw the last major epidemic of bubonic plague that was to hit England during the fifteenth century. There were many deaths and the Paston family was hard-hit. The young Walter reported on his graduation on 30 June but soon after fell ill. He was brought back to Norwich but died on 18-19 August. It seems unlikely that Walter died of plague, which usually killed more quickly, but two days later came the news of the death of old Agnes Paston at London, probably of plague, though she was certainly an old woman. Her death brought a whole new set of disputes, this time within the family.

During her later years Agnes had been under the care of her younger son, William, a successful lawyer who had outdone all his kinsmen in the marriage stakes by wedding one of the daughters of Edmund, Duke of Somerset. Relations between William and his nephews had frequently been cool, and Agnes had made no secret of the fact that she felt her oldest son had defrauded his brothers out of some of the lands that their father had intended for them. Agnes's final will does not survive, but earlier drafts make it clear that she had intended to recompense William from her own lands. In August 1479 the younger Pastons were clearly suspicious that William would acquire not only the Berry lands but also those Paston estates that Agnes had held for her lifetime. A decade and more of dispute and litigation was to follow.

---

Edmund Paston to John Paston III                    21 August 1479
Norwich

Sure tidings have come to Norwich that my grandmother, whom God assoil, is dead. My uncle [William] had a messenger yesterday that she would not survive, and today came another when we were at mass for my brother, Walter, whom God assoil. My uncle was about to come to make an offering [to the Church], but the second messenger made him return hastily and he at once took horse to inform others of our bereavement. My sister [Anne ?] is delivered but the child has passed to God, who send us His grace.

Docking told me privately that my uncle has ridden in haste to my Lady of Norfolk to have 3 score persons, whether they are to convey my grandmother here or not he could not say: I suspect it is rather to put them in possession of some of her lands . . .

The plague was worst of all in London; Sir John was aware of the dangers, but he was also concerned at the activities of his uncle. It was necessary to lobby powerful figures to ensure that the Norfolk escheator did not return an inquest on his grandmother's lands which would affect his own title.

---

Sir John Paston to Margaret Paston                29 October 1479
London

Please you to know that I have been here in London a fortnight, the first 4 days of which I was in much fear of the sickness, and I also found my chamber and stuff not so clean as I thought, which much troubled me. And, as I told you at my departure, I was not well off for money. For I had not more than 10 marks, of which I parted with 40s. to be rid of my bedfellow; and then rode beyond Dunstable and there spoke with one of my chief witnesses, who promised me to labour to get me writings touching this matter between me and the Duke of Suffolk, and I rewarded him with 20s. And then, as I informed you, I paid 5 marks directly I came here to get out of pledge my velvet gown and other gear . . .

Item, I understand that my Uncle William has made labour to the escheator . . . I have written to the escheator about it on my own behalf. If my uncle had his way in that, he would be no nearer to having the land, but he would, in effect, have this advantage, what is needed for a weak claim, that is some colour or cloak [a prima facie case].

But on Tuesday I was with the Bishop of Ely [John Morton, Master of the Rolls in Chancery], who showed himself good and worshipful. And he said that he would send to my Uncle William that he should not proceed in any such matter till he spoke with him, and, moreover, that he should make sure he was here shortly . . .

---

# Plague and Pestilence

'It first betrayed itself by the emergence of certain tumours in the groin or armpits . . . then spread itself in all directions . . . black or livid spots making their appearance . . . now few and large, now minute and numerous'. Boccaccio's description of the onset of bubonic plague in 1348 and his comment that these symptoms were 'an infallible token of approaching death' helps us to understand the horror produced by the 'pestilence' from which Sir John Paston and probably his grandmother died in 1479.

The first visitation of the Black Death in 1348-9 and its subsequent outbreaks in the later fourteenth century had halved the population of England. Fifteenth-century epidemics were usually more limited geographically and there is no way of measuring mortality accurately. They could clearly be devastating, however. In 1433, for instance, the chroniclers tell of 'a great pestilence' in London and throughout England when 'the people died sore, both poor and rich'; there was 'a sickness called the pestilence', especially in Northern England, in 1438-9: according to Margaret Paston the pestilence was 'fervent' in Norwich in 1465 and in 1471 Sir John was concerned about 'the most universal death that ever I knew in England'. But the 1479 outbreak seems to have been the worst of the century, forcing the closure of the courts at Westminster during the summer. There was a 'huge mortality and death of people . . . not only in the City, but also in many other parts of the realm,' wrote a London chronicler; this is confirmed by a massive increase in the number of wills proved in East Anglia in that year.

Chroniclers are rarely specific about the symptoms of 'the pestilence' and other diseases, such as smallpox, typhus, dysentery, enteritis and influenza, which had epidemic episodes in the fifteenth century. One chronicler associates the King's expedition to France in 1475 not only with an epidemic of the 'French Pox' but also with the 'stitch' and the 'flux' as well as 'pestilence'. Medicine had no cure for any of these diseases but, from most of them, many recovered. It was the very high mortality of the plague that made it so special. Sir John Paston recognized in 1479 that clean surroundings might make infection less likely but the only real answer was to flee from centres of infection. 'Here is great pestilence. I purpose to flee into the country', wrote William Paston from London in 1454. His nephew, Sir John, took the risk of returning to London in 1479 to pursue some business matters, and paid the penalty.

A fifteenth-century woodcut of the martyrdom of St Sebastian, a protector against epidemics, and below, two prayers for protection against the plague.

Sir John's worries about the plague were justified. He died in London on 15 November. Perhaps because of the long entanglement with Anne Haute, he had never married, and thus his heir was his brother, John, now aged about 36 years. A fragment of a will made by Sir John some two years previously survives. This seems to have made his brother his main heir but, as with his father and grandmother, no registered copy survives.

John Paston III to Margaret Paston — November 1479

. . . Mother, John Clement, the bearer hereof, can tell you that, the more pity it is, if it had pleased God, my brother is buried in the White Friars at London. I did not think that this would have been so, for I supposed that he wished to be buried at Bromholm and that caused me to ride so soon to London to have arranged his bringing home; and if it had been his will to have lain at Bromholm I had intended, as I rode on the way, to have brought home my grandmother and him together – but that purpose is now void. But when I come to London I intend to speak with my Lord Chamberlain [Hastings] and to win over through him the Bishop of Ely, if I can . . . I think that Sir George Browne [husband of his Aunt Elizabeth], Sir James Radcliffe, and others of my acquaintance who wait most upon the King and lie nightly in his Chamber, will give their good wills . . .

Also, mother, I pray that my brother, Edmund, may ride to Marlingford, Oxnead, Paston, Cromer [all Agnes's manors] and Caister to enter on them in my name, but to let the tenants of Oxnead and Marlingford know that I am seeking no money from them, but only their acknowledgement. So he should not, until he hears from me again, ask them for any money but let him command them to pay nothing to my uncle nor his servants nor to any other to his use, on pain of having to pay again to me. I think that if there were any money asked in my name, it would, perhaps, set my Lady of Norfolk against me, and cause her to think that I was acting more against her pleasure than did my brother, whom God pardon of his great mercy. I have also arranged to enter at Stanstead and Horwellbury [Agnes's Hertfordshire manors] and I have written a letter to Anne Montgomery and Jane Rodon to make my Lady of Norfolk favourable, if possible . . .

The death of Sir John marks the end of the reasonably continuous, though much depleted, series of family letters that began in the late 1440s. Surviving family correspondence is much sparser henceforward – partly, no doubt, because John III was much more frequently in Norfolk than his brother had been. Many of the letters that do survive refer to the continuing dispute with William II over Agnes's lands. It was possibly in 1481 that Margery wrote to her husband to tell him of her proposed visit to the Duchess of Norfolk who was still supporting William. Her manner of addressing her husband remained very different from that of Margaret.

---

Margery Paston to John Paston III                    3 November [? 1481]
Norwich

Mine own sweetheart, in my most humble wise I recommend me unto you, desiring heartily to hear of your welfare, which I beseech Almighty God to preserve and keep to His pleasure and your heart's desire . . . Sir, on Saturday last I spoke with my cousin, [William] Gournay, and he said that if I would go to my Lady of Norfolk and beseech her to be your good and gracious lady, she would be so, for he said that one word from a woman would do more than the words of twenty men, if I could control my tongue and speak no harm of my uncle. And if you command me to do this, I trust I should say nothing to my Lady's displeasure, but only to your profit; for I think, from what is said by them and by your good farmer of Oxnead, that they will soon be ready for a conclusion. For he curses the time that ever he came into the farm of Oxnead, for he says that he knows well that he shall have a great loss, and yet he will not acknowledge whether he has paid or not: but when he sees the right time, he will tell the truth.

I understand by my cousin, Gournay, that my Lady is nearly weary of her part in this, and he says that my Lady will be coming on pilgrimage to this town, though he does not know whether before Christmas or after. And if I would get my Lady Calthorpe, my mother-in-law, my mother and myself and come before my Lady, beseeching her to be your good and gracious lady, he thinks that you will have a conclusion. For she would fain be rid of it, if she could save her honour, but yet she would have money . . .

Margaret Paston was now probably nearing sixty and increasingly thinking of her end. If she had made a will three years earlier she was now to revise it and asked Margery to ensure that her husband would carry out her requests. John was slightly piqued, but his last surviving letter to her reflects the affection and respect he had for her – and which she certainly deserved.

John Paston III to Margaret Paston                                    [? 1482]
Norwich

. . . When I may, I will with as good will be ready to recompense you for the cost that my housewife and I have put you to as I am now bound to thank you for it, which I do in the best way I can. And, mother, it pleased you to have certain words to my wife at her departure touching your remembrance of how short you think your future days will be and also of the intentions that you have towards my brothers and sister, your children, and also to your servants, in which you asked her to be a mediator to me that I would tender and favour the same. Mother, saving your pleasure, there needs no ambassadors or mediators between you and me; for there is neither wife nor other friend that shall make me do what your command shall make me do, if I may have knowledge of it; and if I have no knowledge, in good faith I am excusable both to God and to you.

And if you remember well, I know well that you ought not to doubt me over anything that you would have me do if I outlive you; for I know well no one man alive has called upon you so often as I to make your will and put everything in certainty that you would have done for yourself and for your children and servants. Also, at the making of your will and at every communication that I have had with you touching the same I never opposed anything that you wanted done but always offered myself to be bound to the same. But, mother, I am right glad that my wife is in any way in your favour or trust, but I am right sorry that my wife or any other child or servant of yours should be in better favour or trust with you than myself. For I shall and must give up and put from me all that your other children, servants, priests, workmen and friends to whom you will bequeath something will be given for themselves. And this I have and ever shall be ready to do, while I live, on my faith, and never thought otherwise, so God be my help, whom I beseech to preserve you and send you such a good and long life that you may do for yourself and for me after my decease. And I beshrew the hearts that would or shall cause you to mistrust or be unkind to me or my friends.

At Norwich this Monday, with the hand of your son and truest servant, John Paston.

John Paston's status in the county was recognized by his appointment to the Norfolk commission of the peace in 1480 and he was active in county affairs until the end of Edward IV's reign. His relationship with Lord Hastings seems to have strengthened and, soon after the death of King Edward, he was sent to Calais to support Hastings's sick brother, the lieutenant of the subsidiary fort of Guisnes. He was summoned back late in April to attend upon Hastings, and was elected for the city of Norwich to the parliament of Edward V which never sat. The murder of Hastings and the usurpation of the throne by Richard of Gloucester was a blow to his prospects. That he was not trusted by the new regime is clear from his omission from the commission of the peace and other commissions during the reign of Richard III. He did not get involved, however, in any conspiracies and the new Duke of Norfolk who, as John Howard, had quarrelled so violently with his father a quarter of a century before, seems to have been favourably disposed: in 1484 Norfolk and the other co-heir to the Mowbray estates, the Earl of Nottingham, released all rights that they might have claimed in Caister, which finally brought to an end the twenty-five years of disputes over the Fastolf estates.

John's 'livelode' was greatly increased in November 1484, when his mother died. Her will, made two years earlier, makes provision for her younger children and for her grandchildren, including the family of Margery Calle and Sir John's illegitimate daughter. John was not only the chief executor but he also inherited most of her lands. At the last, however, she looked back primarily to her Mauteby ancestors rather than to her Paston connections: she was to be buried at Mautby, not by her husband at Bromholm, and her tomb was to illustrate above all the importance of her own ancestry.

John was a wealthy man with a considerable stake in the country when, in August 1485, Henry Tudor landed at Milford Haven. Among his chief followers was John, Earl of Oxford, who had escaped from eight years of captivity at Calais. Although John was summoned by the Duke of Norfolk to serve against the invasion, it is extremely unlikely that he did fight at Bosworth against his old patron.

The triumph of Henry VII at Bosworth and the death of the Duke brought Paston new standing in the county and, indeed, in the country at large. The Earl of Oxford virtually became the King's lieutenant in East Anglia and John became steward of his large Norfolk estate. He was also appointed an Esquire of the Body to the King and his brother, William, whose activities since Eton are obscure, entered Oxford's service as one of his secretaries. John was appointed sheriff of Norfolk and Suffolk after Bosworth and his power is shown by a letter from the Countess of Surrey, who fifteen years before had been seen by John as a possible bride. Her husband, heir to the Dukedom of Norfolk, was in the Tower.

The Countess of Surrey to John Paston III          3 October 1485
Isle of Sheppey

My right worshipful cousin, I recommend me heartily to you, thanking you for your great kindness and loving disposition towards my Lord and me at all times, which, I pray God, I may see requited, and I pray for its continuance.

Cousin, I showed you my mind, that I would have my children taken to Ashwellthorpe [Norfolk], and you were pleased to say that I should have horses from you to help to convey them there. But now I understand that my Lord Fitzwalter [of Attleborough, Steward of the King's Household] has discharged my Lord's [Surrey's] servants there, saying that they had had unfitting language about the King . . . I would not have thought my Lord Fitzwalter would have taken such displeasure at my keeping 10 or 12 men at Thorpe . . . I trusted to have found my Lord Fitzwalter better lord to me, seeing that when I was with my Lord of Oxford . . . he promised to be good lord to my Lord and me, and I pray you to remind him of that and trust that by your means I find him better lord hereafter.

I have found my Lord of Oxford singularly very good and kind lord to my Lord and me, and steadfast in his promise, whereby he has won my Lord's service as long as he lives . . . I pray you, good cousin, that by your means I may continue to have his good lordship, and to my poor power I trust to deserve it. I pray you, cousin, that this bill may recommend me to my Lady Brews and to my cousin, your wife . . .

The dispute with William Paston continued well into the new reign. Since William had also been an old and loyal counsellor of the Earl of Oxford, John was not able to use his new patronage to force a settlement to his liking. The dispute seems to have been settled by arbitration before William's death in 1496. Oxnead, at least, remained in the possession of John Paston and his successors. But it is probable that John had to pay a large sum to William in recompense, and this produced financial embarrassment for a number of years. Many of the letters of this period refer to John's official business and his relations with the Earl of Oxford, or are requests for favours. His brother, William, was a useful friend in Oxford's household and gave him news of high politics and the Court. In March 1487 he encouraged John to put on a good show during the King's first visit to East Anglia and showed a proper pride in his native county.

---

William Paston III to John Paston III                    7 March 1487
Sheen

. . . As for the King's coming into the country, on Monday fortnight he will lie at the Abbey of Stratford and so to Chelmsford, then to Sir Thomas Montgomery's [at Faulkbourn], then to Hedingham [the Earl of Oxford's seat], then to Colchester, then to Ipswich, then to Bury, then to Dame Anne Wingfield's [at East Harling, Norfolk] and so to Norwich. He will be there on the eve of Palm Sunday and so tarry there all Easter and then go to Walsingham. Wherefore you need to warn William Gogyne and his fellows to provide themselves with enough wine, for everyone assures me that the town will be drunk dry, as was York when the King was there.

Sir, Master Sampson . . . has required me to write to you that it would be best for you to provide yourself with some gentlemanly things for the coming of the King, for he will certainly bring you guests enough, so provide for them now. He also sends you word that it is my Lord's mind that my sister [John's wife] with all other goodly folk thereabout should accompany Dame Elizabeth Calthorpe, at the King's coming, because there is no great lady thereabouts and my Lord has made great boast of the fair and good gentlewomen of the country, and the King had said that he would like to see them.

Sir, my Lord has sent unto the greater part of the gentlemen of Essex to wait upon him at Chelmsford, where he intends to meet with the King, and has ordered them to be so well appointed that the Lancashire men may see that there are gentlemen there of so great substance that they are able to buy all of Lancashire. Men think that you should do the same among yourselves. Your country is greatly boasted of, and also its inhabitants.

I beseech you to remember the horse that you promised me . . .

# Travel and Roads

The constant movement of the Pastons and their servants is apparent from their correspondence and, in this, they were far from unusual. Fifteenth-century roads were thronged with travellers of all sorts. There were streams of messengers bringing writs and letters from the King and from the departments of state to sheriffs and other local officials; sheriffs' messengers making returns to London; lawyers, litigants, judges and juries journeying to the courts; merchants and their servants carting their goods to markets, fairs and ports; farmers driving cattle and sheep; nobles and their retinues with carts loaded with furnishings moving from one house to another or on their way to court or to parliament; pilgrims and friars on religious business; county or town levies on their way to the King's army; pedlars and intinerant workmen, minstrels and entertainers; and, all too often, vagabonds and robbers. There was always someone available to take a letter, at least to London, just as 'Harry Wilton's man' took a letter from Margaret Paston in 1465.

As the fourteenth-century Gough Map shows, the main road system in medieval England radiated from the capital and these roads were the best-kept, the most secure and the best provided with inns and ale-houses. Other routes traced the development of new markets and the growth of religious houses and castles by forming a series of interlocking networks. From the towns and market-villages on these main roads fanned a maze of roadways and tracks which connected nearly every settlement with its neighbours. Coastal and river-shipping also played a part in the transport of bulky commodities and passengers; burgesses from Lynn, for example, began their journey to London by sailing up the Ouse to Cambridge before taking horse. But from most parts of East Anglia, road transport was the norm for people and goods. English roads were the 'King's highways'; land-owners had, in theory, to maintain their surface and to clear the land to within 200 feet of either side of the road in order to deter robbers. When William and Agnes Paston wished to change the line of a local road they had to obtain a licence from the King – and even then faced difficulties with their neighbours. Rural roads – and many town roads – were unmetalled and local landowners often allowed them to deteriorate quite quickly. The roads were usually wide however and, with the cleared land on either side, carts and carriages, as well as horsemen and pedestrians, could normally pick

*East Anglia and London from the* Gough Map of the British Isles, *dated 1360. (North is to the left).*

their way around the worst of the pot-holes and puddles. The maintenance of roads, ferries and bridges was seen as a pious as well as a social duty. Religious houses and guilds had been associated with their upkeep for centuries and, in the later Middle Ages, it became common for people to leave money for their improvement in their wills; the wealthy Thomas Spring left no less than £200 for the upkeep of roads around Lavenham, in Suffolk in 1486.

Travel for gentlemen and their servants, and for many of the lower classes, was usually on horseback, since horses could be hired if not owned. Carts were also used for passengers and some noble families owned litters or carriages. Speed of travel varied, of course. News of the Battle of Towton, sent by the King's messenger, was carried 192 miles to London in four days; the news of Bosworth was taken by one of the City's contingent 120 miles to York in less than 48 hours. More normal, perhaps, would have been the three days that William Worcester took to travel from Norwich to London in 1478. The normal route from Norwich to London was via Thetford, Newmarket, Ware and Waltham, but the Pastons often made detours; in 1479, for example, John Paston III was prepared to take his pregnant wife along country lanes in midwinter to visit relatives. Clearly the state of the roads, however much complained about, was no major handicap to the political, military or social activities of the able-bodied person.

John Paston was knighted soon afterwards, at the Battle of Stoke, the last pitched battle of the Wars of the Roses, and his political career continued to flourish. He was a JP until his death, and on a number of other local commissions, and he was active on Oxford's business in Norfolk. He probably sat in parliament, but the names of few MPs are known for this period. Domestically things seem to have been peaceful and happy, at least for the first few years of the new reign. His oldest surviving son, William, had been born around 1480 and, by the time he was about ten years old, possible marriages were being discussed. The potential dowry was an important factor, particularly since John was considerably in debt to the Norfolk lawyer, Roger Townshend, and the London merchant, Henry Colet, as well as to his uncle. His brother Edmund, by now married and living at his wife's manor of Clippesby, advised on a suitable match.

---

Edmund Paston to John Paston III                              [circa 1490]

Right worshipful sir, I recommend me to you. Yesterday I was with my cousin [Robert] Clere . . . and he moved me of the marriage of my nephew, your son, and these folks would be more glad to bargain over this than you realise. He showed me that you would have as much as Sir Edmund Bedingfield promised, which was 500 marks, and he pointed out that Sir Edmund would part with it to Sir Roger Townshend or Harry Colet which he knew you would not want, but rather to have the money at your own disposal. And it seems by what he said that he knows well that if you deal with Sir Henry Heydon he will ensure that the money that he parts with should go to the redeeming of your lands and to pay your other debts . . . I know well that this gentleman bears you as good will as any man alive, and my mistress, his mother, and my mistress, his wife, likewise; and it seems to me that he does not make the reservations about delivering you his money that other men do . . .

Merchants and new gentlemen will, I know, proffer generously but, while not dispraising others, you know the ancestry of this man and how well he is connected. I know well that if you go to London you will have large offers, but if your journey is only to ease yourself in this matter my poor advice would be to wait for 3 or 4 days, for I do not think I would have been spoken to about it so openly [if they] did they not intend to speak of it to you soon . . .

I pray God that you do as well for your honour as I would do for myself. If you will wait this little while I know well that you may have the matter more fully discussed ; and if you tarry till Monday, I will await on you at Hedingham, with God's grace, who ever preserve you and yours . . .

John chose to marry his son to Bridget Heydon, the grand-daughter of his old enemy. He did, however, marry his daughter, Elizabeth, to Clere's son and heir. John and his family seem to have moved to Oxnead, no doubt a more comfortable if less magnificent home than Caister, and it was to there that John addressed the last of the surviving letters to his wife. Margery, like many housewives, had by this time become something of a medical expert, and John hoped that she could cure the rheumatism affecting James Hobart, the Attorney-General and one of the most powerful men in the kingdom. An old and seemingly helpful acquaintance, Hobart had long been, like John, a servant of the Dukes of Norfolk.

---

John Paston III to Margery Paston [1487/95]

Mistress Margery, I recommend me to you. And I pray you in all haste possible to send me by the next sure messenger that you can get a large poultice of your flos unguentorum [flower of ointments] for the King's Attorney, James Hobart, for his disease is but an ache in the knee. He is the man who brought you and me together, and I would give £40 that you could with your plaster part him from his pain. But when you send me the poultice, you must send me writing how it should be laid to and taken from his knee, and how long it should abide on his knee without removal, and how long the plaster will last and whether or not he must wrap any more clothes about the plaster to keep it warm. And God be with you.

---

Margery died in 1495 and was buried in Norwich. John married again, but had no further children. His relationship with the Earl of Oxford continued to the end of his life and probably the last surviving letter addressed to him came from the Earl to report bad news of his brother.

---

Earl of Oxford to John Paston III 26 June 1503/4
London

Right worshipful and right entirely beloved, I commend me heartily to you. And whereas your brother, William, my servant, is so troubled with sickness and crazed in his mind that I may not keep him about me, wherefore I am right sorry, I at this time send him to you, praying especially that he may be kept surely and tenderly with you to such time as God fortune him to be better in himself and his mind more soberly disposed, which I pray God may be in short time . . .

---

John Paston died on 28 August 1504. No will or inquisition of his lands survives and it is not known where he was buried. His second wife died in 1510 but her will makes no reference to the Paston connections. John's Uncle William, his Aunt Elizabeth, his brother Edmund, and his sisters had all pre-deceased him; it is not known when his brother, William, died. John and Margery had two daughters and a younger son who survived until adulthood, but it was only through their elder son, William, that the Paston family survived and proliferated in the male line. William lived until a ripe old age and saw Bromholm, the friaries where his mother, great-grand-mother and his uncle, Sir John, lay and so much else that has featured in these letters swept away at the Reformation. But the work of his ancestors had laid a sure foundation for the future prosperity of the Paston family. Ironically, the Pastons, who had first come to eminence through the first William, the Judge, ended with another William, the 2nd Earl of Yarmouth, whose death in 1732 saw the end of the family and the dispersal of the estates and archives.

# Further Reading

*Effigy of Katherine Paston,
wife of Sir Edmund Paston,
who died in 1628,
in St Margaret's Church,
Paston, Norfolk.
The monument was made by
Nicholas Stone.*

A large number of books and articles have been consulted in the preparation of the introduction and features and only a general acknowledgment can be given here to the many scholars, past and present, whose writings have been drawn upon. Guidance on the politics and society of the fifteenth century can be found in the following general works on aspects of the period.

J.A. Thomson, *The Transformation of Medieval England, 1370–1529* (Longman 1983)
B.P. Wolffe, *Henry VI* (Eyre Methuen 1981)
C.D. Ross, *Edward VI* (Eyre Methuen 1974)
C.D. Ross, *Richard III* (Eyre Methuen 1981)
S.B. Chrimes, *Henry VII* (Eyre Methuen 1972)
A. Goodman, *The Wars of the Roses* (Routledge 1981)
R. Vaughan, *Valois Burgundy* (Allen Lane 1975)
P.S. Lewis, *Later Medieval France* (Macmillan 1968)
N. Orme, *From Childhood to Chivalry* (Methuen 1984)
J.L. Bolton, *The Medieval English Economy 1150–1500* (Dent 1981)
Barbara Hanawalt, *The Ties that Bound* (Oxford U.P. 1986)
J.C. Dickinson, *The Later Middle Ages* (A. & C. Black 1979)

The following are the main editions and commentaries on the Paston Letters.

*The Paston Letters*, ed. J. Gairdner (Library edition, 6 vols, 1904: reprinted Alan Sutton, 1984)
*Paston Letters and Papers of the Fifteenth Century* ed. Norman Davis (Oxford U.P. 2 vols, 1971, 1976)
H.S. Bennett, *The Pastons and their England* (Cambridge U.P. 1937)

C. Richmond, 'The Pastons Revisited', *Bulletin of the Institute of Historical Research*, LXVIII (1985), pp. 25–36
C. Richmond, *John Hopton* (Cambridge 1981) is a fascinating study of a Suffolk contemporary of the Pastons.

The following primary sources have been referred to in the introduction and features.

*The Stonor Letters and Papers 1290–1483*, ed. C.L. Kingsford, Camden Society, 2 vols, 3rd series XIX–XXX (1919); *Supplementary Stonor Letters and Papers, 1314–1482*, ed. C.L. Kingsford, Camden Society, 3rd. series XXXIV (1924)
*The Plumpton Correspondence*, ed. T. Stapleton, Camden Society, Original Series, IV (1839)
*The Cely Letters 1472–88*, ed. A. Hanham, Early English Text Society, 273 (1975)
Sir John Fortescue, *The Governance of England*, ed. C. Plummer (Oxford 1885)
Sir John Fortescue, *De Laudibus Legum Angliae [In praise of the Laws of England]*, ed. S.B. Chrimes
*The Book of Margery Kempe*, translated by B.A. Windeatt (Penguin 1985)

# Glossary

*Church of St Peter and
St Paul, Mautby, Norfolk.*

This Glossary is in two sections. The first lists words which are still in use, where the fifteenth-century meaning differed from today's normal usage. The second lists some technical words which are not explained in the text.

## SECTION 1

**Assoil** to absolve from guilt; to pardon.

**Cheer** disposition or mood; hospitable reception.

**Cunning** knowledge or skill.

**Demean(ing)** behave; behaviour or bearing.

**Ease** opportunity; enjoyment.

**Governance** control; way of life.

**Heavy** sorry; causing sorrow or regret; burdensome.

**Labour** to try to influence; to take trouble.

**Lewd** unlearned or ill-bred, or, simply, bad.

**Liegeman** faithful or sworn follower.

**Likely** capable; suitable; handsome.

**Livelode** income; property which yields income.

**Lordship** authority (with implication of patronage).

**Mean** mediator; mediation or intercession.

**Move** to urge or appeal to someone.

**Rule** good order; conduct; power.

**Sad** serious; trustworthy.

**Speed** to succeed or attain one's purpose.

**Strange** unfriendly or cold in manner.

**Tall** goodly; handsome; bold.

**Treaty** discussion with a view to a settlement; a settlement.

**Troth** pledging one's faith – usually a form of emphasis.

**Vouchsafe** usually employed as a polite way of asking a favour.

**Wit** cleverness; skill or talent.

**Worship** honour; renown or dignity; good name.

## SECTION 2

**Assizes** bi-annual visitation by two judges to each county to try civil and criminal cases.

**Bond** a legally enforceable document guaranteeing action of payment, with penalty for default.

**Commission of Oyer and Terminer** appointed by the Crown to try and punish specific offences or general crime in a specified area.

**Commission of the Peace** group of lords, judges and local gentry and lawyers appointed by the Crown in each county to keep the peace and punish offenders. Justices of the Peace usually held office for a number of years, most of their work being done at 'Quarter Sessions' which met four times a year.

**Disseise** to expel from land or other property.

**Distraint/Distress** legal device to enforce fulfilment of obligation by seizure of goods.

**Enfeoffment to Use** grant of legal ownership of land to 'feoffees' or trustees, to hold to the use of the donor, who continued to have actual possession and draw the income.

**Indenture** written contract in two or more parts, one held by each party.

**Indictment** criminal charge put before a local jury who decided whether it provided a case to answer.

**Jointure** settlement of land at marriage on husband and wife to hold for their lifetimes.

**Pardoner** one licensed to sell papal pardons or indulgences for sin.

**Sanctuary** church or other privileged place where a fugitive was safe from arrest.

**Writ** written order issued from a court ordering some action by its recipient.

# The Selection of Letters

Of the thousand or so letters and other documents printed by Gairdner it has been necessary for the purposes of this edition to choose something under one-fifth and, of these only a few are printed in full. Generally, substantial extracts from a limited number of letters have been preferred to snippets from many so consequently some themes and episodes are only lightly touched on. In selecting the extracts and linking them by brief comments I have tried to tell the story of the Paston Family during the period from about 1440 to 1490 largely in their own words and to illustrate the personalities of the writers and the relationships between them. The selection does not, therefore, do justice to the tens of thousands of words in the originals dealing with economic and financial matters, central and local politics and, above all, with the law and litigation, though enough samples of these have been included to illustrate such matters.

In dating their letters the Pastons and their correspondents rarely give the year, at least until the 1470s, when the two Johns frequently date by regnal year, for example, 'the 16th year of King Edward IV'. Therefore, it is usually necessary to date the documents from internal evidence, such as references to datable events. This is not always easy. Many of Gairdner's suggested dates have been corrected by Professor Davis and other scholars and these have been followed here, but the dates of some letters remain very doubtful. Within the year dating is usually by feast-day, rather than by day of the month, so Margaret Paston's letter of 14 December 1441 is dated 'the Thursday before St Thomas's Day [18 December]'; showing that sense of time was closely related to the calendar of the Christian year. Such dates have been given the modern form in the text.

Letter-writing was highly conventionalised and treatises on the art taught a number of formulae to be used when addressing different types of correspondent, particularly in the opening address and in the ending. These have almost all been omitted from the extracts printed here, except for a few included as specimens. 'I recommend me to you' was frequently the abrupt opening, though Margaret usually precedes this with some variation of 'worshipful husband' or, to her sons, 'I greet you well'. Her sons usually open with 'mother' or 'brother' Margaret normally ends letters to her husband with 'The Holy Trinity have you in His keeping', and to her son 'I send you God's blessing'. Variations on these are the most common forms throughout the correspondence.

In adapting the letters for modern readers I have tried to maintain as much of the rhythms, language and grammatical structure as possible in order to represent the flavour of the original. Spelling and punctuation have been modernised throughout but word-order and grammar have been retained except when they might produce confusion or ambiguity. Certain usages have been modernised even where no confusion arises, because the Pastons did not employ them consistently; for instance 'you be' has been changed to 'you are' and modern practice in the use of 'shall' and 'will' has been adopted. Roman numerals have been altered to Arabic throughout.

Problems of vocabulary have been dealt with in one of three ways. Obsolete words have been silently given their modern equivalent: for instance, 'wete' is translated 'know'. Words that have changed their meaning but have no clear equivalent that would not be anachronistic have been left as in the original and explained in the glossary. Technical or unusual words which occur only rarely have been left in the text but are explained in square brackets. Other editorial comment is also put in square brackets.

Omissions of text are represented by dots but no attempt is made to signify the extent of the omission.

It is unlikely that these practices have been followed with total consistency but I hope that the text presented does provide a reasonable representation of the tone and style, as well as the contents of the original letters. In the close reading necessary to select and adapt the text I feel that I have come to know and like the Paston family and their circle. Even Agnes and her sons, John and William, appear as understandable, if not always very sympathetic, personalities, but inevitably we know far more about those who wrote most of the letters, Margaret and her sons. The sense of comradeship and mutual support among the sons of John and Margaret produce some of the most attractive letters, but it is Margaret who is the linchpin of the family throughout nearly the whole period of this correspondence. Serving the family interests in Norfolk, often at considerable exertion and risk, bringing up her children and trying to keep the peace between them and their father and later their uncle; trying to reconcile her husband with his mother; running a large household and still having time to write – or dictate – probably hundreds of letters – it is no wonder that late in middle life a note of exasperation with unsatisfactory children creeps in and she finds the company of her old servant, James Gloys, more satisfactory. She was no heroine but she was an admirable woman and, in spite of all the activity of her husband and sons in administration, law, politics and war, she seems to me to be the central character of the Paston story.

# Index

# Picture Credits

1   MS FR. 598, f. 31, Bibliothèque Nationale, Paris/ Marie Thérèse Souverbie.
3   MS Harl. 2897, f. 160, British Library, London.
5   Brandiston Hall, Norfolk/Sonia Halliday and Laura Lushington.
8   MS FR. 599, f. 40, Bibliothèque Nationale, Paris/ Marie-Thérèse Souverbie.
17   Norwich Cathedral/Michael Holford.
21   Mauteby Family Tree, 17th-century copy, University Library, Cambridge.
26   MS Cotton Jul. EIV, Art. 6, f. 4v, British Library, London.
28   MS Latin. 1158, f. 27v, Bibliothèque Nationale, Paris/Marie-Thérèse Souverbie.
33   MS Add. 36619, f. 5, British Library, London.
37t   MS Add. 42130, f. 170, British Library, London.
37b   MS Gough Liturg. 7, f. 10, Bodleian Library, Oxford.
39   Photograph by John Meek.
42   MS 5087, f. 144, Bibliothèque de l'Arsenal, Paris/ Marie-Thérèse Souverbie.
43t   Victoria and Albert Museum, London, no. E. 1700-1931.
   Victoria and Albert Museum, London, no. E. 5397-1911.
   Victoria and Albert Museum, London, no. E. 3443-1928.
   Victoria and Albert Museum, London, no. E. 4828-1911.
43b   Devonshire Tapestries, Victoria and Albert Museum, London/Michael Holford.
46t   British Museum, London.
46c   British Museum, London.
46b   British Museum, London.
51t   Photograph by A.F. Kersting.
51b   Photograph by John Meek.
56   Photograph by Michael Holford.
60   MS Cotton. Roll 11, 23. membr. 7, British Library, London.
62   MS Add. 43490, f. 48, British Library, London.
67   MS Harl. 4205, ff. 31v-32, British Library, London.
72   Victoria and Albert Museum, London.
74   MS Egerton. 2019, f. 157v, British Library, London.
76tl   Museum of London.
76tr   Museum of London.
76b   The Wallace Collection, London.
79   By courtesy of the National Portrait Gallery, London.
83   MS 188, Library of the Inner Temple, London/ Godfrey New Photographics.
86   MS Royal 16 Fii, f. 73, British Library, London.
87   Print taken from facsimilie edition, published by The London Topographical Society, 1881-82. Original drawing in the Ashmolean Museum, Oxford.
90t   Church of St Chad, Shropshire/Sonia Halliday and Laura Lushington.
90b   The Wallace Collection, London.
93   MS Ashmole 13, Bodleian Library, Oxford.
94-5   MS Mun. KC-18-N1, King's College, Cambridge/Christopher Hurst.
98   MS 1130, f. 83, Bibliothèque Ste. Genevieve, Paris/Garnier, Artephot.
100   MS Add. 48976, fig. 50, British Library, London
104   MS Bodleian 13, f. 8-11, Bodleian Library, Oxford.
109t   MS 722, f. 203, Musée Chantilly/Giraudon, CRL 14.062-LAC 150451.
109b   MS Douce 104, f. 46, Bodleian Library, Oxford.
111   MS Add. 48976, fig. 57, British Library, London.
119   By courtesy of the National Portrait Gallery, London.
124   MS Harl. 642, f. 79v, British Library, London.

126   MS Harl. 4605, ff. 94v-95, British Library, London.
130   MS Add. 27695, f. 14, British Library, London.
135   MS Add. 42130, f. 196v, British Library, London.
139   Victoria and Albert Museum, London, L.475-1918. L139.
152l   MS Buchanan, e. 13, f. 97, Bodleian Library, Oxford.
152r   From The Flowering of the Middle Ages, edited by Joan Evans, courtesy of the publishers, Thames and Hudson Ltd, London.
156   Photograph by John Meek.
157   MS Cotton Dom. A XVII, f. 150v, British Library, London.
159   Brandiston Hall, Norfolk/Sonia Halliday and Laura Lushington.
161   Woodcut map by William Cunningham, 1558, British Library 59. i. 28.
163   MS Cotton Jul. E1V, Art. 6, f. 3, British Library, London.
168t   MS Douce. 365, f. 115, Bodleian Library, Oxford.
168b   Aachen Cathedral Treasury/Bildarchiv Foto Marburg.
170   MS 265, f. 6, Lambeth Palace Library, London.
171   British Library, London.
172-3   MS Lansdowne, 285, British Library, London.
176   The Wallace Collection, London.
179   Canterbury Cathedral/Sonia Halliday and Laura Lushington.
182t   MS Cotton Tib. A. VII. f. 90, British Library, London.
182b   Museum of London.
184   MS Lansdowne 451, f. 230, Britisn Library, London.
185   Devonshire Tapestries, Victoria and Albert Museum, London.
191   The Board of Trustees of the Royal Armouries.
192-3   MS Royal 14. E. IV, f. 210, British Library, London.
197   Photograph by John Meek.
201   St Mary's Ewelme, Oxfordshire. Photograph, F.H. Crossley and Canon M.H. Ridgway, from The Mediaeval Face, by Amanda Tomlinson, National Portrait Gallery, London.
204   MS 236, University of Ghent.
207   Essex Record Office, D/Dml Ml.
211t   St Mary's, Warwick. Photograph, F.H. Crossley and Canon M.H. Ridgway, from The Mediaeval Face, by Amanda Tomlinson, National Portrait Gallery, London.
211b   Church of St Mary's, Norbury and Roston, Derbyshire. Photograph Courtauld Institute, London.
220   MS Egerton 3127, f. 1v, British Museum, London.
225   MS Douce 208, f. 1, Bodleian Library, Oxford.
227   Maps Department, British Library, London.
231   The Mansell Collection, London.
232-3   Maps 23807. (I), British Library, London.
237   MS 236, University of Ghent.
238-9   MS Harl. 7353, fig. 10, British Library, London.
242   MS Harl. 3719, ff. 158v-159, British Library, London.
245   Photograph courtesy of English Heritage.
256   MS 18, f. 109, Nantes/Giraudon, Paris, LAC 45112.
264   Eton College Collections, Eton College, Windsor.
265   MS Eton 178, Eton College Collections, Eton College, Windsor.
269   Ost. Nationelbibliothek, Vienna.
276   MS Gough Gen. Top. 16-8E, Bodleian Library, Oxford.
280   St Margaret's Church, Paston, Norfolk, photograph by John Meek.
281   Photograph by John Meek.
283   St Margaret's Church, Paston, Norfolk, photograph by John Meek.

**ENDPAPERS**

MS Add. 43490, f. 18, British Library, London. Original size 8¾ x 5½in.

**FRONT COVER**

Top left:
The Blessing of a Marriage, 15th century, MS Lansdowne 451, f. 230, British Library, London.
Top centre:
King and Queen entertained by Courtiers, 15th century, MS Roy. 20. C. 11. f. 159, British Library, London.
Top right:
Christine de Pisan, Writing, French, 15th century, from Collected Works of Christine de Pisan, MS Harl. 4431, f. 4, British Library, London.
Bottom left and right:
Threshing and associated sign of the zodiac, Virgo, Occupation of the Month, August, Book of Hours, French, 15th century, Fastolf Master, MS Auct. D. inf. 2. 11, f. 8r, Bodleian Library, Oxford.
Bottom centre:
The Battle of Barnet, detail from Ghent Manuscript MS 236, University Ghent.

**BACK COVER**

Lady Sweeping, French, 15th century, from Livre des Propriétés des Choses, Barthelemy l'Anglais, MS Fr. 9140, f. 107, Bibliothèque Nationale, Paris/Marie-Thérèse Souverbie.